EMPEROR
FRANCIS
JOSEPH

ALSO BY JOHN VAN DER KISTE

Published by Sutton Publishing unless stated otherwise

Frederick III, German Emperor 1888 (1981)
Queen Victoria's family: a select bibliography (Clover, 1982)
Dearest Affie: Alfred, Duke of Edinburgh, Queen Victoria's second son, 1844–1900 [with Bee Jordaan] (1984)
Queen Victoria's children (1986; large print ISIS, 1987)
Windsor and Habsburg: the British and Austrian reigning houses 1848–1922 (1987)
Edward VII's children (1989)
Princess Victoria Melita, Grand Duchess Cyril of Russia, 1876–1936 (1991)
George V's children (1991)
George III's children (1992)
Crowns in a changing world: the British and European monarchies 1901–36 (1993)
Kings of the Hellenes: The Greek Kings 1863–1974 (1994)
Childhood at court 1819–1914 (1995)
Northern crowns: The Kings of modern Scandinavia (1996)
King George II and Queen Caroline (1997)
The Romanovs 1818–1959: Alexander II of Russia and his family (1998)
Kaiser Wilhelm II: Germany's last Emperor (1999)
The Georgian Princesses (2000)
Gilbert & Sullivan's Christmas (2000)
Dearest Vicky, Darling Fritz: Queen Victoria's eldest daughter and the German Emperor (2001)
Royal visits in Devon and Cornwall (Halsgrove, 2002)
Once a Grand Duchess: Xenia, sister of Nicholas II [with Coryne Hall] (2002)
William and Mary (2003)

EMPEROR FRANCIS JOSEPH

LIFE, DEATH AND THE FALL OF THE HABSBURG EMPIRE

JOHN VAN DER KISTE

SUTTON PUBLISHING

First published in the United Kingdom in 2005 by
Sutton Publishing Limited · Phoenix Mill
Thrupp · Stroud · Gloucestershire · GL5 2BU

British Library Cataloguing in Publication Data
A catalogue record for this book is available from the British Library.

ISBN 0-7509-3787-4

Typeset in 11/13.5pt Sabon.
Typesetting and origination by
Sutton Publishing Limited.
Printed and bound in England by
J.H. Haynes & Co. Ltd, Sparkford.

Contents

List of Plates

Preface

'I am spared nothing', Emperor Francis Joseph of Austria is reputed to have said in June 1914, soon after being told the news that his nephew and heir, Archduke Francis Ferdinand, and his wife had been assassinated at Sarajevo. It was an echo of the words attributed to him almost sixteen years earlier after another assassination in the family, that of his own wife Empress Elizabeth, in Geneva.

The Emperor had indeed been spared little in his personal life. The violent murders of his wife and nephew had been preceded in 1889 by the suicide of his only son, Crown Prince Rudolf, and in 1867 by the execution of his brother Maximilian, Emperor of Mexico. In the longest reign of any European monarch of the last three centuries, almost sixty-eight years, he had also suffered two ignominious defeats in war, with Italy in 1859 and with Prussia in 1866. Both had done immense damage, albeit of a temporary nature, to his personal standing and that of the house of Habsburg, so much that he even feared abdication might be necessary. 'Never was martyrdom borne with greater dignity and resignation', wrote Walburga, Lady Paget, wife of the British ambassador to Vienna towards the end of the nineteenth century. 'His one fault is his weakness, but why this accumulation of terrible misfortunes, of which none of Shakespeare's tragedies equals the horrors!' Yet he weathered the storms, and by the time of his diamond jubilee in 1908 he had come to personify his empire in the same way that his contemporary Queen Victoria embodied hers.

A conscientious, well-meaning ruler and a kindly man, he has often been dismissed as dull and unintelligent if not stupid. Beside his more mercurial, wayward and tragic relatives, at first glance his long life may look uninteresting to some. Consequently, as a subject for biography he has often been neglected. One only has to compare the number of books published about his contemporaries in England

and Germany, Queen Victoria and Emperor William II, to appreciate the difference.

This book intends to show him as a man against his family background – the son of a forceful mother, the husband of a difficult, wilful wife, the father of three very different children (not including a daughter who died in infancy). It is also the portrait of a ruler who presided against the decline of the Austrian empire and a man of generally peaceful intentions, who ironically bore some responsibility for the start of what was at the time the most momentous conflict in European history, a war the consequences of which he did not live to see.

Acknowledgements

I wish to acknowledge the gracious permission of Her Majesty The Queen to publish extracts from material of which she owns the copyright; and the staff of the Public Record Office to quote from material in their possession. Sue and Mike Woolmans have been extremely helpful with regard to supplying illustrations and information during the writing of this book, while Coryne Hall, Karen Roth, Katrina Warne and Robin Piguet have also given invaluable advice and encouragement at various stages. As ever I am also indebted to the staff of the Kensington & Chelsea Public Libraries for access to their collection; and to my editors at Sutton Publishing, Jaqueline Mitchell, Jane Entrican and Anne Bennett.

Last but not least, many thanks to my wife Kim, who cheerfully accepted my afternoons, evenings and very early mornings 'in Habsburgland' on the computer (to say nothing of hours spent trying to fix computer problems – thanks also in this regard to Hannah, Caroline, James, Andy and Phil). She and my mother Kate provided unfailing encouragement and interest throughout, and without their work in reading the manuscript in draft form, the end result would surely be much the poorer.

The House of Habsburg

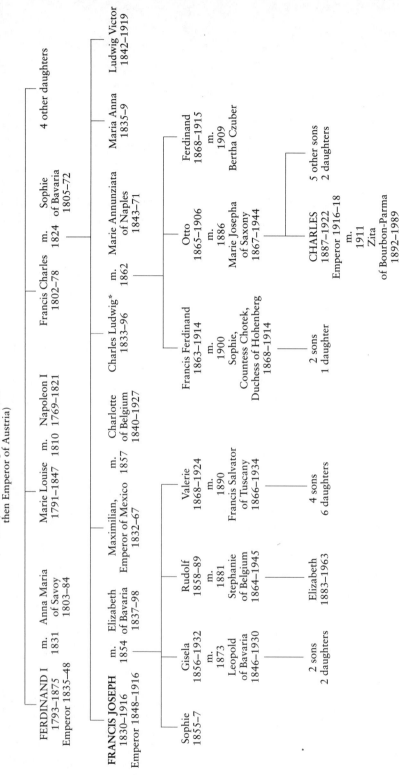

* Only the wives of Francis II and Charles Ludwig whose children were of major dynastic significance are included in this table.

ONE

Sovereign in Waiting

Archduke Francis Joseph was born on 18 August 1830, third in line to the imperial throne of Austria after his uncle, Emperor Ferdinand, and his father, Archduke Francis Charles. This was the infant on whom would rest the future of the house of Habsburg, a dynasty which could trace its lineage back through several centuries, but with an increasingly chequered history by the early nineteenth century.

In 1792 Emperor Francis had been crowned Holy Roman Emperor in Frankfurt, the Holy Roman empire being in effect a hereditary possession of the Habsburgs. With the proclamation of a republic in France that year, and the rise of Napoleon Bonaparte, Francis sought a title to assert his superiority over the upstart Frenchman and also his authority over his Habsburg dominions. When Napoleon proclaimed himself Emperor of France in 1804, Francis thought it politic to take an hereditary imperial title, which would appear stronger than the 'elected' office of Holy Roman Emperor, and he accordingly became Emperor of Austria. His country's defeat at the battle of Austerlitz in 1805 resulted in a settlement which left Austria considerably diminished in prestige, and the creation of the Confederation of the Rhine a year later led to the final dissolution of the Holy Roman empire, as well as Francis's renunciation of the now redundant title. At the Congress of Vienna in 1815, summoned to determine the shape of Europe after the defeat of Napoleon's France, the constituent territories of the Austrian empire were agreed. In addition to Austria and Hungary, they included Bohemia, Moravia, Galicia, Silesia, Slovakia, Transylvania, the Bukovina, Croatia-Slavonia, Camiola, Gorizia, Istria, Dalmatia, Lombardy and Venetia.

Though the empire comprised eleven nationalities, with little geographic and economic unity, it emerged from the Congress of Vienna greatly enriched. It was the intention of the statesmen who had met in Vienna, particularly the Austrian foreign minister Prince Clemens von Metternich, to maintain the European status quo. Austria, he maintained, had a historic right to be the major standard bearer of the principle of legitimacy, of leadership on the continent. After more than two decades of conflict the major European powers were exhausted, and anxious to ensure that France should no longer be in a position to threaten Europe again. They did this mainly by surrounding her with states of equal if not greater power. The Austrian and Russian autocracies had survived, and Prussia was now more powerful, having absorbed some Saxon territory and with a new commanding position on the Rhine, in order to forestall French expansion across the northern Alps. With its possessions of Lombardy and Venetia in Italy, Austria likewise acted as an obstacle against French designs in the south. In addition, it assumed leadership of the confederation of German states.

Emperor Francis had been married four times and fathered thirteen children, but only two sons and five daughters survived infancy. All were the issue of his second wife, Maria Theresa of Bourbon-Naples, a first cousin twice over. Though not generally recognised at the time, such inbreeding was to have serious implications for the family, some members of which were physically or mentally deformed. At the time, the blame for such shortcomings was attributed to other factors that sound less credible today. For example, the mentally deranged and extremely ugly Archduchess Marie's problems were said to be a result of her mother having been chased during her pregnancy by an orang-utang from Vienna's Schönbrunn zoo.

The elder son and heir, Crown Prince Ferdinand, was a well-meaning, simple-minded soul and a victim of epilepsy. With his ugly shrunken figure and unnaturally large head, he could barely utter two connected sentences, lift a glass with one hand, or descend a staircase without assistance. In December 1830 the court physician Dr Stifft told him there was no medical reason why he should not marry, but warned the rest of the family that it was unlikely he would or could ever make any effort 'to assert his marital rights'.[1] Two months later he married Princess Anna Maria of Savoy, who was said to be 'white as linen', and with a voice that shook perceptibly at the marriage ceremony. He reputedly suffered several seizures on the wedding night. The second in line to the throne, his brother Archduke Francis Charles was mentally and physically sound but regarded as a somewhat lightweight personality.

At one of the regular family gatherings comprising the Habsburgs and the Wittelsbachs (the royal house of Bavaria), Francis Charles became particularly attached to his cousin Sophie, daughter of Maximilian I, King of Bavaria, and his second wife Princess Caroline of Baden. The Bavarian children included two pairs of twin daughters, one of these younger twins being Sophie. She and her five sisters had a reputation for being strong-willed and authoritarian by nature, and the Prussian historian Heinrich von Treitschke would later refer to them collectively as 'the Bavarian sisters of woe'.

Francis Charles was clumsy, shy and not particularly handsome, with a long thin face out of all proportion to his slight body. Well meaning but rather slow on the uptake, he made no impression on Sophie at first. She adored her mother and her twin sister Marie, and at first any thoughts of marriage were far from her mind. But the Archduke would not be put off, and he travelled regularly from Vienna to Munich to be with her. He sent her presents and wrote her affectionate letters, which she answered politely without guessing his intentions. Thus encouraged, he plucked up the courage to ask her for her hand in marriage. She could hardly refuse, but as the time drew near for her to leave home, she was so distraught that she said farewell to all her friends as if she was about to take her leave of them forever. The thought of living far away from her family with a man of whom she was not particularly fond, and whom she did not yet know that well, appalled her. However, the proposal had been made and could not be withdrawn. Being second in line to the throne of Austria, and likely to become Regent when his brother Ferdinand succeeded to the crown, the Archduke was one of the most eligible bachelors in Europe.

The wedding was to take place in November 1824, and Sophie was pleasantly surprised by her rapturous welcome in Vienna. Moreover, she found encouragement in seeing that her diffident husband-to-be clearly acted with more confidence in his own homeland. It touched her that he was always thinking of surprises for his bride, constantly buying her fine dresses, coats, jewellery and ornaments. Soon she was clearly becoming besotted with the suitor whom she had at first regarded with little more than indifference. His mother-in-law, Queen Caroline of Bavaria, liked him but was not blind to his faults, calling him 'a good fellow' who wanted to do well, but in the same breath saying he was 'really terrible' and that 'he would bore me to death. Every now and then I would want to hit him.'[2]

Opinion is divided on Sophie's attitude towards her husband in the early days of her marriage. Some said that at first she barely tolerated him, and only the presence at court of their nephew François, Duc de Reichstadt, the short-lived tubercular son of Napoleon Bonaparte and her sister-in-law Archduchess Marie Louise, proved her saving grace at Vienna. Others suggested that what had at first appeared to be a loveless match developed into a very happy marriage.

As she matured Sophie became ambitious and optimistic, and clearly cherished hopes of becoming Empress. When her mother asked her soon after her marriage if she was happy, she replied, 'I am content', a restrained remark which some misinterpreted as lack of enthusiasm. What did disturb her peace of mind were any threats to the old order elsewhere in Europe. When the Bourbons were deposed in France, she prayed for the divine destruction of revolutionary Paris, and regarded the Orléans regime as 'illegitimate'. She also lambasted her Hanoverian contemporary King William IV for his 'liberal stupidities' in presiding over the Great Reform Act in England.[3]

Personal frustration was probably responsible to some extent for such intolerant behaviour. The couple dearly wanted a family, and during their first five years Sophie had five miscarriages. She underwent a number of cures in Ischl, and when another pregnancy was confirmed early in 1830 the doctors ordered her to take particular care of herself. Despite her longing for some fresh air, they insisted that she stay indoors during the long hot summer months. Some years later, after her name had become a byword for cold-hearted authoritarianism, a story was told that in the later days of her pregnancy, she threw the scalding contents of a cup of coffee in her husband's face, and told him that she would be delivered of a child on only one condition – that a free pardon was granted to some prisoner under sentence of death. The only Austrian subject who fitted this criterion was guilty of some of the worst crimes imaginable, though unspecified, but he was still released from prison as a result of her intervention.[4]

In mid-August the long-awaited son arrived, and was named Francis Joseph, or sometimes 'Franzi' within the family. Almost from birth, he was granted his own apartment in the palace, though the rooms were en suite, with a never-ending procession of relations, servants and friends of the imperial family. His bedroom was situated above the guards' lavatory, and at each change of guard drums rolled and bugles were sounded directly beneath his window.

Franzi was the eldest of five children. In July 1832 a second son followed and was called Ferdinand Maximilian, though always known in the family as Max. Charles Ludwig was born in 1833, and a daughter Maria Anna in 1835. Her brothers were all healthy, but their sister was delicate from birth. Though the doctors did their best to reassure her that the baby girl would probably grow out of her complaint, Sophie realised that she suffered from the hereditary taint of epilepsy. By the time she was four, she was so ill that the physicians recommended her hair should be cut off and leeches applied to her forehead. It was to no avail, and within a few weeks she was dead. Franzi shared in his mother's grief, showing sympathy and understanding beyond his tender years. Max was puzzled at seeing their mother weep openly for the first time. Desperate to console her, he spent a month's pocket money on buying her a pet monkey, and as he presented it to her he apologised profusely for being unable to buy her another little girl.[5]

At the time of her daughter's death Sophie was expecting another child, and gave birth to a stillborn son a few months later. Late in 1841 she knew she was pregnant again, and in May 1842 she had a fourth son, named Ludwig Victor. Having already lost two children, and aware that her childbearing days were probably over, she devoted herself completely at first to this new son, with a maternal love that bordered on the obsessive.

Although their early years were thus not free from sadness, by and large the young Habsburg Archdukes enjoyed a carefree, happy childhood. Francis Charles was a doting father, and enjoyed galloping about the nursery with little Franzi on his back, taking him to the park to feed the deer, or helping him entice pigeons to the windowsills of their apartment in the imperial palace, the Hofburg, by putting out scraps of bread or seed. Every evening the boys would play hide and seek or similar games around the corridors, or sit at their mother's feet while she read aloud to them from such titles as *Gulliver's Travels* and *The Swiss Family Robinson*. When they were a little older, both parents took them for outings, walks, visits to the theatre and exhibitions in Vienna. While the importance of good behaviour in public was impressed on them, they were allowed to move freely and informally around in the family circle, and were never banned from the adults' rooms.

On birthdays and name days the whole Habsburg clan gathered in the Hofburg for family feasts and exchanging of gifts, and the younger members performed in carefully drilled ballets, amateur theatricals, tableaux and recitations. With his gift for mimicry, his fine singing voice and outgoing charm, Max always enjoyed these the most. Sophie ensured that Franzi played the leading role as befitted the eldest brother, even though he had little talent for or love of acting. He was, however, the best dancer, and with his fondness for uniforms and fine clothes he was very proud when allowed to appear at a ball wearing tails for the first time. Max could not resist making fun of him, and after attracting everyone's attention by mimicking the affectations and poses of the dancers, he seized his brother's tails and made them both gallop round the edge of the ballroom.

Each year on Christmas Eve the whole family would gather outside the closed doors of the Emperor's apartments, the younger children trying to glimpse through the keyhole the Christchild leaving gifts. When the Christmas bells rang, the doors of the Red Salon were flung open. There stood an enormous lighted tree with generous imperial gifts: a perfect child-size carriage, large enough to be drawn by a small pony; or a palace guard in miniature, complete with sentry boxes, drums, and toy guns. All evening Francis drilled his archduke uncles. After Christmas, during carnival, there were children's balls, tables laden with sweetmeats, and the gayest of waltzes and polkas. At the end all the adults joined in the fun and games.

After Easter, when the weather improved and the days lengthened, the children could spend more time in the gardens of the Schönbrunn Palace, the imperial summer residence, riding in their donkey cart, swimming in the river, playing in the Indian wigwam one of the gardeners had made for them, or visiting a collection of exotic animals the Emperor had bought from a circus.

As infants, the Archdukes had their own household. Less than two years separated Franzi and Max, and they were entrusted to the same governess, Baroness Louise von Sturmfeder ('Aja'). She was devoted to her charges, and felt sorry for Franzi with his lack of privacy, lamenting that 'the child of the poorest day-labourer is not so ill-used as this poor little Imperial Highness'.[6] Several others worked under her, including an assistant nurse, cook, chamberwoman, two maids and two footmen. Her diary gives some glimpses of the future Emperor in his earliest days. His favourite toys were a tambourine and a drummer girl given to him as Christmas presents when he was very small. A stoical child, he seemed much less concerned than everyone else when he arrived back from a walk in the park one bitter November afternoon with hands blue from cold because nobody had thought to give him any gloves.

Francis, Max and Charles Ludwig all enjoyed good health but Ludwig Victor was a sickly child, and his frequent bouts of illness gave his parents many an anxious moment, fearing they might lose him like his sister. Accidents and infections often kept him confined to bed for days if not weeks at a time. While ailing young archdukes and archduchesses were generally ministered to by nurses, Sophie was unusual in looking after him herself much of the time, rarely leaving his bedside if he was not well. If he was in bed during Christmas, she would postpone the main celebrations until he was able to take part. If the three elder brothers ever resented the fuss made of the baby of the family, they never showed it. On the contrary they were devoted to him, often bought him toys from their pocket money, and sometimes got together to stage small masquerades or theatrical performances for him. He showed his gratitude by regularly interrupting them while they were meant to be engrossed in their homework, and perhaps not surprisingly they were never reluctant to complain.

It was clear from early on that the down-to-earth Francis would be a soldier. Even as a toddler he loved military ceremonial, from sentries pacing beneath the nursery window each day, to the sound of bugle calls and the sight of parade-ground drill at the nearby barracks. From the age of four he enjoyed dressing up in uniform and playing with his toy soldiers. It was not long before he formed a collection in which every regiment of the Austrian army was represented, with the details of each uniform perfectly reproduced, and none of these soldiers was ever broken. By contrast the dreamy, more imaginative Max was always much more interested in the animals, birds and flowers to be seen near the palace.

From an early age, all four brothers were quite different from each other. Franzi was the most handsome and intelligent, with a strength of character and clear sense of self-discipline. Conscientious and hard-working, he had the utmost respect for authority. Max, romantic and given to daydreaming, was Sophie's favourite. As the second son who was unlikely to succeed to the throne, he could afford to be mischievous, the one who could never resist seeking out their tutors' weaknesses and teasing them mercilessly. If Franzi was their mother's strength, Max was her delight. Charles Ludwig ('Karly') was intelligent but lazy, greedy, lacking in self-motivation, interested in nothing but sport and shooting. Ludwig Victor ('Bubi'), weak and effeminate, was often grossly spoilt as the youngest.

The family spent the spring and autumn months at Schönbrunn and their retreat of Laxenburg, outside Vienna. Franzi and Karly preferred the latter where they could go shooting wild ducks and rabbits with their father. Maximilian liked Schönbrunn best, where he could always visit the zoo full of strange animals and the conservatory full of scented tropical plants. Every summer they moved to Ischl, a little mountain resort in the Salzkammergut, where they lived in a rented villa by the River Traun. Sophie believed in the therapeutic qualities of the Salzkammergut's saline springs, which she swore had helped her become pregnant after years of miscarriages.

In February 1835 Emperor Francis celebrated his sixty-seventh birthday with a great court ball. A few days later he and the Empress attended the Burgtheater on an exceptionally chilly evening, with a sharp wind throughout Vienna, and within forty-eight hours he was confined to his bed with pneumonia. Some years before, it was said, Dr Stifft had examined him when he was suffering from a severe cold, but assured him there was no cause for alarm, as he was strong and there was 'nothing like a good constitution'. Presumably with tongue in cheek, the Emperor retorted that he had no wish to hear that word again, on the grounds that he had no constitution and intended never to have one. Nevertheless this time he would not recover and he died on 2 March, to be succeeded by the charming but pathetic Ferdinand. The views of those who did not know him were summed up by Lord

Palmerston, at the time British foreign minister, who called him 'a perfect nullity; next to an idiot'.[7] The Duc de Reichstadt thought him 'a pathetic child, feeble-minded but fundamentally good at heart'.[8]

On his deathbed, Emperor Francis had signed two documents addressed to his son and successor. One entrusted him with defending and upholding the free activity of the Roman Catholic Church, and the other was a political testament in which he insisted that Ferdinand should take no decision on public affairs without consulting Prince Metternich. He also charged his brother Ludwig with presiding over the Council of State that would govern in Ferdinand's name. This was a surprise as three of the Emperor's surviving brothers were considered more able than the Emperor himself. Charles was a capable military commander, Joseph had showed himself a successful governor of Hungary, and Johann was a brave soldier and patron of arts. Francis had chosen the least capable of his brothers to guide his successor throughout his reign, giving Metternich absolute power, since the three Archdukes who had opposed him were put aside.

Such was Sophie's respect for the memory of Francis that she made no criticism of his request, dictated by the wily Metternich, in which Ferdinand had been recognised as his successor. Privately she found it hard to forgive the statesman for thus promoting the succession, which was perfectly lawful but which she felt should have gone to her husband. While she had no illusions as to her husband's ability, she wanted him at the forefront as trustee of their eldest son's interests. All she could do was wait until their children reached manhood, and meanwhile she devoted herself to their upbringing. She strove to impress on them that in spite of the pathetic figure of the Emperor in his sovereign robes, his face distorted by constant epileptic attacks, the Habsburg empire was still the centre of the civilised world. This was easier said than done, when from early days they had to help at the imperial dinner table and watch their uncle Ferdinand. Looking at him, Sophie admitted to her mother, sometimes made her feel physically sick. On the question of her sons' education, Sophie relied on nobody but herself, least of all her ineffectual husband. Although she disliked Metternich as he had excluded Francis Charles from the Council of State, she knew they could not do without his formidable political talents.

In 1836, two of Metternich's closest friends were chosen as governors to Sophia's sons. Count Heinrich Bombelles was appointed to supervise the education of Francis and his brothers. Each of the boys had their own special tutor or personal chamberlain as well, and Count Johann Coronini-Cronberg filled that role with regard to Francis, becoming responsible for the boy's military training. Playmates were chosen for the young Archdukes, namely Marcus and Charles, the sons of Bombelles, and Francis, Coronini's son. Coronini saw that Francis Joseph was timid and anxious and took it upon himself to give him a sense of pride and teach him self-mastery. A true nobleman, Coronini told him gently but firmly, could never yield to the plebeian vice of weariness, but always had to follow 'the example of those self-controlled aristocrats who, in service in the field and the Court, had been able to conquer every weakness of the body'.[9]

Bombelles devised a programme of study for his charge. At the age of six, he was expected to spend eighteen hours a week studying from his books, increasing to thirty-six or thirty-seven at the age of eight, and forty-six hours at eleven. When he was thirteen, he became seriously ill, and the physicians put this down to stress induced by an over-taxing educational regime. After a suitable break he was given additional subjects to study, and by the age of fifteen he was working between fifty-three and fifty-five hours a week. The importance of early rising and punctuality was impressed on him. In the summer, lessons began at 6 a.m., and continued with short breaks until 9 p.m.

Considerable emphasis was placed on learning by rote, and little – perhaps too little – on how to think for himself. Baron von Helfert, a contemporary courtier and historian, thought the teachers could have been chosen better. In his view, they were 'men of no deep culture or preparation, with a weakness for hollow affirmations'. Their standards of instruction were poor, and the boys were inclined to make fun of them. The history lessons, in particular, were 'a spiritless mixture of sacred and profane history, with much scrambling up and down genealogical trees; a dry enumeration of events, with careful avoidance of any stimulus to original thought'.[10] However, while these history lessons imbued Francis with a sense of the divine omnipotence of the sovereign, they also brought him up with the immovable concept that a just monarch was a good monarch; an emperor had obligations towards his subjects, and foremost among his duties was to protect them from injustice.

When seen alongside the more liberal educational regimes and syllabi devised for Prince Albert of Saxe-Coburg and for Francis Joseph's contemporary, Prince Frederick William of Prussia, it was a narrow one somewhat lacking in systematic liberal and scientific or artistic content. Chemistry and technology were taught, but all as a haphazard collection of facts in which the emphasis generally appeared to be part of a process of learning facts for the sake of it, rather than as part of an integrated programme. From necessity there was more provision made for learning the different languages within the empire, and as he would need to be able to converse with peoples outside the empire, he was required to learn French as well, but never English. Otherwise the curriculum had changed little from what the boy's grandfather had been taught in his childhood. In due course, his education was widened to include philosophy and spiritual matters from the court chamberlain, Joseph Colombi, and Abbot von Rauscher, a close friend of Archduchess Sophie. As Francis Joseph was a prospective ruler, it was felt that he would never need to appeal directly in person to his subjects or their representatives, and the art of public speaking was therefore considered unnecessary.

The education followed strict religious lines, and he remained a lifelong, unquestioning believer in the Catholic Church. His attitude to religion, it was said, was that of almost every Austrian gentleman of old nobility. To him, Catholicism was 'as natural and obvious as the mountains of his country or any of the great given facts in the landscape of his life. One does not talk much about it; nothing is less liked in settled Austrian circles than any sort of talk about faith, whether popular or scientific.'[11] Yet he lacked any intense religious fervour, and of all the family, only his brother Charles Ludwig became a passionate Catholic.

By the time of his eighth birthday Franzi was writing letters to his mother in French. At twelve he was learning Magyar and Czech as well as French, with Italian and the rudiments of Latin and Greek later. Unlike Max he never showed much interest in literature or reading, but enjoyed drawing, and made a series of sketches in Italy after his fifteenth birthday. As an adult he showed little interest in the visual arts, taking the view that painters should be decorators, producing meticulous pictures that celebrated military victories or faithfully reproduced familiar landscapes. In boyhood and adolescence he and Max enjoyed regular visits to the theatre, and Franzi liked dancing, though music excited little interest in him, apart from military marches.

Franzi was not a born soldier, and had to be taught to fill the role. Naturally reserved, quiet and shy, he had to be forced to mount a horse, often weeping bitterly from fear. It said much for his self-control and determination, as well as his tutor's persistence, that he became a proficient and fearless rider.

At the age of thirteen he became colonel-in-chief of the 3rd Dragoon Regiment, and a year later he was allowed to ride at the head of his regiment when it was participating in exercises in Moravia. In 1845 Franzi, Max and Charles Ludwig were sent on what amounted to an official tour of Lombardy-Venetia, under the supervision of the respected veteran commander Field Marshal Joseph Radetzky. He staged reviews, firework displays and exhibitions of horsemanship for the young imperial visitors, as well as conducting tours of various defence works. Despite the Italian resentment of Austrian rule in the provinces, they were enthusiastically cheered when they appeared on an excursion down the Grand Canal in Venice, escorted by a small fleet of gondolas.

As adulthood beckoned, Francis Joseph was seen more and more in public. In January 1847 he was sent to Buda, Hungary, to represent the family at the funeral of his great-uncle Archduke Joseph. He had made good progress in learning Magyar, and his tact and apparent interest in everything he saw on his travels made the right impression. On two subsequent ceremonial occasions that year he was in Hungary again, making carefully rehearsed speeches in Magyar. At home there were other family funerals for aged relatives at which he would be seen riding at the head of his regiment, as well as various field exercises and court receptions.

In Vienna economic unrest during the 1840s, with poor harvests throughout Austria, mounting unemployment, and trading competition from Britain and Prussia, sowed the seeds of a depression which gradually spread from the poorer regions to more prosperous areas of the city. By Christmas 1847 Archduchess Sophie was in a state of profound gloom over the outlook for Austria. Her family connections included a half-brother on the throne of Bavaria, a twin sister as consort of the King of Saxony, and an elder sister married to King Frederick William IV of Prussia. She read several of the German newspapers and several French periodicals, and was probably the best-informed member of the imperial family. To her it was clear that younger politicians were impatient with the elderly Metternich's conservatism, and within the Austrian empire the spread of a linguistic, cultural nationalism was creating instability.

Within the first few weeks of 1848, it was clear that events elsewhere in Europe were likely to provide a catalyst for change. There was insurrection in Sicily, liberal agitation in Tuscany and the Papal States, and a constitution was granted in Naples. In February Louis-Philippe, King of the French, was forced to abdicate. Early in March Lajos Kossuth, a Hungarian lawyer and journalist, made a speech to the Diet urging the establishment of a virtually autonomous Hungary with a responsible government elected on a broad franchise. While he spoke respectfully of the dynasty as a unifying force, he still considered it essential to change the character of government in the monarchy in order to safeguard the country's historic rights, with constitutional institutions which recognised the different nationalities.

When reports of his speech reached Vienna, they produced the response of a plea for civil rights and some form of parliamentary government. Petitions were sent to the Emperor demanding the removal of police surveillance, and the dismissal of Metternich and his hated minister of police, Joseph Sedlnitsky. Early next day, a body of students marched on the Herrengasse. The army was sent out to quell the rioting, and four men were killed. Metternich was asked to resign, but refused to go unless his sovereign and the Archdukes in line of succession would personally absolve him from the oath he had taken before the death of Emperor Francis that he would give loyal support to Ferdinand.

This gesture of absolution required the presence of Archduke Francis Charles and his son Francis, and in this way the seventeen-year-old boy was admitted into the inner counsels of government. On agreeing to resign, Metternich protested half-heartedly against calling his action a generous one, saying that he acted according to what he felt was right. Two days later he left Vienna and fled to England.

With some prompting from his wife, known behind her back with a mixture of awe and respect as 'the only man in the Hofburg', Francis Charles emerged as chief spokesman for the government, and urged the granting of an imperial constitution. Once this had been granted, he said, all subsequent political reforms could be deferred until full agreement had been reached on the basic instrument of government. Archduchess Sophie was concerned at this proposal, as she was already aware that their son was likely to ascend the throne before long, and she did not wish his powers to be limited by any concessions which might be seen to have been wrung from the imperial family at a time of desperation. She thought it better that they should wait until the popular agitation and celebrations of Metternich's fall from power had died down. On the next day, Francis joined his father and the Emperor on a carriage drive through Vienna, designed to test the mood of the public. The reaction was mixed, with some cheers for the Emperor, but some sullen faces as well.

There were sporadic uprisings in various parts of the empire, especially in Hungary. Sophie was keen to send her eldest son away from the difficult atmosphere and what she saw as the sorry spectacle of their fugitive court, and in April she thought that sending him to Prague as Viceroy would be a suitable diversion, as well as giving him some official status. However, the unrest in that city put an end to the idea.

Knowing that his time was coming, she wanted to give him some conspicuous position that would put him more in the public eye. If he was closer to 'the victorious and avenging sword', but not too close for danger, somewhere connected with the Italian theatre of war would be ideal. In April the *Wiener Zeitung* announced that the Archduke would be joining Radetzky in order to see for himself 'the Field-Marshal's warlike preparations against enemies and agitators'. As Radetzky's army was immobile at the time, it was merely a way of enhancing the prestige of the youth whom his mother was already grooming as the saviour of the imperial dynasty.

Sophie had made her plans without consulting the Field Marshal who, despite his loyalty to the Habsburgs, was still prepared to speak his mind and vent his indignation. He coldly told the young Archduke on his arrival that his presence only made matters difficult for him. 'If anything happens to you, I am to blame; and if you are taken prisoner, I and my army are lost.'[12] He ensured that Francis Joseph was kept out of harm's way as far as possible, and entrusted him to the care of Lieutenant-General d'Aspre, on whose staff the young Prince remained. He received his baptism of fire on the battlefield in May when the Piedmontese army launched three assaults on the Austrians in the village of Santa Lucia. Almost 400 men were killed in the skirmish, but the young Archduke was said to have remained calm and collected though not far from the cannon fire.

By May workers' and students' demonstrations, fuelled by sympathy for the nationalist aspirations of the Italian territories and Hungary, had made the atmosphere in Vienna so tense that the imperial family were advised to move under cover of darkness from Vienna to Innsbruck, where they remained for the next three months. Soon after their move Sophie's sister Ludovika, Duchess in Bavaria, came to visit them, accompanied by her daughters. Helene was fourteen and Elizabeth ten. It was the first time Francis Joseph had met his Bavarian cousins, but they made no particular impression on him. On 18 August he attained his majority, and his eighteenth birthday present from his parents was a pair of decorated meerschaum pipes.

That autumn Theodore Latour, minister of war, gave orders for part of the Vienna garrison to assist in the subjection of Hungary, where resistance to Habsburg rule had been hardening. This prompted demonstrations by the radicals in Vienna, and violence erupted once more in the city. A mob seized Latour from his office, stabbed him to death and hung his naked body on a lamppost in one of the city squares. Again, the imperial family were advised that temporary retreat would be prudent, and they departed for the garrison town of Olmütz.

In the last week of October Field Marshal Otto von Windischgrätz massed his army to surround the city and subjected it to a prolonged bombardment. The resistance of the radicals soon evaporated, and in the ensuing disturbances between 2,000 and 3,000 were killed. Within a few days the city capitulated to the troops. Over twenty suspected ringleaders of the revolt were shot, and throughout the winter the city remained under strict military control.

Another family conference took place, dominated by Archduchess Sophie whose plans coincided perfectly with those of chief minister

Prince Felix Schwarzenberg, Windischgrätz's brother-in-law. The latter would only accept office under a new emperor, and it was confirmed that, in accordance with discussions held earlier that year, Ferdinand would shortly be asked to abdicate. Through no fault of his own, he was clearly unfit to reign, particularly at a time of such instability, and especially as he was seen as the imperial personification of the system against which the Viennese had rebelled. Archduke Francis Charles had been found wanting. In an age of peace he would have made an adequate Emperor, but in exile he had been a grumbler, indecisive and no match for revolutionaries who threatened the fabric and stability of the empire. Much as she had longed to be Empress, Sophie realised that it was not to be. Instead she would be the mother of an Emperor. Francis Charles was easily persuaded to renounce his place in the succession, doubtless relieved that the responsibility would never fall on his shoulders.

On 2 December 1848 the family and ministers were summoned to appear before Emperor Ferdinand in the salon of the Prince-Bishop's palace at Olmütz. In his halting, at times barely coherent, voice he read out the official act of abdication handed to him by Schwarzenberg. He surrendered his Austrian imperial titles and the crowns of Hungary, Bohemia and Lombardy, while still retaining the personal style and dignity of Emperor. Schwarzenberg then read Archduke Francis Charles's formal renunciation of his place in the succession, announcing that at this moment in the Habsburg history, a younger person was needed. Francis Joseph was untainted by association with the events of the last few months, and could serve as the symbol of a new era in the history of the Austrian empire. The ceremony ended with the new Emperor kneeling to his predecessor and asking for his blessing. Ferdinand laid his hands upon the youth's head, made the sign of the cross, then embraced him as he told Franzi that God would protect him.

Emperor Ferdinand and Empress Anna Maria, doubtless pleased to relinquish their responsibilities, went to hear Holy Mass in the palace chapel, and then left for Prague, where they settled in Hradschin Castle. Ferdinand lived at Prague till his death in 1875, and was known affectionately as '*der Praguer Majestas*', to distinguish him from his nephew.

Meanwhile, Archduke Francis was proclaimed 'by God's grace' Francis Joseph, Emperor of Austria. By not styling himself simply Emperor Francis, but adding the name of his much-revered progressive grandfather Emperor Joseph II, it could be inferred that he was planning to follow in the latter's footsteps and become a constitutional, reforming monarch. He inherited a generous collection of sovereign titles – King of Jerusalem, Apostolic King of Hungary, King of Bohemia, Galicia, Lodomeria, Lombardy, Venetia, Illyria and Croatia, and Grand Duke, Duke, Margrave, Prince and Count of some thirty other territories in the huge Austrian empire with its 35 million inhabitants. Some contemporary wits found this panoply amusing, if not faintly absurd. According to an old Austrian joke, 'The King of Croatia declared war on the King of Hungary, and Austria's Emperor, who was both, remained benevolently neutral.'[13]

A proclamation to the new emperor's subjects, almost certainly drafted by Schwarzenberg, took place with a flourish of trumpets outside the Rathaus (town hall), and a little later on the steps of the cathedral. In it the young monarch announced that they (as opposed to he himself) were

> convinced of the need and value of free institutions expressive of the spirit of the age

and that they entered

> with due confidence, on the path leading to a salutary transformation and rejuvenation of the monarchy as a whole. On the basis of genuine liberty, on the basis of equality of all the nations of the realm and of the equality before the law of all its citizens, and of participation of those citizens in legislation, our Fatherland may enjoy a resurrection to its old greatness and a new force. Determined to maintain the splendour of the crown undimmed and the monarchy as a whole undiminished, but ready to share our rights with the representatives of our peoples, we count on succeeding, with the blessing of God and in understanding with our peoples, in uniting all the regions and races of the monarchy in one great state.[14]

TWO

'Physically and Morally he is Fearless'

According to legend, when Emperor Francis Joseph returned from the ceremony which confirmed his accession to the throne he burst into tears, saying 'Farewell my youth'. The serious young man was already somewhat old for his years. At once he bowed to the demands of his office. Before dawn each morning he sat at his desk to deal with official papers, a routine to which he would adhere for the rest of his long life.

Yet he had not completely bidden farewell to his youth, or at least his youthful spirits. Not long after his accession, his brothers were playing in the audience chamber of the palace with a ball, and Ludwig Victor accidentally threw it straight through a mirrored door just as his mother and eldest brother were entering the room. Dreading a scolding and in tears, he was about to apologise when the Emperor astonished them by turning to Sophie and asking for her permission to help them smash the door down. Like a good subject, as well as an indulgent mother, she allowed them to do so. Her sons proceeded to shatter it beyond repair, the young Emperor leading them with suitably boyish enthusiasm. What would the Bishop think of those vandals who were her sons, Sophie asked herself, not knowing whether to laugh or cry.[1]

It was probably her eldest son's last outburst of high spirits. A few weeks later he, Max and two of their cousins were returning from a military inspection one day in bright sunshine. Max and the two younger boys enjoyed a snowball fight in the gardens but Francis Joseph stood apart, laughing at their antics but stopping short of joining in.

As Emperor, albeit a youthful one, more weighty matters demanded his attention. The Hungarian resistance had to be broken, or at least quelled, if order was to be restored to the empire. By the first week of January 1849 the Austrian forces under Windischgrätz

18

controlled the twin Hungarian capitals of Buda and Pest. In April Kossuth proclaimed 'the deposition of the house of Habsburg' in Hungary and moved his revolutionary government eastwards to the town of Debrecen. A Hungarian delegation offered to discuss a settlement, but the Field Marshal replied that there could be no negotiations with rebels. Two weeks later, he confirmed to the Emperor that victory was theirs.

The young Emperor grew rapidly in self-confidence. His elders had assumed that he would be a mere rubber stamp, content to agree to any ideas put forward or documents put in front of him without consideration, and that he would be a tool of his mother, or of Prince Schwarzenberg. Both exercised a lifelong influence on the autocrat, in theory one of the most powerful rulers on earth, yet still little more than a boy. But he surprised them all by presiding over meetings in person. That spring he decided, against the advice of Windischgrätz and Schwarzenberg, to ask Tsar Nicholas to come to Austria's assistance by despatching a Russian expeditionary force to help put down the simmering rebellion in Hungary. The Tsar met Francis Joseph in May 1849, and wrote to the Tsarina telling her how impressed he was with the young ruler. 'The more I see of him, the more I listen to him, the more I am astonished by his intellect, by the solidity and correctness of his views. Austria is lucky indeed to possess him.'[2]

Nevertheless, six weeks were to elapse between the Tsar's approval of intervention and the despatch of a Russian relief army to Hungary. This allowed General Julius Haynau, Commander-in-Chief of the Austrian forces in Hungary, to take the initiative in a campaign of conquest. Haynau had a reputation for severity, and Radetzky had said of him that though he was a good general, he was like a razor: 'when you have used him, put him back in his case'.[3] In August a Russian force crossed the border into Hungary and received the surrender of the Hungarian revolutionary army commander, General Arthur von Görgei. This speedy conclusion was bad news to the Austrians, who had worked hard to defeat the rebel state, only to see the Romanovs save the Habsburgs – a favour which would surely have to be repaid with interest before long.

Meanwhile, Francis Joseph ordered that no death sentences should be carried out without authority from Vienna. Tsar Nicholas advised that showing mercy to the leaders at this stage would be prudent in securing Magyar goodwill for the future. Schwarzenberg responded cynically that it was a good idea, 'but we must have some hanging first'.[4] In the name of their Emperor, he and Haynau had nine of the leaders sent to the gallows, and another four shot. Nearly 400 officers were sentenced to imprisonment. Some 114 death sentences were passed, and another 1,765 rebels were imprisoned. Between 1848 and 1853, Francis Joseph signed and confirmed more death sentences than any other European ruler throughout the whole of the nineteenth century.[5]

The execution which shocked the world most was that of Lajos Batthyany, a former Hungarian prime minister, of whom the military wished to make an example although they could not find sufficient incriminating evidence against him. His wife appealed for clemency to Archduchess Sophie, who never answered her letter. Batthyany tried to kill himself in prison, with either a blunt penknife or a dagger, and was shot instead of being hanged, as it was thought that dragging a wounded man to the gallows might have outraged opinion too far. General Görgei was spared thanks partly to the personal intervention of the Tsar, and partly because he had shortened the conflict by ordering his regiment to lay down its arms. He was banished abroad, and returned to Hungary some twenty years later. All magnates, deputies, officials and clergymen who had served under the revolutionary government in Hungary were dismissed from their posts and punished.

Schwarzenberg, who worked closely with his sovereign, was quick to see his virtues and his failings. In a letter to Metternich, he praised Francis Joseph warmly for his intelligence and diligence, noting that he worked at his desk for at least ten hours a day, and sent back many a ministerial proposal for revision.

> His bearing is full of dignity, his behaviour to all exceedingly polite, though a little dry. Men of sentiment – and many people in Vienna lay claim to kindliness – say that he has not much heart. There is no trace in him of that warm, superficial goodheartedness of many Archdukes, of the wish to please, to strive for effect. On the other hand he is perfectly accessible, patient, and well disposed to be just to all.

Above all, the minister maintained, he had great courage. 'Physically and morally he is fearless, and I believe the main reason he can face the truth, however bitter, is that it does not frighten him.'[6]

Those who worked with Francis Joseph noticed that he had an excellent memory, a keen desire to solve problems as soon as possible, and a lack of patience with people who would have liked him to consider decisions more deeply. In his early years he showed an unwillingness to hear anything disagreeable, though in the years ahead there would be more than enough unpalatable news which could not be kept from him. Some accused him of a lack of imagination, considering him generally hostile to any change in the existing order, with a tendency to overestimate respect for tradition.

His insularity and the fact that he had never mixed socially with a wider class of people were also seen as disadvantages. Ernest, Duke of Saxe-Coburg, met Francis Joseph for the first time in 1852 and called him

a young man of great promise, who combines a noble build & grace with a princely bearing & tact unusual in one so young. . . . In addition he undoubtedly possesses a talent for organising which is greatly helped by a quick comprehension & an unusually good memory. Had the young man had a wider education & if he had been allowed to travel abroad, especially in Germany & acquire information on his own account, he would already through his own natural ability carry far more weight.[7]

As Emperor, Francis Joseph would abide by his military principles. Having come to the throne at a time of revolution, he never forgot that he owed his position on the throne to his generals and troops, and their maintenance of law and order. Early in his reign, a senior general on manoeuvres carried out a small variation on the imperial orders on his own initiative, only to be called up in front of the whole military staff by the sovereign and sent back to do it again as he had been instructed, with the words, 'I command to be obeyed!'[8] ringing in his ears. On learning of the coup d'état carried out by President Louis Napoleon in Paris in December 1851 he approved wholeheartedly, saying that 'the man who holds the reigns of government in his hands must also be able to take responsibility. Irresponsible sovereignty are, for me, words without meaning; such a thing is a mere printing machine for signatures.'⁹

As the head of the Habsburg dynasty and Emperor of Austria, called by God to the throne at the age of eighteen, he had been brought up to believe that he was the divinely chosen leader. While intending to be a benevolent autocrat, he found reassurance in the simple maxim that order and discipline could normally be relied on to solve problems pertaining to government as on the parade ground. He nearly always appeared in public wearing military uniform. Had he done so a bit less often, he might have become more popular with the masses in Vienna. Much as they respected their Emperor, they would not have been averse to a sight of his more human side, instead of a ruler clearly obsessed by all things military and nicknamed 'Lieutenant Red Legs' because of the scarlet trousers of his livery.

Civilian uniform was generally restricted to private journeys abroad, such as his visit to the Paris Exhibition in 1867, or courtesy calls on royalty from other countries. He paid little attention to informal attire, and one of his valets was astonished to see that he thought nothing of wearing a blue tie with a green lounge suit. The only article of civilian clothing from his wardrobe which he really liked was the *Bratenrock* or morning-coat. While being fitted for a dinner jacket by his tailor, he remarked scornfully that he saw most men wearing one at the theatre, and found it a very ugly fashion.¹⁰

Francis Joseph's love of military attire, and the shyness with which he dealt face to face with those of lower status, tended to make him appear unapproachable if not impossibly remote. His two predecessors had had a reputation for sociability and kindliness, two qualities in which he was lacking. His upbringing had imbued in him a stiff formality, often taken as coldness, which he would never lose. One of his generals complained of his sovereign's distant manner, that he demanded devotion from others 'and is annoyed if it is lacking, but does nothing to win the love of his people or attract affection'.

On a visit to the Bohemian Theatre, Prague, he barely acknowledged his reception. It made an unfortunate contrast with the demeanour of his predecessor Emperor Ferdinand, who may have been weak in the head, but was kindly and 'rouses far more feeling in Prague than the young Emperor did'.¹¹ He was well aware that any remarks or personal opinions which he aired would soon spread throughout the court, and probably the whole of Austria as well, and he never let his guard slip.

In April 1852 Schwarzenberg unexpectedly passed away from a stroke, while changing for a ball at which he planned to dance with his latest lover, the wife of a Polish army officer. Francis Joseph was summoned at once, arriving just in time to witness the statesman's last moments, and his mentor's death moved him to tears. On regaining his composure, he ordered that the Prince's study should be locked, and took the key away with him. Refusing to appoint a new president of the ministerial council, he said that now he and he alone would chair its meetings; he would have to do more things himself, as he could not rely on anyone else.

For the next seven years, the Emperor ruled effectively without a prime minister. Next to him the most powerful figure was now Alexander Bach, minister of the interior, but he exercised less authority than Schwarzenberg. The Emperor had once told Windischgrätz that, now his name stood alone under all decrees, criticism of those measures was high treason. There spoke the autocrat, who was beginning to sound like a man prematurely aged by the responsibility of high office. The future German chancellor Otto von Bismarck noticed this, as well as the more relaxed side of his character which still sometimes showed through: 'the fire of the twenties, coupled with the dignity and foresight of riper years, a fine eye, especially when animated, and a winning openness of expression, especially when he laughs'.[12]

Throughout these years, Archduchess Sophie, the First Lady of the empire, was to a certain extent the power behind the throne – or at least the court. The Emperor's daily timetable was submitted to her for approval, and she dictated where and when meals were to be served, as well as such details as the imperial table guest list, or floral decorations for state and court balls during carnival time. She saw it as her business to take care of the trappings of royalty, such as coordinating the roles of functionaries like Grand Master of the Household, and Master of the Horse, to ensure that the Emperor rode in smartly refurbished carriages, with coachmen and postillions resplendent in their imperial livery. It was vital that the people of

Vienna should see the imperial house undertaking its rightful ceremonial functions. Her son's role was to be head of the government and head of the army, and it was her duty – as she saw it – to take the strain off him in making sure that the Habsburg image was properly maintained in public.

To Sophie, the revolution had been little short of an outrage. To the end of her days, she would recall the turbulent moments of 1848 with shame. One year after them she remarked that she could have borne the loss of one of her children 'more easily than the ignominy of submitting to a mess of students'.[13] Yet although a resolute conservative, efficient, methodical and painstaking, she was no puritanical killjoy, committing her son to an existence of unremitting toil. Court balls at which he and the rest of the Archdukes could relax and enjoy themselves were to be savoured to the full. The young Emperor worked hard, and played hard. He clearly relished such functions, as Baroness Scharnhorst, a contemporary observer at Vienna, would testify. 'The Emperor thoroughly enjoys dancing, and is an excellent performer,' she wrote to a friend.

> Without flattery, he is the best dancer and also the most in-defatigable. It is impossible to say where this will lead. The officers dance out of duty and inclination to the best of their abilities; the countesses swoon with delight when the Emperor singles them out. They rush there as though inspired by Oberon's horn, and drink in their luck with full draughts.[14]

Lady Westmoreland, wife of the British ambassador to Berlin, was also impressed by the young ruler. The Emperor, she remarked, was 'not handsome, but has a well-built, active figure and a most intelligent and expressive face', while his mother was 'a very interesting person, and is wrapped up in this son, who seems likely to justify the pride she takes in him'. Such approval did not extend to his father, 'a very poor creature, who cares for nothing but having his leisure unmolested'.[15]

There was always the risk of a potentially uncomfortable entanglement for such an eligible young bachelor. Any married woman who seemed to be getting too close to His Imperial Majesty was liable to be warned off. Countess Elizabeth Ugarte, a lady of twenty-nine and regular guest, wrote to a friend how she was

> greatly taken up with the Court balls, as I dance each time with our delicious Emperor. It created quite a sensation, as you may well believe, when I danced twice with him in the cotillion, and it flattered my vanity. I am charmed by our most delightful monarch, who combines in his person all the virtues one can think of. He is also agreeable in conversation, and improves each time one talks to him.[16]

If Francis Joseph found her amusing company, the Archduchess strongly disapproved. So did Baroness Scharnhorst, who sniffed that the Countess danced like a girl of eighteen, but 'lacks the talent to retain his affection', and she soon fell out of favour.

Yet it was time for Francis Joseph to look towards the perpetuation of the dynasty. At a time of war, or of uprisings and scattered military campaigns, an emperor's life could not be guaranteed. His visits to Hungary, Transylvania and Croatia, and other constituent parts of the empire, were all overshadowed by the threat of assassination. His life and that of his heir Max might have been lost during the storm they weathered on the Adriatic in 1852, and their third brother, Archduke Charles Ludwig, would have to be groomed for the throne in a hurry.

Archduchess Sophie knew how much her son needed a wife and children. It was important for the state, and also for him as a man. As he was old and serious beyond his years, the right companion and a family life of his own might soften him. He had probably had his initiation into earthly pleasures, like many archdukes before him, not through any explanation of 'the facts of life', but more through the experience of barrack life when attached to the Hussars. A little assistance was also doubtless forthcoming from his Chamberlain and aide-de-camp, Count Karl Grünne, who undertook to find a 'hygienically pure' countess to teach him what he needed to know. Grünne was an aristocratic cavalry officer who soon became Francis Joseph's most respected mentor and confidant. Apart from his mother and Schwarzenberg, few other individuals had a greater influence on the character of the young ruler, and some of his more reactionary views could be ascribed to Grünne's presence.

The first princess to be seen as a likely Empress of Austria was Elizabeth, widow of Ferdinand d'Este, Duke of Modena. A daughter of Archduke Joseph, Palatine of Hungary, she was five months younger than Francis Joseph, with a daughter aged two. In the spring of 1852 he appeared at a state ball in Hungarian Hussar's uniform and allowed the Czardas, the traditional Hungarian dance, to be danced at court at Vienna for the first time since the revolution. But the entrenched anti-Hungarian prejudices of Sophie and the court forestalled any serious romance, and two years later she was married to Archduke Charles's second son.

That autumn Francis Joseph visited Berlin. At the courts of both Austria and Prussia there was talk of a possible marriage with Anna, a niece of King Frederick William IV. It would have met with approval from the Austrian foreign minister, Count von Buol-Schauenstein, as a step towards easing Austro-Prussian relations. Anna was a staunch Lutheran, but this was not considered an impediment; her aunt had embraced the Orthodox Church in order to marry Tsar Nicholas I of Russia. But she was already betrothed to Frederick William, Landgrave of Hesse, whose wife Alexandra had died suddenly at the age of nineteen. Moreover, some of the Prussian conservatives looked askance on a marriage alliance with Austria, and the plan was soon dropped. Next Archduchess Sophie urged him to consider Princess Sidonia, a sister of his friend and cousin, Albert of Saxony. However, her health was poor, and she seemed low-spirited and lacking in character. Nevertheless, Francis Joseph was only twenty-two, and the matter did not yet seem urgent.

An alarming event early the following year put matters into a different perspective. On 18 February 1853 the Emperor was strolling around the old fortifications of Vienna, a casual break in routine which nearly proved his undoing. Janos Libényi, a 21-year-old tailor's apprentice, threw himself on the Emperor and stabbed him in the neck. The heavy golden covering embroidered on his collar deflected the blow, but left him bleeding profusely from a deep cut. A civilian passer-by came to his assistance while his military aide Count Maximilian O'Donnell seized Libényi and held the latter, who was shouting in Hungarian 'Long live Kossuth!' until police guards came.

The young Emperor's popularity rapidly soared, and the churches were full that evening as prayers of gratitude were offered up for the saving of his life. At first he made light of the attack, sending a message to his mother not to be too frightened as 'I was in no greater peril than my brave soldiers in Italy'.[17] But as Lord Westmoreland reported to Queen Victoria, 'this atrocious attempt' on his life had been serious.

> His escape is almost miraculous, for the knife was bent on the bone of the skull, having been aimed at the back of the neck, which would have been quite fatal. The wound bled very much, & for a little while he was blinded by the effects of the blow. He was able to walk home, but is being kept in bed as he has a little fever.[18]

Francis Joseph also suffered from delayed shock and loss of blood, and he and the doctors feared his sight might be affected. For three weeks he was confined to the Hofburg.

One of his first visitors was Max, who was so worried about his brother that he left his naval squadron at Trieste to return to Vienna and see him at once. From his sickbed the Emperor told him sternly that he had no right to leave his fleet without permission. In pain and frightened of going blind, he might have felt that his ambitious younger brother had his eye on the throne, should he himself not make a full recovery from his injuries. Max was sensitive and deeply hurt by this reaction, but magnanimously he launched an appeal for subscriptions to build a thanksgiving church next to the site of the attack.

The Emperor had begged the police not to handle Libényi too roughly on the spot, but when he was condemned to death he did not reprieve him, though on Archduchess Sophie's advice he granted a small pension to the man's mother. The would-be assassin, who was executed on 26 February, had belonged to a Hungarian regiment that had fought during the rebellion of five years earlier. His father had done likewise and gone to the gallows for his pains. On 12 March Francis Joseph drove in a carriage to St Stephen's Cathedral for a service of thanksgiving to celebrate his recovery, and crowds cheered him much of the way. Thereafter he resumed his full duties as Emperor, and in May he was host to King Leopold of the

Belgians on a visit to Vienna. The latter wrote afterwards (3 June 1853) to his niece, Queen Victoria, that he liked the Emperor:

> there is much sense and courage in his warm blue eye, and it is not without a very amiable merriment when there is occasion for it. He is slight and very graceful, but even in the *mêlée* of dancers and Archdukes, and all in uniform, he may always be distinguished as the *Chef* [most important figure].[19]

The attempt on Francis Joseph's life accentuated the none-too-friendly rivalry and differences with his brother Max, who had decided to become a naval officer. In the past the Habsburgs had paid little attention to the fleet, and Max did what he could to interest his elder brother in the service. The latter took a keen interest for a while in the Adriatic squadron until one night in March 1852, when the Emperor and his heir were caught in a violent storm on a voyage in the northern Adriatic aboard a steam-powered warship. The naval authorities were blamed for allowing both to go to sea at a time of such danger. Thereafter the navy was regarded as only a minor force, and not for another two years, when Max was appointed Commander-in-Chief, were any serious efforts made to modernise the imperial fleet.

Even so, Max was suspected of harbouring ambitions unbecoming in a younger brother, and the fact that he gave every impression of being their mother's favourite caused further problems. Francis Joseph suspected he might be using the navy to try and further his aspirations. With his enthusiasm for literature, painting and the arts, and his less military inclinations, Max was more popular with the Viennese than Francis Joseph. Even if he was the weaker character of the two, and something of a dreamer, he might prove a more popular Emperor if the occasion was to arise.

The attempt on her son's life intensified the Archduchess's resolve to see him married. In June she sent an invitation to her sister Ludovika, Duchess in Bavaria, to bring her two elder daughters to Ischl for a few days in August, so they could join in celebrations for the twenty-third birthday of their cousin. At nineteen Helene, known in the family as Nené, was just the right age for marriage.

On the afternoon of 16 August, Nené, the Duchess, and her second daughter Elizabeth (Sisi), took rooms at a hotel in Ischl, where they were joined by Archduchess Sophie, her elder sister Elizabeth, Queen of Prussia, and her sons, for tea.

What happened next was a prime example of how the best-laid plans can go terribly wrong. Nené was a mature, intelligent young woman who had been lightly groomed as the next Empress of Austria, and was well aware of her destiny. If she did not relish the prospect – and posterity has no way of telling what her opinions might have been on the matter – she, like her aunt Sophie before her, was evidently dutiful enough to go along with family expectations. However, face to face with the cousin whom she knew was supposed to become her husband, she became embarrassed and tongue-tied. All she could do was make strained small talk with Francis Joseph.

Elizabeth was quite unconcerned, had no such inhibitions and treated him as a friend. Her gaiety was self-evident, her conversation unforced, and her eyes sparkled. With a younger sister's sense of mischief, she probably found this little pantomime rather amusing. It was hardly surprising that she made a far more favourable impression on the young Emperor.

Another, perhaps less accurate version of this momentous family gathering says that when Francis Joseph dined with his Aunt Ludovika, only Helene was allowed to join them. Elizabeth, who he had not seen, was ordered to eat alone with her governess. When she was forbidden to leave the hotel afterwards there was a scene, and she was called into the room. Francis Joseph saw her for the first time, and was instantly smitten.[20]

Whatever the truth of this episode, which has inevitably been much retold and romanticised over the years, everyone involved except possibly Nené would long rue the day. At their first evening meal together, Francis Joseph could not take his eyes off Sisi. Charles Ludwig was said to have nursed hopes of eventually asking for the girl's hand in marriage. He seemed mildly jealous that his brother was about to deny him such a prize, and told his mother that Franzi was clearly enchanted with her. The Archduchess was dismissive, insisting that her eldest son knew better than to look twice at 'that little scamp'. Yet the besotted suitor lost no time in proving his mother wrong. When he saw Sophie before breakfast next morning, he could talk of nothing but Sisi's beauty. She told him gently that the younger of his cousins might be beautiful, but at fifteen she was far too young. Nené was the right age, was more intelligent, and would be far more suitable in every way.

Yet Francis Joseph would not be swayed. At the first ball in Ischl, he made his intentions clear by dancing with Sisi, and presenting her with the bouquets he had been expected to give to her tongue-tied sister. Elizabeth was flattered but embarrassed by his intentions. She knew that her sister was supposed to be the one chosen as an empress in waiting, and only now did it dawn on her that the plans had gone somewhat awry. From childhood she herself had been less well educated, thoroughly spoiled and indulged by her father.

Duke Max in Bavaria was no conventional prince. Though he was a general in the Bavarian army, his interests were less military than artistic. He enjoyed the company of circus performers and gipsies, spending his time in taverns where he sang songs usually of his own composition, accompanying himself on the zither. He and Ludovika had five daughters and four sons, though he was never the most faithful of husbands and sired several more children by various women. Ludovika sometimes lost patience with his infidelities, but proved an ever-forgiving wife. He was idolised by his children, all of whom became fine and fearless riders. As he was away from home so much they did not miss him greatly, and when a lady asked Sisi whether she had seen him on his return from one of these frequent absences, she replied, 'No, but I have heard him whistling!'[21] He took great pride in teaching his daughters deportment; they had to walk like angels with wings on their ankles.

Sisi was always his favourite; he was captivated by her attractive looks, her high spirits and the impulsive streak in her which so mirrored his personality. Like Max she was a romantic at heart, given to daydreaming, and wrote verses in her spare time. She was both fascinated and repelled by her apparent hold on her imperial cousin. When discussing the possibilities with her governess, it was said that she remarked sadly, 'If only he were not an Emperor!'[22]

Though Duchess Ludovika and Archduchess Sophie were both disappointed that their strategy had gone wrong, they were disinclined to do anything to discourage the match. It was, after all, close to the family alliance on which they had set their hearts.

Sophie considered her niece young and pliable enough to be eased into her role as a model empress and consort, and vowed that she would take her in hand. She watched the girl carefully on their family expeditions during the rest of the visit, and noted with concern the fact that she resented the presence of the Chamberlain, Count Grünne; her awkwardness and diffidence; and her response to the good wishes of the Court Mistress of the Robes, Countess Sophie Esterhazy-Liechtenstein, saying that she would 'need a great deal of indulgence at first' if the palace at Vienna was to be her ultimate destination. The one person who might have persuaded her to reconsider, her eccentric father, was away at the time. But he was too flattered by the prospect of being the Emperor's father-in-law, even if His Majesty had fallen for the wrong bride. He was asked for his consent by telegram and quickly answered in the affirmative.

One other royal matriarch was convinced that he might have chosen better if he had looked further afield than his Wittelsbach relatives. 'What say you to the Emperor of Austria's marriage?' Queen Victoria wrote to Leopold, King of the Belgians. 'I am so disappointed as I had hoped for dear Charlotte. Your prognostications – that the 4 Mighty Sisters – would not let him wait – but try to get *one* of their *own Princesses* for him – have come true!'[23] In fact 'dear Charlotte', the King's daughter and Queen Victoria's cousin, was also destined to become a Habsburg Empress consort by marrying Francis Joseph's brother Maximilian.

From then on, there could be no turning back. On Sunday 19 August, the family attended Mass in the parish church at Ischl. The building was packed to overflowing as the family arrived, and the national anthem struck up. At the end of the service the priest came down the altar steps to dismiss the congregation with his blessing. He was forestalled by Francis Joseph, who took Elizabeth by the hand and led her up to him, asking him to give them his blessing, as this was his future wife. As the couple left the church they were received with a torrent of flowers from well-wishers. Sisi grasped his hand nervously, her face a mask of confusion, as if unable to come to terms with the turn of events. That afternoon they went for a drive through the forests in the neighbourhood.

The next few days were probably the happiest they ever spent together. He was besotted with her, almost unable to believe his good luck, and while she might be fearful of the future, she seemed genuinely content and very much in love with him. Sophie had accepted the situation with good grace, though she could not resist telling her son that Sisi might be very pretty but she had yellow teeth.[24]

From this idyllic sojourn, Francis Joseph went back a little sadly to his desk at Vienna. He wrote to his mother that it had been hard, if not depressing, 'to take a leap from the earthly paradise of Ischl to this writing-table existence and masses of papers with all my cares and troubles'.[25] A crisis loomed, with Russia threatening to invade the Ottoman empire. He was reluctant to join Tsar Nicholas in a formal military alliance, as was his neighbouring sovereign, King Frederick William IV of Prussia, even though all three came together for what turned out to be a rather unproductive meeting at Warsaw.

As soon as he could get away, he returned to Bavaria to see his future bride at Schloss Possenhofen, her family home on the Starnbergersee. He planned to go with her family to Munich and pay his respects to another cousin, Maximilian II, King of Bavaria. Possenhofen was fairly private, and they could spend much of their time riding together. He discovered what a fine and fearless horsewoman his wife-to-be was. Less welcome was the first sight of her reaction to the formalities which would surround her in her new life. At Munich she was required to receive the diplomatic corps, members of whom had come to congratulate her on her forthcoming marriage, and she did so with great reluctance, unhappy at being the centre of attention. She was overwhelmed by shyness when she and the Emperor had to enter their box at the opera house.

Though Francis Joseph remained clearly smitten by her, he found the informality and casual way of life at Possenhofen an astonishing contrast to what he had been brought up with at Vienna. Once he had returned to his capital, he became every inch the Emperor again. He was such a stickler for doing everything the correct way that he wanted to send a formal demand to the court at Munich for the hand of HRH the Princess Elizabeth, and had to be persuaded by his minister in Munich that it was not necessary.

The months leading up to the wedding found Francis Joseph increasingly preoccupied with a crisis in European affairs. In June 1853 Tsar Nicholas had marched into the Balkan principalities of

Moldavia and Wallachia, then part of the Turkish empire, and Turkey declared war on Russia. Anxious to keep the Russians from Constantinople, England and France did likewise six months later. Prussia remained neutral, but Austria played an indecisive hand which would cost it dearly in the long term. The government was subjected to considerable diplomatic pressure on both sides, and while the Emperor was anxious to safeguard commercial and strategic interests on the Danube, he had no intention of committing the empire to a potentially crippling war. He was torn between Count Buol, who intended that Austria should stay clear of the conflict, at least until intervention would be decisive and victory assured, and the pro-Russian element in the military who saw the virtues of siding with Russian autocracy as a bulwark against liberalism in the empire. In the end he backed Buol, while agreeing to partial mobilisation against Russia and permitting the stationing of troops along the empire's eastern frontiers. In April 1854 an offensive and defensive alliance between Austria and Prussia, with the aim of containing and helping to localise the Crimean war, was concluded in Berlin.

Meanwhile, in December the Emperor was back in Munich to join the family as they celebrated Elizabeth's sixteenth birthday, which fell on Christmas Eve. On that day the young couple exchanged portraits of each other on horseback, and when they gathered round the Christmas tree he gave her a bouquet of magnificent flowers which had arrived by courtier from the conservatories at Schönbrunn barely half an hour earlier, and a green parrot from the palace menagerie. Among her other presents was a garland of roses sent by the Archduchess.

During the next few weeks there were various formalities to be settled. Sisi was related to her husband-to-be in the second degree on the maternal side, and in the fourth degree on the paternal side. As these ties of consanguinity formed an impediment in canon law, and the former in civil law as well, a dispensation from the Pope was required, and easily obtained. As part of the marriage settlement, Sisi was granted a dowry of 50,000 gulden (florins) by her father, to which the Emperor promised to add a sum of 100,000 gulden, supplemented by a *Morgengabe* of 12,000 ducats, in accordance with an ancient custom by which the bridegroom was obliged to offer his wife as a gift on the morning after their nuptial night, in compensation for the loss of her virginity. He also presented her with an allowance of 100,000 gulden per annum for her unrestricted personal use, to cover such expenses as clothing, charities and unspecified minor expenses. All other expenses would be his responsibility.[26] Finally, the King of Bavaria was required to make a solemn declaration that no obstacles to the Princess's marriage existed.

In March 1854 Francis Joseph was back in Bavaria to present Elizabeth with the tiara, necklace and earrings of diamonds and opals which the Archduchess had worn at her own wedding, and which she wished her future daughter-in-law to wear. The bride was bewitched by these magnificent gifts, which equalled in value all the rest of her jewels and ornaments put together. However, there was a sting in the tail, for at the same time Francis Joseph mentioned to her that his mother had been a little shocked at being addressed as 'thou' in Sisi's last letter. He told her firmly that this must not be done; even he wrote to his mother as 'you', out of the respect and veneration due to an older woman.[27] Already it was clear that Elizabeth's future life would be full of archaic formalities and petty reprimands.

The following month Elizabeth arrived in a Vienna sparkling with festivities for the wedding. Many of the streets and squares were decorated with flags and flowers, ready to be illuminated on the eve of the wedding and the day itself, and church charities were given 200,000 florins. The Magyar nobility were invited to send delegations to the marriage ceremony and receptions, wearing what the disapproving Archduchess Sophie called 'fancy dress costumes', while the Emperor-bridegroom granted an amnesty for nearly 400 political offenders and promised that, from the start of the next month, martial law would be lifted in Lombardy-Venetia. It had been arranged for Elizabeth to come down the Danube aboard a paddle-steamer, named after the Emperor. He would welcome her to Austrian soil at Linz on the evening of 21 April, and return to Vienna in time to greet her on Saturday afternoon at an ornate landing stage erected for the occasion on the quayside at Nussdorf. At the latter, the boat took half an hour to moor because of an unexpectedly strong current in the Danube. As soon as the landing bridge touched the vessel, Francis Joseph ran eagerly on board and, in the presence of an enthusiastic crowd, he tenderly embraced and kissed his bride, then escorted her to the carriage in which she drove with the Archduchess to Schönbrunn. *The Times* correspondent noted that she 'smiled and bowed to her future subjects as if every face on which her eye rested belonged to an old and valued friend'.[28]

At the palace, Elizabeth found that all her staff had been chosen for her by Archduchess Sophie. While this was hardly unusual for a royal bride, it was an unwelcome reminder that her life would no longer be her own. Countess Esterhazy-Liechtenstein, who was to be her chief lady-in-waiting, wasted no time in handing Elizabeth a large document on ceremonial procedure for the official progress of 'Her Royal Highness, the Most Gracious Princess Elizabeth', which had to be studied that evening.

Next morning bride and groom were taken to the Theresianum, the old castle from which Habsburg brides emerged for their first ride through the city. From here they made their grand entry into Vienna, taking two hours to cover the densely packed route of just under two miles to St Stephen's Cathedral.

The wedding took place at four in the afternoon on Monday 24 April, in the Augustinerkirche, the fourteenth-century court church in the shadow of the Hofburg. It took nearly an hour for the glittering procession to pass through the palace corridors and courtyards, and down the street leading to the church. About 1,000 people were present in the building where several thousand candles gleamed on the embroidered vestments of the prelates, the collars of the Knights of the Golden Fleece and the jewel-encrusted costumes of the Hungarian magnates. Escorted by her mother and mother-in-law, Elizabeth looked pale and nervous. Her face was unveiled and her wedding dress of white and silver, strewn with myrtle blossom, was surmounted by her opal and diamond crown.

As the bride was led up the aisle, the Emperor, attired in the uniform of a field marshal, gave his bride the tenderest of adoring looks. At the altar she turned shyly towards her mother before whispering her vows almost inaudibly, in contrast to Francis Joseph's bold confident response. As they exchanged rings, saluting cannon on the Augustinerbastion fired the first salvoes to join the pealing church bells in letting the people of Vienna know that Austria had a new Empress.

Officiating at the ceremony was the Emperor's old tutor and the Archduchess's spiritual adviser, Joseph Othmar von Rauscher, Cardinal-Prince Archbishop of Vienna, known behind his back as 'Cardinal Plauscher' (loquacious). He delivered a lengthy address on the virtues of family life, informing the bride loftily that among other things she would be to her husband 'an Island of refuge amid the raging billows, an Island where roses and violets grow'.[29] It was noticed that by now the bride looked bored and weary as she turned towards the groom, better schooled than her in the art of enduring such tedium in the name of imperial duty.

After the ceremony there was a 50-yard procession down the carpeted street to the Hofburg, where for two hours the Emperor and Empress had to receive the loyal homage of their guests: princes and princesses, dukes and duchesses, the old aristocracy and the new and the veteran commanders, Radetzky, Windischgrätz and Count Jellacic. Between 10 and 11 p.m. the family were served with dinner, but Elizabeth had little appetite. Until now she had seen Habsburg court life only when she had been on family holidays in Ischl, and the reality of what she had just encountered in Vienna astonished her.

One traditional part of the ceremony remained. Sophie and Ludovika escorted the bride to her room, where the former left them and waited in the anteroom, next to the great chamber with the marriage bed. Sophie then fetched her son and led him to his bride, to wish them a good night, in more sense than one. 'She hid her natural loveliness,' Sophie wrote in her journal, 'for only a wealth of beautiful free-flowing hair buried in her bolster caught my eye, like a frightened bird lying low in its nest.'[30] She saw nothing intrusive in observing such intimate details, and gave Elizabeth's shy discomfiture not a second thought. Such modesty was only to be expected of an innocent young bride on her wedding night. That the high-spirited young girl from Bavaria might have fiercely resented the embarrassment, the lack of privacy on their wedding night and at breakfast with her husband in the mornings, and the lack of any honeymoon, counted for little. There was to be no escape from time-honoured Habsburg protocol, least of all from a young Emperor who clearly lived his life according to his mother's instructions. Though both her father and father-in-law were present at the ceremonies in Vienna, they were apparently content to let their wives take control.

Yet in one way, if her mother-in-law's journal is to be believed, Elizabeth stood her ground. Not for another two nights was the marriage consummated. On the morning of 27 April, the Archduchess recorded in her journal that after the young Empress excused herself from the communal breakfast, the Emperor came to see her in private, and assured her that 'Sisi had fulfilled his love'.[31]

Though international affairs precluded any chance of a honeymoon, on 29 April Francis Joseph took Elizabeth to the Prater to see a command performance by the Circus Renz. She had often heard her father mention the showman Ernst Renz with great respect, and now father and daughter alike were enthralled by the displays of horsemanship, fireworks, and balloons released into the night sky. The proceedings, she said, were 'too lovely for words', and that she really must get to know Renz. On learning of her daughter-in-law's enthusiasm, her mother-in-law was not amused.

Next morning Elizabeth's parents and sister left Vienna to return to Bavaria. Too honest to conceal his feelings, her father told her that he could not take any more of the court etiquette at Vienna; in future she would have to come and visit him at Possenhofen. Her mother was similarly relieved to be going back home, and while her heart went out to her sister, Nené was obviously glad to have escaped such a destiny. Francis Joseph saw that his bride was close to physical and nervous collapse, and that afternoon he decided that it was time for them both to take a short break from their formal residence in the capital.

According to the timetable there were still some ceremonies and receptions for them to attend, but he braved Sophie's disapproval and cancelled them. Instead he took himself and Elizabeth fifteen miles out into the country at Laxenburg to stay for a while. From here he travelled every morning into the Hofburg, returning to his wife each evening. Sisi, he warned his mother, was overtired. Though he knew better than to tell her, he realised that the combination of a week's festivities, formality and life at the Hofburg had grated on his wife.

Significantly, as soon as husband and wife were at the more picturesque Laxenburg, with its grotto and Gothic bridge and the small wooded lake dotted with artificial islands, she seemed herself again. It might be just another Habsburg palace, a summer home on a smaller scale than the Hofburg, with the same dreary formality, but had the benefits of a more attractive setting. After more than a week of life in Vienna, she could get on horseback and be herself once more. Sparing no effort to try and make her feel at home, the Emperor had had her dogs and parrots from Possenhofen brought to keep her company, and ensured that the finest horses from the imperial stable were hers to ride.

Even so, after a couple of weeks, Laxenburg began to pall. She missed her husband, who left for Vienna before she was awake and did not return until dinner at 6 p.m. Apart from her beloved animals, the only company she had were the courtiers and palace ladies, all much older than her. She was still very naive and shy, taking refuge in keeping her distance, yet still too ready to express her own opinions which would find their way to the Archduchess and be repeated against her. Sophie was in some ways the stereotype of a mother-in-law, constantly nagging at her daughter-in-law and eager to correct her in almost everything.

Yet she was not the monster that Elizabeth and her defenders later made her out to be. According to Elizabeth's biographer Conte Egon Caesar Corti, the Archduchess 'with her vigorous and uncompromising personality, was in the habit of crushing the individuality of everybody about her'.[32] This verdict is a little un-gracious. At heart Archduchess Sophie was a generous woman who knew that sometimes one had to be cruel to be kind. Though she may have been tactless and indiscreet, this was often the way of royal matriarchs. She had grown up in a hard school with a nonentity of a husband far less clever than her, devoting herself to her four sons and their ambitions for the future, particularly that of her eldest. The girl whom she had made into an Empress – notwithstanding the fact that her elder sister had originally been selected for the honour – needed to be schooled in her role, and the Archduchess saw it as nothing less than a sacred duty to guide her through these first testing years.

Elizabeth, the obstinate rebel, was too young to see that all this was being done for her own good. She was like a stubborn child who never really matured. She was very much her father's child, a wayward headstrong girl who resented following rules and conforming to the expectations of what everyone else wanted her to be. When she was involved in something which really interested her, like visiting Hungary or riding her horses, her enthusiasm and gaiety were obvious. If asked to do anything she disliked, she withdrew into herself and acceded reluctantly or else made herself scarce.

Her husband was the Emperor of Austria, and could evidently do as he liked, though he always put duty before pleasure. She could play the autocrat; when possible she too could, and would, do as she pleased. It was her good fortune that she had found such a compliant, indulgent husband. It was his misfortune that he had chosen a most wilful, self-obsessed wife.

THREE

'A Firmness of Purpose'

Emperor Francis Joseph was required to be a perfect husband, a dutiful son, and a masterful Emperor at a time of serious international tension. It would have taken a remarkable human being to have accomplished all three, and posterity can easily forgive him for having been less than successful in each role.

Throughout other European courts, excellent reports of the young couple and their marriage were circulated. Five days after the wedding, Queen Victoria

> received an interesting & charming account . . . of the reception & marriage of the young Empress Elizabeth. The young Emperor looked so happy, for he is much in love & adores his pretty & very pleasing young Bride of 16! May God bless them. I am sure the poor young man requires to be happy.[1]

A month later the Queen's brother-in-law the Duke of Saxe-Coburg was in Vienna, and thought the sovereign's nuptials had rejuvenated him; he found

> a great change for the better in the Emperor, since I saw him last; he has become much stronger, more free and definite in his movements. Despite the dark outlook and the political frost, one felt a sort of joyful excitement about the bright young monarch: his domestic happiness seemed to have had a most happy effect on his temper.[2]

Nevertheless, the couple's domestic happiness would not last for long. The Emperor was a kindly man if not perhaps an especially perceptive one, but severely torn between conflicting loyalties. The Archduchess continued to advise him on matters concerning the

40

Austrian empire and government, as well as on domestic affairs. These were undoubtedly concerns which she considered beyond her daughter-in-law's comprehension and interest. Had the Emperor taken his wife – who was also now Empress, albeit an inexperienced and immature one – more into his confidence, it would have flattered her and also done wonders for marital harmony. It would also have boded better for them had they not been surrounded by individuals such as Elizabeth's particular *bête noire*, Count Grünne, who owed his position entirely to the Archduchess. The Empress felt he was a spy reporting every little detail of gossip back to her mother-in-law.

As she became older, the Archduchess's dignity turned into haughtiness. Having been brought up to believe that class distinctions were everything, she could not unbend sufficiently to shake hands with a coachman. She probably envied, as well as despised, the way in which Elizabeth could effortlessly banter with her riding master. To her, the young girl's impulsiveness and spontaneity were tiresome if not offensive to her sense of time-honoured Habsburg etiquette. For her part, Elizabeth resented the lack of privacy anywhere in the Hofburg, and was disgusted to discover that her ladies-in-waiting had to use a toilet hidden behind a screen in a passage guarded by male sentries. A request that something might be done about this was apparently met by a retort from the Archduchess that her daughter-in-law evidently thought she was still in the Bavarian mountains.

Although expected to eat heartily every day, Elizabeth was content with little, preferring a simple intake of white bread, broth and fruit at the official banquets. Her husband likewise thrived on a fairly spartan but regular diet, and retained his slim figure. His wife dreaded becoming fat, weighed herself every day, and subjected herself to a punishing regime of exercise and dieting. Her main indulgence was a passion for iced fruit, but she also enjoyed drinking beer, and smoking cigarettes or cigars, despite (or perhaps partly because of) the Archduchess's disapproval in an age when ladies were not expected to smoke. At her first state dinner, contrary to custom, she removed her gloves. An elderly court lady quietly reproved her, and when she asked why she should not do so, she was told it was a deviation from the rules. 'Then let the deviation henceforth be the rule,'[3] she retorted.

Meanwhile, the Emperor was distracted by the worsening relationship with Russia. Some of the Viennese aristocracy and military were convinced that in the coming conflict in the Crimea, Austria should intervene on the side of Russia out of gratitude for Tsar Nicholas's part in helping to put down the Hungarian insurrection in 1849. Most of the ministers considered that it was time they called a halt to the over-mighty Tsar's ambitions. They believed that an alliance with the western powers would probably safeguard Austria's Italian provinces and also help to strengthen its position in the German confederation against the increasingly ambitious Prussia. Torn between both, the Emperor believed that the most pragmatic solution was neutrality. It was a decision for which the Tsar never forgave him.

Peter von Meyendorff, Russian ambassador in Vienna, blamed Francis Joseph for the decision. Just before the final breach between both emperors, he wrote to the Russian chancellor, Count Karl Nesselrode, suggesting the only possible explanation of the Austrian monarch's behaviour was that he had made it a rule to take nobody's advice and listen to nobody. There seemed, he said, 'to be a curse from heaven on this Habsburg race. The only one among them who has the stuff in him to make a ruler is blinded by his self-will and the foolish assumption that he can judge and decide everything entirely by himself.'[4]

Though less critical, Lord Westmoreland also saw danger in the sovereign's virtues. He spoke in glowing yet slightly guarded terms on the subject to Queen Victoria, who noted in her journal after an audience with him in July of Francis Joseph's

> great straightforwardness & honesty, which perhaps had been carried a little too far, as he would not do anything for the sake of popularity. No one influences him, he thinks. The Emperor's devotion & attention to his mother are great, but he does not allow her to interfere in politics. He is wrapt up in his young wife.[5]

In June 1854, about six weeks after their wedding, the Emperor and Empress paid a state visit to Bohemia and Moravia. Away from the tedium of court life and the Archduchess's constant supervision, Elizabeth became much more her old self. She was fascinated by the people and picturesque landscape of Bohemia, and instantly made to feel at home in Prague, where the kindly former Emperor Ferdinand and Empress Anna Maria treated her like the daughter they never had. Francis Joseph was delighted to see how she revelled in some of her ceremonial duties as Empress, visiting churches and convents, almshouses, hospitals and orphanages. Her approachable demeanour and simple manner struck a chord with those she met, and everyone was full of praise for her. These few weeks were almost like a belated honeymoon for husband and wife.

Soon after their return, the Emperor went on manoeuvres to Galicia, while the Empress remained behind at Laxenburg. The court physician, Dr Johann Seeburger, was summoned to examine her, and informed the family that she was with child. The Archduchess was thrilled at the prospect of being a grandmother. She intended to watch over her daughter-in-law, for the birth of an heir – as everyone hoped it would be – would mean endless attention and a total lack of the privacy which the young expectant mother craved. Sisi, Sophie wrote to her son, should pay less attention to her parrots; if a woman looked too much at animals in her first months of pregnancy, the children would probably grow up to resemble them. 'She had far better look at herself in her looking-glass, or at you. *That* would have my entire approval.'[6]

On 5 March 1855 Elizabeth gave birth to a daughter. The infant was baptised with all due pomp and ceremony, and without any consultation with her mother she was named Sophie. Representatives of every European power except Russia appeared at the baptismal feast. Archduchess Sophie had chosen the nursery staff, including the wet nurse and cook. The baby's quarters were set up next to her own rooms in the Hofburg, and whenever Elizabeth wanted to see her firstborn, she had to climb a long staircase; when she reached the nursery, her mother-in-law was usually present.

As a result Elizabeth's resentment of Sophie's interference hardened. She was not maternal by nature, and resented the inconvenience of pregnancy, to say nothing of what she feared it would do to her beauty. Having given birth, her main priority was getting back on to her horses. Yet it was only natural that she wanted some time with the child herself, without having to endure such inconvenience.

43

Francis Joseph was delighted at being a father. He did not in the least mind his first child being a daughter, though Elizabeth realised with resignation that she would be expected to give him a son before long.

Yet he had other things on his mind besides fatherhood. After the allied landings in the Crimea in 1854 he signed a treaty of alliance with the western powers, so vaguely worded that it gave him ample opportunity to evade any obligations. By doing so he alienated his uncle and hitherto firmest ally, King Frederick William IV of Prussia, and forfeited for Austria the allegiance of the Confederated German States, as most of the kings and grand dukes were related by marriage to the Tsar. Though refusing to commit Austrian forces to war, his policy and apparent display of ingratitude deeply angered Tsar Nicholas. In March 1855, shortly before Sophie's birth, the Tsar died after a short illness, or as contemporaries said, a broken heart at his empire's reverses in the conflict. Despite ordering four weeks of court mourning and sending a letter of condolence to his successor, Tsar Alexander II, Francis Joseph received a withering answer. Alexander told him bitterly that his father had loved the Emperor like his own son, only to see him 'follow a political course which brought you ever closer to our enemies and which will still bring us inevitably, if that course does not change, to a fratricidal war, for which you will be accountable to God'.[7]

Other contemporaries spoke or wrote more benignly. It was at around this time that Lord John Russell wrote from Vienna to Lord Clarendon, praising the Emperor's manner as 'singularly agreeable', and his countenance 'open and prepossessing'. While the sovereign might not be 'one of those men who at once prove themselves qualified to hold the rudder, and guide the ship through a dangerous navigation, he seems to show an intelligence and a firmness of purpose which may enable him to rule this great Empire with ability and success'.[8] He could hardly foresee that in the sphere of foreign policy, Francis Joseph's limited abilities were to bring him scant success.

When her husband left on a tour of military inspection in Galicia that summer, Elizabeth wept bitterly at his departure. Anxious that she might be lonely, he allowed her to visit her family at home in Bavaria. The Archduchess disapproved, saying she should stay in Vienna to represent the court during her husband's absence. Yet Elizabeth was keen to return to Possenhofen, albeit briefly, and when the Archduchess insisted she leave baby Sophie behind, the mother offered no resistance. On her return to the Hofburg, she found her infant did not seem to recognise her, and that the nurses and doctors were taking orders only from the Archduchess. To add to her gloom, shortly afterwards she found that she was pregnant again. On 15 July 1856 she had another daughter, whom they named Gisela.

The little Archduchess's birth was a disappointment to family and Austrian empire alike. Should the Empress continue to have only daughters, the succession would then pass to the Emperor's brothers and any male descendants they might have, and the Archduchess redoubled her efforts to help find wives for her other sons. On his first voyage abroad Max had fallen deeply in love with Princess Amalia Maria of Brazil, who could claim the Wittelsbachs and Empress Josephine among her ancestors. Unhappily she was not robust, and soon afterwards died from consumption.

Saddened but undaunted, Sophie urged that her son should visit Brussels and make the acquaintance of King Leopold's pretty daughter Charlotte, whom her cousin Queen Victoria had once seen as a possible Empress of Austria. Meanwhile, Charles Ludwig was betrothed to one of his cousins, Princess Margaretha, daughter of Sophie's sister Queen Amalia of Saxony, and they married in Dresden in November 1856. That left the youngest brother Ludwig Victor, a spoilt and indulged boy of fourteen who was still thought too young to be interested in girls. It was a state of affairs which, his detractors maintained rather unfairly, would not change throughout a life of seventy-seven years. Despite a tendency to indulge in cross-dressing, to which a few photographs still in existence testify, and involvement in one or two homosexual scandals, he also had passing affairs with women, though none would lead to matrimony.

Elizabeth insisted that her children were to be moved to rooms adjacent to hers, her anxiety exacerbated by the fact that Sophie was a sickly baby, and the Emperor supported her. The Archduchess reacted bitterly, declaring that Elizabeth was more interested in her horses than her children, and unfit to be in charge of them or their education. Declaring that she was no longer wanted, Elizabeth threatened to leave the Hofburg altogether. Harassed almost beyond endurance by trying to mediate between wife and mother, the

Emperor wrote firmly to the latter, deploring her habit of having the girls more or less confined to their own rooms and brought out to show off to visitors like display pieces instead of normal children. He also begged her to be a little more indulgent with and understanding of Sisi, who for all her faults was a devoted wife and mother.

Soon the time came for Emperor and Empress to pay a visit to Italy. Francis Joseph was determined not to cede any of his territories in Lombardy-Venetia, while Italian nationalists aspired to a united country. A visit to the Provinces could only improve Habsburg standing there, especially if the people saw and fell for the charms of their beautiful Empress. Elizabeth saw it as a chance to travel somewhere new, and as an escape from a depressing winter in the Hofburg. She insisted on taking little Sophie, to benefit from the milder Italian climate. In vain did the Archduchess protest that Italy was more an armed camp than a health resort, and not the place for a delicate child.

Elizabeth had her way, and they reached Italy in November 1856. Overall the progress was a brave but foolhardy gesture. In Venice, the streets and squares were packed with crowds who came to gaze at them, almost in silence. When they visited the towns, they found the peasantry and most of the citizens friendly enough, but the upper and middle classes were distinctly hostile. At a reception things looked ominous when several leading Venetian families suddenly found that they had important engagements elsewhere, and only 30 of the 150 patrician families invited actually appeared. However, the Emperor and Empress went through with their programme, Elizabeth making a particular effort to be gracious to all. Five days after their arrival, at her suggestion, the Emperor issued an amnesty for a number of political prisoners. Almost at once, when the news broke, there was a marked improvement in the people's attitude towards them, and they were greeted with applause in the streets.

Matters went less smoothly at Brescia, where the brutality of Haynau was still a recent memory, and they were received in icy silence. Francis Joseph was unable to conceal his distress, and Elizabeth could barely hold back her tears as her heart went out to him in their shared ordeal. On going to the equally hostile Milan, they won plaudits from other crowned heads. King Leopold considered he had 'acted wisely', and thought that 'his presence at Milan has produced a good effect'.[9] Nevertheless, again the people obstinately refused to cheer them. A gala performance at the opera house was to be attended by members of aristocratic families, who promised to come, then instead sent their servants to show up, wearing red or black gloves as a sign of mourning. The Emperor's amnesty for political prisoners failed to create a good impression, and it was said that the Empress had only brought their infant daughter along with them to shield them from possible assassination attempts.

Soon after this episode, Francis Joseph decided to replace military dictatorship with benevolent civilian rule. Maximilian was appointed governor of Lombardy-Venetia, but his best liberal intentions were not enough for the patriots who declared that they did not want the Austrians to become humanitarian; they wanted them out.

Meanwhile, the ministers decided to send Francis Joseph and Elizabeth on a visit to Hungary, and despite Archduchess Sophie's misgivings, baby Gisela joined them, with Dr Seeburger among their suite. They arrived at Buda via the Danube on 4 May 1857. Elizabeth was immediately entranced by Magyar life, and captivated by the picturesque aura of Budapest, where they were given an enthusiastic reception.

However, at Budapest Gisela fell ill. She was a robust child and soon recovered, but within a week the more delicate Sophie also became unwell. Seeburger tried to explain her troubles away by saying they were caused by teething, but when the child began to vomit blood and bile, it was clear that she had something more serious, possibly typhoid or measles. When the parents reached Debreczin on 28 May, he sent a telegram recommending their return as soon as possible. Her condition had deteriorated, and they hurried back anxiously to the palace at Budapest, but it was too late. Elizabeth could only sit by the bedside of her helpless elder child, aged two years and two months yet fading fast before their very eyes, while a crestfallen Seeburger was unable to answer her questions and could only say that he had not yet given up hope. That evening Sophie's struggles were over. Sadly, the Emperor telegraphed to his parents that 'our little one is an angel in Heaven', and that Sisi was 'full of resignation to the will of the Lord'.[10]

His words were far from the truth, for Elizabeth was in utter despair. For twenty-four hours after her daughter's death she insisted on staying next to the body, until she fainted from fatigue. She blamed herself for having brought her to Hungary, and took a sudden violent aversion to Seeburger, against whom nothing could be said except that he had been the bearer of bad tidings to the soon-to-be-bereaved mother. The Emperor refused to dismiss him, telling her that the doctor had done his best, and there was no reason why she should not remain under his care.

Elizabeth dreaded returning to Vienna and coming face to face with her mother-in-law, but to her relief, the Archduchess showed remarkable tact and uttered not one word of reproach. She too had been devastated at the loss of the child, and as she had been through similar bereavement as a young mother herself, was full of sympathy towards them. Little Sophie was buried in the Habsburg crypt in the church of the Capucines. Every day that summer the Empress drove from Laxenburg in a closed carriage with the blinds drawn down, then went to the crypt to weep and pray by the tomb. Back at the palace she spent hours crying alone in her room, or going for solitary walks or rides, only allowing grooms and detectives to follow her at a distance.

In August an end had to be brought to court mourning. Max and Charlotte had been married in Brussels on 27 July, the bride looking radiant in her wedding dress and the groom dashing in the uniform of an Austrian admiral, with the Order of the Golden Fleece around his neck. They returned to a warm welcome in Vienna, the Archduchess delighted with her new daughter-in-law whom she found charming as well as pretty. She could easily have been forgiven for thinking that this new bride, once thought to have been a suitable wife for Francis Joseph, might still be the saviour of the Habsburg succession after all. If the Empress failed to bear a male heir, she probably would. Elizabeth made only the most perfunctory appearance at the festivities laid on to greet them, and overcome by further grief, returned to her room in tears as soon as she conveniently could.

The Emperor returned to Hungary later that summer to complete the tour, but Elizabeth was clearly in no state to accompany him, and remained behind to continue mourning her daughter. Once her husband had gone, she refused to eat, and even talked of taking her own life. Certain people at court, she was convinced, were blaming her for her daughter's death.

At length Francis Joseph was so alarmed at the reports of his wife that he wrote in despair to Archduchess Sophie, asking that Elizabeth's mother and sisters should be allowed to visit in order to help lift her spirits. Ludovika, Nené and Marie were invited and descended on her in Vienna. The sisters were now betrothed, the former to Maximilian, hereditary Prince of Thurn and Taxis, the latter to Francis, Duke of Calabria, heir to the kingdom of Naples and the Two Sicilies. They helped to cheer Elizabeth, who was now determined to confound those at court who had given up on her, and produce an heir.

Early in the new year her third pregnancy was confirmed. On the afternoon of 21 August, she went into labour. Unlike the previous two occasions, it was a long and painful confinement, and courtiers in the adjoining rooms could hear her screaming in agony. Just before midnight, the Emperor was given the good news that he was the father of a son. Weak and exhausted, Elizabeth was sure it must be another girl, and would not believe them when they told her, until she was allowed to see her baby son. The little Archduke, born Crown Prince of Austria, was christened Rudolf, after the first Rudolf of Habsburg. Francis Joseph did not think him very good-looking, but 'magnificently built and very strong'.[11]

Unhappily, the arrival was overshadowed by tragedy within a month. On 15 September, Charles Ludwig became a widower when his wife of less than two years, Margaretha of Saxony, succumbed to fever, aged eighteen, while on a visit to Monza.

Austria's half-hearted neutrality during the Crimean war had gained it no friends in Europe, and it came away from the peace conference at Paris in March 1856 empty-handed and isolated. Francis Joseph had succeeded in offending Turkey, France and England as he had not joined their alliance, while Russia had been angered at large numbers of its troops being pinned down along the Danube. This isolation would lead to a grave defeat three years later, and it would not be the last.

In July 1858 Count Cavour, prime minister of Piedmont, heavily disguised with a false beard and false passport, met Napoleon III at Plombières, and between them they reached a secret agreement that France would come to the aid of Piedmont if the latter was attacked by Austria. The main condition was that neither France nor Piedmont should appear to be the aggressor. A campaign in the press, and a little fermenting of revolutionary elements against the unpopular Habsburg despots, would surely provoke the Austrians into retaliation. In return for French aid, Napoleon would be allowed influence in certain Italian territories, with Nice and Savoy being ceded to France.

Events soon played into their hands. Emperor Francis Joseph was much under the influence of the war party headed by Count Grünne and the foreign minister Count Buol. They persuaded him that Austria needed to retain her sovereignty in Italy, the army had to be strengthened, and General Francis Gyulai was entrusted with the supreme command. Max's appointment as governor-general of Lombardy-Venetia soon proved to be a crown of thorns. The Archduke was seen as too much of a liberal, while Francis Joseph was jealous of his brother and distrusted him, thinking him too much under the sway of his wife Charlotte and his ambitious yet far-seeing father-in-law King Leopold. Max's anxious letters to Francis Joseph, warning him in April 1858 that the Italian territories had 'just cause for complaint', and that 'a just, sage and wherever possible mild treatment is to be recommended'[12] were disregarded. An even more urgent letter the following January, holding out the hope that 'If we don't provoke and show determination without fear, then we will perhaps be able to solve the present catastrophic crisis'[13] also went unheeded.

Emperor and ministers were convinced that the small state of Piedmont would never dare to take up arms against Austria, or that Napoleon – whose secret agreement had at last been rumbled by Austrian diplomats – would honour his word. Russia proposed that differences should be arbitrated by a conference to which all the European powers would be invited, a rallying call which Queen Victoria in England readily endorsed. In February she wrote a long letter of appeal to the Emperor, which was handed to him by Lord Cowley. Having considered the circumstances which appeared to threaten the peace in Europe, she wrote, she could find

> nothing which a prudent diplomacy might not surmount, if the principal parties interested are animated by the mutual desire of facilitating its action. The present state of Italy is that which constitutes the real danger; but even this danger would not be

such that general tranquillity ought to be menaced, if there existed no antagonism executed by the real or supposed interests & engagements of Austria & France.

As a 'mutual friend of both Sovereigns and as having fortunately no personal interest', Victoria agreed to offer her 'good offices & perhaps open amicable negotiations relative to the questions now threatening'.[14]

At the suggestion of Buol, Francis Joseph insisted that Piedmont – which had taken up a position of 'permanent aggression' against the empire – would have to disarm before Austria would participate, and on 23 April he sent an ultimatum to Cavour. When the Emperor discussed it with the elderly Metternich, the latter insisted 'above all, no ultimatum' – only to be told it had been sent the day before.

The war was swift and inglorious. On 4 June the Austrian army, commanded by Gyulai, superior in numbers and equipment, met and attacked the French near the town of Magenta. After an indecisive battle during which they suffered over 10,000 casualties the Austrian forces retreated and conceded victory to their foes. Gyulai was relieved of his command and the Emperor hurried to the front in order to take command personally. When he told Elizabeth of his intentions she burst into tears, fearing she might never see him again. To assuage her loneliness she took to spending most of the day on horseback, unable to settle to more sedentary pursuits indoors. Dr Seeburger, with whom her relations had never recovered after the death of her firstborn, complained that she was unfit for her position as Empress and wife, 'and though she grieves and weeps over the noble Emperor's absence, she goes out riding for hours on end, ruining her health'.[15] She begged her husband to let her join him at his headquarters, but in his reply he said that much as he would love to have her company again, women would be out of place in such an environment, and he could not set his men a bad example. He begged her not to grieve so much for him, 'but to take care of yourself; try to find plenty of distractions, go for rides and drives in moderation and preserve your dear, precious health, so that when I come back I may find you thoroughly well and we may be as happy as can be'.[16] The Emperor assured his wife that rather than join him on the battlefield, she would do more good by showing herself to the people of Vienna, paying visits to hospitals. 'You do not know what a help you could be to me if you would do this. It will raise the spirits of people in Vienna and maintain the good atmosphere which I so urgently need.'[17]

The decisive conflict took place on 24 June. On a plain near Solferino, for the last time, three European monarchs – the Emperors of Austria and France, and the King of Sardinia – faced each other at the head of their armies in battle. After several hours of fighting in the sweltering midsummer heat, a violent thunderstorm burst overhead just as the Austrian forces had decided to retreat. Within days it was ascertained that they had suffered at least 20,000 casualties, and the Franco-Italian forces perhaps as many as 17,000.

Francis Joseph wrote to Elizabeth with great sadness of the horror of it all, 'a confused mass of wounded men, fugitives, carriages and horses'. It was 'the sad story of a horrible day, on which great things were done, but fortune did not smile upon us. I am the richer by many experiences and have learnt what it feels like to be a defeated general.' His only ray of consolation, he added, was that he was returning home to his 'angel'. He told her not to despair, but put her faith in God. 'He is punishing us sorely and we are only at the beginning of still worse trials, but one must bear them with resignation and do one's duty in all things.'[18]

Napoleon and Francis Joseph were so shattered by the sight of this wholesale carnage and slaughter in the name of war that, now the conflict was over, they embraced each other with ill-concealed relief. An armistice was concluded at Villafranca in July. Napoleon was astute enough to realise that he should not be over-zealous in his demand for the victor's spoils, in case he needed Austrian support in the future. In front of the tent where they had arranged to meet, he stood waiting patiently, his plumed hat in his hand, allowing Francis Joseph to take precedence, as he 'would never think of preceding a Habsburg'.[19] A little flattery could go a long way. Lombardy was to be ceded to the French, who would in turn cede it to Piedmont; Austria would retain Venetia; and the other Italian states would form a federation. The kingdom of Italy was proclaimed less than two years later.

Throughout much of Europe there was considerable sympathy for Francis Joseph. Queen Victoria commented in her journal that she felt 'very much for the unfortunate Austrian army, but otherwise think the Emperor Francis Joseph has done very wisely'.[20] But in Austria the damage to his personal reputation was immense. The empire's newspapers were subject to strict censorship and anything which smacked of *lèse-majesté* was unlikely to find its way into print because of dire penalties against those responsible. Yet veiled criticism of the monarch, his ministers and court was impossible to suppress, and out of the question to keep all such papers from the eye of the diligent monarch himself. Queen Victoria learnt that on his return to Vienna the Emperor had 'issued a proclamation to the effect that he has concluded Peace, because he saw he could expect no support from his old natural allies, & because he thought he should obtain better terms, if he treated directly with the Emperor Napoleon, than by the mediation of the neutral Powers'.[21] The proclamation evidently did not go down well, for when he appeared at a military review crowds in Vienna were heard to call for his abdication.

Maximilian was openly if briefly spoken of as a more suitable Emperor of Austria than the failed autocrat. The Emperor had been jealous of his brother since his marriage, when Elizabeth had discovered that Maximilian was a fearless rider who loved being on horseback, and made it evident that she would much rather go out with him on her mounts than with her husband, who had so little enthusiasm for such an activity.[22]

When Napoleon proposed that Venice should become an independent state under the Archduke's rule, Francis Joseph told him bluntly that Austria would continue the war rather than see this happen. At the peace conference signed at Zurich in November, King Leopold asked for Maximilian to have the governorship of Venice, only to be told in no uncertain terms that the administration of Austrian provinces was strictly a matter of internal policy. Bitterly Maximilian wrote to Leopold of his depression at seeing the great and once-powerful monarchy slowly sinking into decline 'through incompetence and muddle-headedness for which there is neither excuse nor explanation'.[23]

Austria was in a state of acute crisis, its future threatened by bankruptcy and fear of revolution. Scapegoats for the disaster were needed, and accordingly found. Well might the ever-loyal but worldly Count Grünne remark that 'Their Majesties change their best servants as readily as their gloves'.[24] He himself was removed from his post as Adjutant General, and instead made Master of the Horse, where he would have no voice in military policy. Count Stephen Szechenyi, who had been one of the Emperor's most loyal magnates and spokesmen in Hungary, wrote a bitter letter to the government in Vienna about the impossibility of keeping the Magyars loyal, and then killed himself. So did General Eynatten, the Quartermaster-General, who had been arrested during the course of an inquiry about corruption in the supply services of the army, and the minister of finance Baron Bruck, after being wrongfully indicted in a case of embezzlement of army funds. Several generals and ministers, notably the hated Buol, were either dismissed or demoted.

While Emperor Francis Joseph had been preoccupied with affairs of state, at home the atmosphere between his mother and wife had deteriorated even further. Elizabeth was thinner and more nervous still, deeply sensitive to the slightest word of criticism, and seeing enemies everywhere. Sophie understood better than her daughter-in-law that the last thing the Emperor wanted at this stage was a new round of family rows.

A further cause of friction was provided by the matter of Rudolf's upbringing. His attendants were driven to distraction by contradictory orders from both women. Elizabeth was a possessive mother, but in her nervous state temperamentally unsuited to look after the sickly infant on her own. Despite her domineering nature, the experienced Archduchess knew better what was good for her grandson, and was genuinely upset that the Empress was behaving so unreasonably. While Elizabeth would fight to try and wrest control of her children from their grandmother, once she had done so she was incapable of acting as an attentive mother to them herself, as she was only intermittently interested in them. She would visit them in the nursery and make a fuss of them, but lose interest when it came to supervising or taking part in the routine of their daily upbringing, and would readily leave this to the nursery staff. If she was indignant at hearing comments from her children that Sophie was their real Mama, or from courtiers that the Archduchess was the real Empress, she lacked the willpower to change the situation. Tactless though it might have seemed, Francis Joseph allowed his mother to supervise Rudolf's education, defending his decision by saying that nobody was better qualified to do so as she had prepared him for the throne. It was a move which Elizabeth contested bitterly, but to no avail.

Nevertheless, despite her emotional immaturity, at this time Elizabeth gave every impression of being still very much in love with her husband. She knew how deeply he took to heart Austria's loss of prestige after the Italian defeat, and how desperately he needed comfort and reassurance. At times of crisis she was capable of drawing on inner reserves of strength. This was proved by the visits to soldiers in hospitals which her husband had encouraged her to make, knowing how she needed a purpose in life and fully aware of the comfort her presence would bring the wounded.

As is often the case, there were conspicuous faults on both sides. She was incapable of making a sustained effort; spontaneous affection and generosity one day could be replaced by paranoia and tantrums the next. She was also too proud to admit that her mother-in-law might be right, that the hectoring advice Sophie gave about her duties as a mother, wife and above all Empress, was kindly meant if perhaps clumsily given.

Francis Joseph's greatest fault as a family man was that he lacked imagination. The qualities of dedication to duty which served him well as Emperor were not those required for a successful husband. In his way he loved her deeply, as his anxious letters from the front in Italy showed, but it took him time to understand his wife's complex, sensitive character, or realise that there was anything of value in her ideas, that she had a vivid and active mind sorely needing a useful outlet.

On their visit to Hungary in 1857 Elizabeth had been fascinated by the country and people. She loved the vitality of Magyar life, music and horses, while the Hungarians immediately saw that they had a genuine friend at court. When she first asked Francis Joseph to give serious thought to making concessions to the Magyar constitution and national aspirations, the most he would concede was that 'there are some good points in what you say'. Initially he was too ready to agree with his mother that the only reason Sisi took an interest in them was because they appealed to her sense of the picturesque. But he soon came to understand her point of view, and he was impressed with her rapid progress in learning Magyar.

One evening they attended the theatre, taking their seats in the central compartment of the imperial box, while Sophie sat in the one next to them. Elizabeth was wearing a gold-embroidered headdress as generally worn by the wives of Hungarian magnates. At the sight of this Sophie stared at her daughter-in-law coldly through her lorgnette, standing up and bending over the front of the box to get a better view, then returned to her chair, shaking her head. The audience looked on in amazement, paying more attention to this little drama than the one they had paid to see on the stage. Eventually they began whispering among themselves, and Elizabeth was so irritated that she got up and left, closely followed by her husband.

Francis Joseph had been brought up to believe that his status as Emperor would be compromised by allowing the subject of a more representative system of government in the empire to be raised, let alone adopted. In June 1860 he warned his council of ministers that he would not be party to any curtailment of monarchical power through a constitution. But with his prestige weakened by the loss of Italy, he was powerless to resist calls to modernise. That autumn the Reichsrat (imperial council) presented him with two alternative recommendations: either federal government, or centralised administration under a larger parliamentary body. When given the reports to read, he was warned by Count Nicholas Szecsen, a spokesman for the Magyar Old Conservatives, that he risked unleashing further unrest in Hungary if he did not give the Reichsrat a clear answer. On the other hand, Szecsen assured the Emperor that if his compatriots knew their historic Diet was to be restored, they would probably cooperate with the other nationalities and treat the monarchy as a unitary state.

As Francis Joseph was about to meet Tsar Alexander II of Russia and William, Prince Regent of Prussia, at Warsaw, he did not want his authority tarnished by reports of trouble in Hungary, which would be a painful reminder of the Magyar revolution during the early months of his reign. He accordingly commissioned Szecsen to produce a new settlement for the empire as a whole, based upon recommendations sent to him by the majority in the Reichsrat. This, he instructed, must be ready within twenty-four hours, before his departure for Warsaw – a deadline the diligent Szecsen duly met. It resulted in what became known as the 'October Diploma', a fundamental law which strengthened the provincial Diets, giving them legislative authority over matters previously determined by ministers of the interior, and making provision for them to send delegates to the parliament, which would be recognised as the principal law-making body of the empire. Supplementary to the basic Diploma were more than twenty 'Sovereign Rescripts' which established electoral bodies to prepare for the Diets in the various provinces. At last open discussion was allowed where an aura of benevolent dictatorship in all but name had precluded genuine debate for some years.

'Now we are going to have a little parliamentarianism,' Francis Joseph informed his mother, just before leaving for Warsaw, 'but all power stays in my hands, and the general effect will suit Austrian circumstances very well indeed.'[25] His confidence did something to reassure the Archduchess, who had read details of the October Diploma earlier that day with some misgivings. On paper, at least, Francis Joseph had relinquished absolutism, even though the measures fell short of full democratic or constitutional government.

In January 1859 Elizabeth's sister Marie had married Prince Francis of Naples, who ascended the throne of the Two Sicilies four months later. His reign was to last for less than two years. In June 1860 Giuseppe Garibaldi and his army of 1,000 volunteers descended upon Sicily and invaded Naples. The King and Queen were driven into their last remaining stronghold at Gaeta, with an increasingly tenuous hold on their throne until it was relegated to history with the proclamation of a united Italy in February 1861. The Queen begged Elizabeth to try and intercede with her husband on their behalf. Plagued by internal difficulties with his government and still suffering from the loss of prestige after Solferino and Villafranca, Francis Joseph could do little. After Austria's crushing defeat in Italy he knew better than to embroil himself again there, and he could only offer his dispossessed relations sympathy and a safe haven if necessary.

With the possibility that Vienna might become a home for exiled royalties from Italy and other neighbouring states, the nineteen-year-old Archduke Ludwig Victor remarked one night at a dinner that all the royal highnesses who were expelled from their dominions came to them. 'I wonder where we will go when we are driven away?' he asked disingenuously. This *faux pas* was received in silence by all except Elizabeth, who gave a high nervous laugh and left the room in tears. The chamberlains later commented that the Archduke 'must have the mind of a street urchin to make such a remark'.[26]

As a child, the youngest brother had been petted and spoilt by the family. He hero-worshipped Francis Joseph, to the extent of wanting to be seen beside him in public on occasions such as visits to the theatre, with none of the other family around. Francis Joseph was unwise enough to indulge him, with the result that Ludwig Victor became more and more convinced of his own self-importance. Precocious and self-confident, without siblings close to him in age, he had been brought up almost exclusively in the company of adults. As his witty conversation was encouraged by his elders, particularly Elizabeth who immediately took to him and his mischievous personality, any tendency to bad taste was perhaps not properly checked.

Adding to Francis Joseph's woes was the sudden arrival of two of Elizabeth's brothers, Dukes Ludwig and Charles Theodore, on a private visit to Laxenburg. The three of them spent several days in conference discussing ways in which they might help the unfortunate dispossessed sovereigns. Elizabeth became more nervous and excited, and the Emperor feared that they might become involved in extraordinary schemes which might involve and therefore compromise his position. It happened at a particularly inopportune moment, as Duke Ludwig had disgraced the good name of the family by contracting a morganatic marriage with an actress, Henriette Mendel, in the face of their strong disapproval. Elizabeth had been the only one to support him, and Francis Joseph looked on with misgivings when she invited them to Schönbrunn.

As Emperor, his main preoccupation that autumn was with the Warsaw meeting between himself, Tsar Alexander and William, Prince Regent of Prussia, who would succeed his seriously ill brother Frederick William IV as king three months later. Their aims were to restore good relations between each other after their differences over the Crimean war, and lay the foundations for a new triple alliance between their countries which would present a united front against the Italian Risorgimento and other manifestations of national liberalism throughout Europe. King Francis of the Two Sicilies and his supporters hoped that they might also give approval for armed intervention in Italy which would secure his throne, and try to hold back the momentum leading to the creation of a united Italian kingdom.

Others thought that the Northern Powers, as they were collectively known, would demand revision of the 1856 Treaty of Paris, in order to safeguard Austria from attack in Venetia or Hungary, and perhaps even try to effect the isolation of England from the other European powers.[27] Queen Victoria and the Prince Consort were planning to visit the Princess Royal and Prince Frederick William of Prussia in Germany, and Count Rechberg, Austrian foreign minister, wanted to take the opportunity presented by their travels 'to see an interview between the Queen and his Emperor, but that perhaps there would have been difficulties in the way'.[28] Lord John Russell, the Queen's foreign secretary, had no enthusiasm for the idea, writing to Julian Fane, secretary at the embassy in Vienna, that

> although it would give the Queen great pleasure to meet H.I.M. there are crises (?) in the present state of Europe which would make it inexpedient for her government to favour such an interview. In fact too many busy bodies are at work to invent, embitter and circulate significant phrases. The contradiction is often as mischievous as the promulgation of such stories.[29]

Against her better inclinations, the Queen had to accept her government's verdict that they should 'nip this project in the bud', but 'care should be taken to do this in such a manner as not to let it appear that there was any disinclination on the Queen's part to meet the Emperor of Austria'.[30]

At the same time Francis Joseph and William hoped to align themselves against Napoleon III, an aim that conflicted with Alexander's desire for an alliance with France, albeit with Austro-German participation. This would entail the exclusion of England, something which the German sovereigns were not prepared to countenance. However, throughout Europe it was generally expected that Austria and Russia would settle their differences after the mutual ill-feeling that followed the Crimean war. Yet the Russian foreign minister Count Gorchakov was even less forgiving than the Tsar, who was too preoccupied by his empire's internal affairs to concern himself unduly over any revival of a Holy Alliance to crusade against liberalism in Italy. The sudden death of his ailing mother gave him an excuse to return to St Petersburg sooner than expected. Once he had gone, the old rivalry and mutual suspicion between Francis Joseph and William resurfaced. Within a few days both monarchs and the sovereign-in-waiting were all back in their respective capitals with nothing to show for their efforts.

Szecsen's assurance that the October Diploma would be popular in Hungary proved over-optimistic. The group of Magyar Old Conservatives at the Vienna court had no following in Hungary, and when self-government was reintroduced into the Hungarian counties, many people refused to pay any taxes unless the validity of the constitutional concessions granted in April 1848 was acknowledged. Some districts in Hungary made fun of the whole system by nominating absentees or frivolous choices such as Kossuth, Napoleon III and Cavour for their 'elected' representatives. Other national groups within the empire were disappointed by the October Diploma; the Germans found it too feudal, too clericalist, and too sympathetic to the Czechs, who in turn complained that the Diploma failed to acknowledge Bohemia's historic State Rights; and the Poles felt aggrieved because they did not acquire the privileged status which they maintained Szecsen had won for Hungary.

It was impossible to please everyone, and Francis Joseph's 'little parliamentary life' proved a valiant but unsuccessful experiment. In December 1860, eight weeks after the Diploma was announced, Goluchowski and Szecsen were asked to resign their posts. A few weeks later Francis Joseph held discussions in Vienna with two liberal Hungarian reformers, the lawyer Ferenc Deak and the novelist Baron Josef Botvos. They intended to give their sovereign some insight into genuine Hungarian hopes and fears, rather than the rarefied feudalism of the Old Conservatives.

As Francis Joseph was not prepared to discard the October Diploma, he chose instead to have its proposals clarified by a supplementary series of ratifications announced on 27 February 1861, known as the 'February Patent'. These were primarily the work of Goluchowski's successor, Baron Anton von Schmerling, a liberal who had once chaired the Frankfurt parliament. They preserved the institutions proposed by the October Diploma but changed their composition and responsibilities, to make the new system more centralised. A two-chamber Reichsrat was created, the upper house comprising the adult archdukes, large landowners, ecclesiastical magnates and various life members nominated by the crown, the lower house comprising 323 delegates sent to Vienna from the provincial Diets under an indirect electoral college system of representation. Much to the horror of the professional army officers, this nominated chamber of deputies was intended to have control over the military budget. The February Patent of 1861 decreed a genuine constitution and handing substantial powers over to parliament. Though the new body had not grown from the people but was set up by imperial decree and could thus be abolished by the same means, it was a genuine legislative institution. It was opened on 1 May with a speech from the throne in the ceremonial *Redoutenhalle* of the Hofburg.

But the Emperor was not surrendering his prerogatives, and again he insisted that real power remain in his hands. He told his Ministerial Council that the February Patent marked the uttermost limits of the curtailment of the sovereign power, demanding from each of them

the solemn pledge to defend the Throne with all your energy and the most single-minded purpose against demands for further concessions. In particular you will, as a matter of duty, keep Parliament from trespassing beyond its proper field and repulse decisively any attempt on the part of this body to concern itself with the management of foreign affairs and of army affairs and the business of the Higher Command.[31]

Never, he told his ministers when the February Patent was under discussion, must they let the lower chamber concern themselves with matters best left to the foreign ministry and the army High Command. He retained a right of veto over contentious legislation and used it freely. While he neither liked nor trusted parliaments, he was prepared to let public opinion have a safety-valve if it minimised the risk of a democratic explosion. It was a step towards the constitutional government at which his predecessors would have been astonished.

FOUR

'Going Down with Honour'

Within seven years of his marriage, Emperor Francis Joseph was facing a major personal crisis, the consequences of which he would have to live with for much of his life. He was about to discover just how ill-matched he and Elizabeth really were.

While he was in Warsaw, it was rumoured in Vienna that one reason for his travels abroad was to renew acquaintance with a Polish countess whom he had known before his marriage, and who fulfilled his physical needs in a way the Empress could or would not. This has been given as one reason for the complete physical and mental breakdown that Elizabeth suffered at this time. A more likely though equally unproven explanation is that for some time her wrists and knees had been disfigured by unsightly swellings at the joints, and court doctors could not diagnose or cure them. Seeking a more honest opinion elsewhere, heavily veiled and under an assumed name, she consulted another doctor who did not recognise her, and told her that she was suffering from an unpleasant contagious disease, probably gonorrhoea.

Whether it was the discovery of her husband's infidelity, the plight of her sister, her inability to take any more from her mother-in-law, a suspected tuberculous infection of the throat, the belief that she had a 'shameful' infection, or a combination of them all, will never be known. Nevertheless the Emperor returned home to find his wife in a state of acute distress, insisting that she must leave and go as far away as possible. She decided on Madeira, which had been described to her by Maximilian as a veritable paradise, and had the added advantage of being sufficiently remote from resident or neighbouring royals and Austrian officials.

The Emperor asked her to delay her departure, as there was no imperial yacht ready or capable of such a journey in winter. She asked Queen Victoria to lend her a vessel, and the sympathetic monarch generously placed her yacht *Victoria and Albert* at Elizabeth's disposal. With it came an invitation for Elizabeth to visit Victoria in England on the way, but this was the last thing she wanted. Through Lord Bloomfield, British ambassador to Vienna, she declined on the grounds of ill health and the fact that she was travelling incognito.

On 17 November the Emperor and Empress left for Munich en route for Bamberg, whence she and her retinue were to go to Antwerp for the voyage to Madeira. Stormy weather accompanied them, but she was unaffected by seasickness, enjoying the excitement of rough sea, and by the time they arrived at the island she was looking better. For four months she surrounded herself with her dogs, ponies and books, and free from the tedium and tensions of court life she found the peace and relaxation she had craved since her marriage. Adding to her new-found contentment was the news that Marie, ex-Queen of the Two Sicilies, was safe in exile. Occasionally Elizabeth would be overcome by melancholy and long to see her husband and children again, and issue orders to depart at once, only to cancel them moments later.

Francis Joseph wrote regularly, entreating her to return. He obtained a detailed map of Madeira, to try and follow her movements on it from the descriptions in her letters. By the end of April 1861 she was on her way back to Trieste to meet him. In May, with tears in his eyes, Francis Joseph met and embraced his wife off the isle of Lacroma in the Adriatic Sea. Following a brief visit to Maximilian and Charlotte, rendered none too happy by jealousy between the sisters-in-law, they returned to Vienna.

After a few days back at home, giving interminable audiences and attending both a ball at court and a state dinner, Elizabeth informed her husband that life in the Hofburg was impossible. Everywhere she looked, whether it was the drawing up of lists of ladies for presentation at court or the furnishing of her private apartments, she could see the hand of her mother-in-law. The reunion with her children had been spoilt by her seeing how much they had fallen under their grandmother's influence. It was only to be expected, for Sophie had been the obvious person to take charge of everything during the Empress's absence. Yet Elizabeth told her husband she was exhausted and must retire to Laxenburg. Sophie had little patience with such demands, and family relations were strained further by the behaviour of Archduke Ludwig Victor. Much amused by the malicious wit of her effeminate young brother-in-law, Elizabeth was unwise enough to confide in him. He took great pleasure in repeating her indiscretions to his mother, and relations between the two women deteriorated still further.

On 23 May Francis Joseph and Elizabeth went to Laxenburg. All official functions and state dinners announced for the next few days were cancelled, as was their proposed journey to Munich for the wedding of another of the Empress's sisters, Mathilde, to Count Ludwig of Trani on 5 June. By mid-June Elizabeth appeared once again in the throes of a rapid decline, with a severe cough, no appetite and extreme weakness. Her physician, Dr Joseph Skoda, was alleged to have said that she had only six weeks to live. Some at court were convinced that she was not nearly as ill as she pretended to be, and their sympathies were with the harassed Emperor who was overworked and distracted by worry over his impossible, spoilt young wife. However, the Archduchess was genuinely fearful at the thought that they might never see each other again.

On 23 June Francis Joseph escorted Elizabeth back to Trieste, and she went on to Corfu, brushing aside warnings from those who claimed that it was no place for somebody in her state of health. Lord Bloomfield commented derisively that he had never before heard of Corfu, notorious for its prevalence of malaria, being recommended by doctors as a summer resort for invalids. Nevertheless, once there her spirits soon lifted, her hacking cough went, and she spent much time walking, swimming and sitting on the beach, with her dogs for company. Soon Vienna was agog with rumours of a definite break between Emperor and Empress. In order to forestall this, and as he still missed his wife desperately, Francis Joseph sent Count Grünne to Corfu to beg her to return.

It was a bad choice, as there were few people she hated more. At first she refused to see him, and when she relented he told her of the gossip, only to have her accuse him and Archduchess Sophie of being responsible for everything that had gone wrong; for making her life a misery, and robbing her of her children. He withdrew and returned to his arguments another day, only to have her accuse him of trying to destroy her marriage by introducing her husband to 'other women'. At length she realised she had gone too far and apologised, but he saw he was wasting his time there, and he might as well return home. Back in Vienna he reported to the Emperor that he had failed, but in private conversation with friends he said that the Empress was mentally ill, the longer she stayed away from Austria the better, and she was quite unsuited for her position as Empress. His comments found their way back to the Empress through the usual source, the ever-mischievous Ludwig Victor.

A solution came from Elizabeth's own family. Duchess Ludovika had been appalled by reports from Vienna, and sent the Princess of Thurn and Taxis, the woman who would have been Empress of Austria but for a quirk of fate, to Corfu. Nené was horrified by the change in her younger sister, hardly recognising the pale, listless, puffy-faced young woman who was deliberately starving herself yet insisting she was putting on too much weight. Her ladies-in-waiting, grateful for the Princess's arrival, confirmed what she had seen for herself. She took charge, persuading her sister to eat sensibly and regularly, accompanying her for walks while she poured her heart out about her grievances and miseries. By the time Nené had gone, Elizabeth was in a more cheerful frame of mind, ready to see her husband and children again.

Grateful beyond measure to his sister-in-law, on 13 October Francis Joseph arrived in Corfu, and found Elizabeth in far better health than the last time he had seen her. He begged her to return home for his sake and for that of the children. Her absence, he stressed, was bad for them, for the empire and the dynasty. When they were back in Vienna together, he promised, he would take her part more actively than before in matters concerning their upbringing, and would stand up for her against his mother if necessary. She held out for a compromise; she would not yet return home to the domestic regime of the Archduchess, for her health and nerves would not permit it, but she agreed to go somewhere within the borders of the monarchy, and spend the winter in Venice.

Francis Joseph had no choice but to agree, and after staying a little longer at Corfu, mainly to inspect military fortifications created by the English, he went back to Vienna. It was in no sense a personal defeat, for he could see that for the Empress to visit Venice and stay there during Christmas could have important political advantages. He had refused to acknowledge the new kingdom of Italy, and believed that Venetia was not irrevocably lost to the Austrian empire. Elizabeth arrived in the city at the end of October and stayed there for six months.

On 3 November Gisela and Rudolf were brought to visit their mother, but they came with their governess Countess Esterhazy, who made it clear that in all matters relating to the children's care and education she was following their grandmother's instructions. Almost at once the women quarrelled bitterly. Francis Joseph arrived in Venice later that month, and courtiers thought that he and his wife seemed as devoted to each other as they had been in the first days of their marriage. But the Emperor's pleasure at being reunited with his wife and children was overshadowed by the antipathy between the women and also by the evident hostility of the Venetians. They had regarded their Empress as an outsider and, unlike the Magyars, showed no interest in her. The Emperor knew the people had nothing but contempt for Austrian rule, and were only quiet because they were kept in order by the troops. He was disappointed to find that not only the middle classes but also the aristocracy remained aloof, and efforts made to invite some of them to visit the palace were in vain. Elizabeth was relieved not to have to entertain them or be drawn into their circle, but she was disturbed by their hostility, particularly for her husband's sake. Moreover Venice was damp and misty, a cold forbidding place after the summer paradise of the Mediterranean.

After the Emperor left she became profoundly depressed, and her ladies-in-waiting reported that she spent hours weeping alone in her room, so irritable that she could not bear to have anybody with her. In January 1862 she persuaded her husband to dismiss Countess Esterhézy, and in future she would only have women around her whom she had chosen herself. Her symptoms, particularly a puffy face and swollen ankles, appeared once more. Her mother came to visit, and was disturbed more by her daughter's mental state than her physical problems. She had begun to collect colour photographs of attractive women, and had instructed the Austrian ambassadors at other European courts to obtain them. The ambassador in Constantinople was asked to find her likenesses of famous Oriental beauties and also of the women in the Sultan's harem. It took a certain amount of subterfuge on his part to acquire these and send them secretly to her. She studied them with apparent admiration and envy. Her aversion to marital relations with Francis Joseph, coupled with such an extraordinary hobby, prompted at least one recent writer to question whether it was 'an expression of unconscious lesbianism'.[1]

The Duchess took her daughter back with her to Bavaria, where she could be examined by her childhood physician, Dr Fischer. As he had known her far longer than the Viennese doctors, he considered himself better qualified to pronounce on her troubles. There was nothing wrong with her lungs, he said; all she required for her anaemic condition was a hydropathic cure at Kissingen.

On 14 August, accompanied by her favourite brother Charles Theodore, she returned by train to Vienna. Her ladies-in-waiting were not expecting her and had to be summoned by telegram. Maybe she delighted in causing minor consternation at the court where all routines were planned rigidly in advance, but not surprisingly the long-suffering Emperor was pathetically grateful to have her back again. She was at Schönbrunn for the celebrations of his thirty-second birthday and those for Rudolf's fourth three days after that. Even the people of Vienna received her warmly, thanks largely to the more liberal newspapers giving the impression that their Empress was at heart a progressive young woman who could bring some influence on their Emperor and counteract that of his clericalist, reactionary mother. On the eve of his birthday, the couple were serenaded by a choir of 300 singers, and after dusk there was a torchlight procession of around 15,000 people.

For the next few months, Elizabeth insisted on having either her brother or one of her sisters nearby to keep her company. Every moment the Emperor could spare from his work was spent in accompanying her on walks and drives, and the Archduchess tactfully stayed out of their way. As Empress, Elizabeth made it clear that she was back on her own terms, which included greater personal independence and the minimum attendance at court functions and festivities. She did attend a court ball in January 1863, wearing a crinoline of white tulle, with fresh camellias in her hair. The foreign ambassadors were captivated by her appearance, and thought she must be fully recovered.

Among the other guests at Vienna during that season were Crown Prince and Princess Frederick William of Prussia, who attended a family dinner party in December 1862. The Princess, eldest daughter of Queen Victoria, wrote to her mother afterwards to say how charmed she was with the Empress. 'Nobody could be more kind and amiable than she was – it is impossible not to love her,' she noted. 'The Emperor seems to *dote* on her – but I did not observe that she did on him.' About the Emperor, she was less flattering. 'He is most insignificant, *very* plain to begin with (which you would not suppose from his pictures and photographs), he looks so old and wrinkled and his reddish moustache and whiskers are very unbecoming, he has little or no conversation, and is altogether exceedingly *unbedeutend* [insignificant].' All the same, she admitted that he and the Empress had been extremely amicable to both of them.[2]

Relieved to have his wife home, the Emperor was more than eager to accommodate her every wish. It was as if he felt himself indebted to her for some reason, a debt which he could never repay. This might lend some credence to the theory that he had infected her venereally and felt a lifelong sense of guilt. Alternatively, it could have been the chivalry of a man who was perceptive enough to acknowledge that she was temperamentally ill-equipped for her station in life, and whose love for her made him strive to do what he could. Yet another possibility was that he feared her Wittelsbach inheritance and the danger that too much stress might deprive her of her reason.

His dilemma was that of a straightforward, ordinary man in an extraordinary position. A devoted son and husband at heart, he held family life in high regard and was devoted to his children. Gisela was a placid, well-tempered child, who lacked her mother's beauty and also showed no signs of Wittelsbach eccentricity or paranoia, while Rudolf was the mischievous, disobedient one. At the age of five he fell off a ladder and hit his head while climbing a tree. While he sustained no major injuries, the incident was alarming enough to bring his father back to Vienna from a conference outside the empire's borders, while Archduchess Sophie interrupted her holiday at Ischl. In order to shield his wife from bad news, the Emperor gave orders that the Empress, taking her cure at Kissingen, should not be informed until their son was out of danger. Sadly, such well-meaning actions only increased her sense of isolation from the family. By the time she returned to Vienna, bringing him expensive toys, he was convalescing. She treated him indulgently, laughing at the tantrums of a child bored by weeks of enforced inactivity, but her frequent absences had told against her. The light which appeared in his eyes when his grandmother entered the room said it all.

The Emperor had been brought up with an unquestioning acceptance of his responsibilities towards the empire of which he was the figurehead. He was a thorough conservative, yet not a blindly reactionary one, unfailingly conscientious, hardworking to a fault, and anxious to rule his subjects as fairly and effectively as possible. Throughout his long reign he never altered his attitude to the high position to which he had been born. As F.R. Bridge suggests, 'his toughness and perseverance were combined with a certain inelasticity of mind and lack of imagination',[3] which helps to explain why he changed so little as an Emperor over nearly seven decades. Still only in his early thirties, he saw that moderate change and reform were necessary for Austria's survival. When the Reichsrat ended its session just before Christmas 1862, he gave his assent to the reform of imperial legislation regarding personal civil rights, freedom of the press and reform of local government administration.

Defeat in Italy, acceptance of the February Patent, and the appointment of Bismarck as minister-president of Prussia in September 1862, had helped to impress on Francis Joseph the wisdom of tempering traditional Habsburg autocracy. He was beginning to see that the various parts of his empire could no longer be controlled by absolute monarchy, especially if the absolute monarch had himself paid the ultimate penalty of being defeated in battle against another nation.

Francis Joseph had first met Bismarck in 1852, when the latter was briefly in Vienna as acting Prussian ambassador. Though the future Iron Chancellor made no impression on him then, during the Crimean war and again during the war of 1859, he and his ministers became aware that Bismarck and his Junker conservatives were largely responsible for Prussia's failure or refusal to respond to Austrian initiatives. Soon after Bismarck came to power, he suggested to the Magyar ambassador in Berlin that the time had come for Austria to 'shift her centre of gravity' from Germany to

Hungary. If the Emperor of Austria was to comply, he could rely on Prussian support in Italy and south-eastern Europe if needed, but if Austria rejected his overtures, Prussia would side with France in any future European crisis.

Vienna looked askance on Bismarck's bullying attitude towards the smaller and less martial German states, especially when he proposed a commercial treaty for them with France which appeared to jeopardise Austrian interests. The Austrian ministers advised the Emperor to support a reform programme, aimed at reasserting Habsburg leadership of a modernised German Confederation by bringing together delegates from the German and Austrian legislative bodies in a federal parliament. By seizing the initiative they might be able to counter the ambitions of Bismarck. Though he had the natural nineteenth-century conservative's reservations about advancing the interests of parliamentarianism against those of divinely appointed crowned heads, Francis Joseph was persuaded by Prince Maximilian of Thurn and Taxis, Nené's husband, to invite the reigning monarchs of the German states to Frankfurt for a *Fürstentag* or 'conclave of princes', to discuss the future of the German Confederation. As the Emperor wrote to Archduchess Sophie, it might be the last chance for them to save themselves 'before they are swept away by the growing tide of revolution'.[4]

Prussia, it was foreseen, might not be prepared to cooperate. King William felt as obliged to attend as his fellow sovereigns and grand dukes but Bismarck, spoiling for a fight with Austria at the least provocation, told him that to do so would be to acknowledge Habsburg leadership in Germany; besides, the invitation to Prussia had arrived so late that it was an insult. The conference opened on 17 August, but without King William and Crown Prince Frederick William, who declared that the honour of Prussia and the Hohenzollerns had been insulted. The conference achieved nothing, and in summing up, Francis Joseph expressed his hopes that their efforts might be crowned by another meeting at the earliest possible opportunity. Nevertheless, in private he agreed gloomily with the Duke of Saxe-Coburg that it would be the last time German princes would meet as friends and not as foes.

Queen Victoria had been visiting Coburg, partly to call on the widow of her mentor Baron Stockmar. While there she accepted a request from the Crown Prince and Princess of Prussia, her daughter Victoria and son-in-law Frederick William, to try and persuade King William to attend the Frankfurt conference. In this she failed, but before returning to England she cordially invited Francis Joseph to pay a courtesy call on her at Schloss Rosenau, the ancestral home of the late Prince Consort. He had had to forego similar requests on her previous journeys to Germany, in 1858 and 1860, and felt obliged to accept this time, while making it clear that this was merely to be '*la visite de politesse*'.

They met on 3 September, the first time Queen and Emperor had ever come face to face. She found him 'very quiet, simple and unaffected, not talkative, but very dignified'. Afterwards she wrote to the Crown Princess that she told him of 'the necessity of Prussia's being put upon a footing of equality', that he told her this was his wish, and he was anxious to assure them all 'of the very friendly disposition of Austria'. While he regretted King William's failure to appear at the conference, he realised that Bismarck was to blame.[5] In a memorandum in Victoria's private journal, she said she hoped German unity would be achieved, as did the Emperor, 'but Prussia was a great difficulty'. Despite the 'great pretensions' raised by the government at Berlin, they agreed that it was important for Europe to 'keep the Emperor of the French quiet'.[6]

As Francis Joseph probably realised, Napoleon was less of a threat, at least to Austria, than Bismarck. At the same time, he was almost certainly unaware of the poor state of Austria's army. Though he had his reservations about parliamentary interference in foreign affairs and the management of the army, he had already conceded to parliament some control over the military budget. Between 1861 and 1866 the army estimates were fiercely contested and reduced by the liberals in the Reichsrat. Prussia was strengthening its army and equipping it with modern weaponry, including the new rapid-firing breech-loading rifle. The Austrian army had been offered this gun in 1851, but Francis Joseph had been advised to reject it in favour of more traditional tried and tested weapons. It was characteristic of the Austrian government to let its own fighting forces be weakened, turning down new armaments for reasons of economy. Moreover, as he would soon discover to his cost, Francis Joseph had no equivalent of Bismarck in his political ranks to help the sovereign get his way in the face of opposition from fractious democrats who governed in his name.

While Francis Joseph was faced with an unsettling future regarding Austria's place in the German confederation, Maximilian was likewise at the crossroads. After the empire's expulsion from Italy in 1859, Max and Charlotte had resided in splendour and boredom in their palace, Miramare, on the Adriatic coast near Trieste. Though Maximilian was prepared to accept that his brother would probably never offer him employment again, his wife longed for responsibility and power. They were ideal candidates for any vacant throne which might be offered them in the unstable world of nineteenth-century European diplomacy.

Napoleon appreciated the wisdom of restoring good relations with Austria after the Italian war, and in 1861 he offered Maximilian the prospect of the Mexican crown. Mexico had been a Spanish colony until 1821 and then briefly a constitutional monarchy for three years until the establishment of a republic. The country had been ravaged by civil war, leading to occupation by French troops brought in on the pretext of unpaid debts. By 1861 they had apparently succeeded in routing troops under General Juarez, and Napoleon planned to establish an empire under French patronage, with the continuing presence of his army as a guarantee of security. Maximilian welcomed the idea of independence from his brother, not to mention the prospect of reigning over an empire potentially richer and greater than Austria, while the ambitious Charlotte was thrilled at the thought of becoming an Empress. Archduchess Sophie resolutely opposed this hazardous venture. With the sickly Crown Prince Rudolf's survival to maturity looking very much in the balance, she believed that Maximilian and Charlotte or any children they might have would still succeed Francis Joseph on the Austrian throne.

The Emperor was too much of a realist to be dazzled by the spectre of an Austrian archduke wearing a Mexican crown. Having once branded Napoleon as 'that arch-rogue', and bearing in mind his reputation for sober caution, it was strange that he did not reject the offer outright on Maximilian's behalf as being beneath the Habsburgs' dignity. But the chance of ridding himself of this tiresome, too-popular brother who thirsted for power was tempting. He let it be known that acceptance of the Mexican crown was out of the question unless it could be shown that the people themselves really wanted him to accept, and if France, Great Britain and Spain all pledged their unconditional support.

Meanwhile, an existing throne closer to home was also vacant. In October 1862 the Greeks deposed their unpopular, childless King Otto, and to replace him chose Queen Victoria's second son Prince Alfred, who received 95 per cent of the votes in a plebiscite. Under the terms of a London protocol signed in 1830, he was disqualified from accepting. The British prime minister Lord Palmerston and his foreign secretary Lord John Russell thought Maximilian 'far too good for Mexico', and recommended him as a possible King of Greece, hoping to spare him an uncertain fate as Napoleon's pawn. King Leopold, who had been offered the Hellenic throne in 1830 but declined it, prudently waiting for better things (like the Belgian crown, which came his way months later), urged his son-in-law to accept a throne 'of incomparably greater importance than that of Mexico', but in vain. He would not consider a crown which had been hawked around unsuccessfully to several other princes. He asked Leopold if he could secure Palmerston's support for the Mexican candidature, for there, he believed, lay 'a brilliant future', calling Mexico a country of immense natural riches, while Greece was 'poor in men and money'. Negotiations proceeded slowly for two years while Maximilian, frequently accompanied by Charlotte, conferred with Mexican delegations and the French, and reluctantly King Leopold gave his consent.

By the beginning of 1864, Maximilian had formally accepted. Napoleon and Empress Eugenie could not be more fulsome in their affection for Maximilian and Charlotte, but in London Queen Victoria and her ministry made it clear that they could do nothing for the young couple beyond wishing them well, and they did not disguise their view that it was a foolhardy enterprise. Charlotte's widowed grandmother, Queen Marie Amelie, in exile at Claremont, tried to dissuade them from accepting. To her and to the other Orléans princes, it was quite incomprehensible that a Habsburg could agree to take part in such a scheme hatched by the Bonapartes. As they embraced for the last time, the Dowager Queen burst into tears, telling Maximilian that it would surely end in his assassination. Charlotte remained stony-faced, but he broke down and wept.

On their final return to Vienna, an unpleasant surprise awaited Maximilian. Already unnerved by sad looks on his parents' faces and entreaties to reconsider his decision from his other elder relations, among them ex-Emperor Ferdinand, he was presented with an act of renunciation which Francis Joseph ordered him to sign. This made his consent to Maximilian accepting the crown of Mexico strictly subject to his renouncing for himself and his issue all rights of succession and inheritance in Austria. If he did not, he would not receive the sanction of his sovereign to go. In that case, Maximilian retorted, he would dispense with his sovereign's sanction, and start from Antwerp on a French boat. Should he do so, countered Francis Joseph, he would be charged with disloyalty and formally deprived of all the rights which he refused to renounce.

A furious and humiliated Maximilian asked his mother to intervene. She begged the Emperor not to take away his brother's birthright, but Francis Joseph remained obdurate, and she left the meeting, angrily slamming the door behind her. Only the entreaties of Charlotte and Napoleon prevented Maximilian from renouncing his Mexican ambitions for once and for all. After further argument, the most Maximilian could wring from his brother was a guarantee that, should he be deprived of the throne in Mexico and have to return to Austria, the Emperor would take all necessary measures to safeguard his position and presence in the Austrian empire as far as was compatible with the national interest.

At Miramare on 9 April 1864 both brothers signed the 'family pact'. All the imperial dignitaries present noticed the reddened eyes and trembling hands of Emperor and Archduke. As they embraced each other that afternoon, witnesses looked away, for tears streamed down the brothers' faces, as if they were conscious that they would never see each other again. Only Charlotte was as outwardly impassive as ever. Next day, a deputation of Mexicans presented themselves at Miramare and formally offered the crown to Maximilian and Carlota, his wife's new Mexican name. Their fate was sealed.

The Mexican empire had been an unwelcome distraction for Francis Joseph from the ever-present German shadows. In 1864 Prussia and

Austria fought side by side against Denmark over the duchies of Schleswig and Holstein, which King Christian IX of Denmark had claimed on his accession to the throne in November 1863. Most German states championed the Duke of Augustenburg as the duchies' rightful ruler, but in Berlin and Vienna a view prevailed that they should belong to Germany. The Danes were soon defeated, and after the cessation of hostilities, at a conference of the Great Powers in London, Prussia and Austria made a joint proposal that Schleswig and Holstein should be constituted as an independent state, linked only by the person of a joint monarch to Denmark.

It was a compromise that the latter refused to consider. A smaller conference was held at Schönbrunn in August 1864, attended by Francis Joseph, his foreign minister Count Rechberg, King William, and Bismarck. Francis Joseph compared Bismarck's view of the Austro-Prussian alliance to 'a hunting expedition from which each party would return with his own bag',[7] but they dispersed without reaching agreement.

At the convention of Gastein, one year later, it was decided that Schleswig should be administered by Prussia, and Holstein by Austria. Suspicion that this was a temporary measure, and part of Bismarck's long-term strategy to establish Prussia as the leading power in Germany, was soon proved correct. Bismarck had already acquired the goodwill of Tsar Alexander II by refusing to support a Polish rebellion against Russia in 1863, whereas Austria, England and France had jointly supported a measure to give Poland a degree of autonomy. At the same time he had assured French goodwill by promising Napoleon that, if Austria was defeated, she would have to surrender her last remaining Italian province, Venetia, to King Victor Emmanuel. When the time came for the Habsburg empire to be provoked into war, she would be on her own as far as the great powers were concerned.

In January 1866 a telegram arrived in Vienna from Berlin accusing Austria of causing unrest in the Duchies. With King William's readiness to endorse Bismarck's strategy, General Helmuth von Moltke's scheme of campaign for an offensive war, and Berlin's negotiations with France and Italy, it was clearly just a matter of time before conflict erupted. In March Francis Joseph asked the Prussian court whether it really meant to rescind the agreement of Gastein, a move which Bismarck immediately denied. Later that month Prussia openly accused Austria of concentrating troops in Bohemia, and four days later King William signed an order for military preparations. Francis Joseph's ministers denounced the accusation that Austria was herself making warlike preparations as a false imputation by the Prussian government, and declared that the Emperor had no thought of attacking Prussia. In April he proposed that Prussia should withdraw her order for military preparations, reiterating firmly that he was not preparing to attack his neighbour. Prussia agreed to cancel its preparations if Austria should do the same.

Elizabeth dreaded the possible effect on her home and family. She was aware that King Ludwig would never be party to any of Bismarck's schemes for war, but feared that Bavaria was prepared to be a willing or at least subservient ally of Prussia. Longing to pay a visit to her old home, she was also keen to see her sister Sophie happily married. Despite everything she had suffered in her own marriage, she still entertained hopes of seeing an alliance between this sibling and her wayward but entertaining favourite brother-in-law Ludwig Victor. He was given permission by Francis Joseph to ask for Sophie's hand, and in March Ludwig Victor accepted an invitation to stay with the family at Possenhofen, but on closer acquaintance, it was obvious that neither cared much for the other. When the bachelor Archduke returned to Vienna he found his sister-in-law considerably less well disposed to him than before. She thought he had raised her sister's hopes with scant regard for her feelings, and never forgave him.

At a Cabinet Council in Vienna later in April, Francis Joseph declared it was time to decide definitely for or against hostilities with Prussia. 'If war be really considered inevitable,' he announced, 'then, far from interrupting the preparations we have already begun, we must, on the contrary, with all speed complete such measures as are necessary for war. But if war can be avoided, the question then is how to formulate our reply.'[8] The other ministers saw that Bismarck was merely seeking a pretext for the war he clearly wanted, and that it was up to them to ensure that his search was in vain.

Plans for both sides to demobilise foundered, and on 20 April the Chief of General Staff, Alfred Baron von Henikstein, advised the Emperor that if Austria desired to acquit herself with honour, they should put the whole army on a war footing. One week later Francis Joseph gave the order for mobilisation of the Austrian army, and war was declared against Prussia.

On 15 June 1866 Prussian troops crossed the frontiers of Hanover, Saxony and Hesse. Several small battles forced the Austrians and their allies from the German Confederation into retreat. The Austrian commander-in-chief, Field-Marshal Ludwig von Benedek, had been transferred from the Italian front, with which he was familiar, to the unknown terrain of Bohemia. He was no match for Moltke, his wily Prussian opposite number, and on 30 June he telegraphed the Emperor, begging him to make peace as a military catastrophe was inevitable. As no major battle had yet been fought, the Emperor was convinced that for them to lay down their arms in such humiliating circumstances would mean the end of Austria as a major European power. It was impossible to conclude peace at this stage, he answered; if defeat was unavoidable, the army should retreat in good order.

Left with no alternative but to stay and fight, Benedek drew the army up on a plain near the village of Königgrätz, ready to face the Prussians. Battle began at around 7.30 on the morning of 4 July. That evening Francis Joseph received another telegram from his loyal but dispirited commander, telling him that the disaster he feared had just occurred. Some 13,000 Austrians had been killed, 17,000 wounded and another 13,000 taken prisoner, and the rest of their forces were in retreat. Moltke's casualties numbered 9,172, of whom only 1,835 had been slain.[9]

Austria had paid dearly for its mistakes – inferior and outdated artillery, slow mobilisation, inefficient use of manpower and resources, and above all a poorly educated and ill-trained army of largely non-speaking German soldiers, who could not shoot accurately or manoeuvre in open order. A scapegoat was needed, and Benedek was asked to resign his command. As he had tried to warn his Emperor and the ministers of the army's grave deficiencies, he was asked to give a written promise that he would not publish any of the correspondence which had passed between himself and his generals or himself and the Emperor, or make any effort to vindicate himself publicly in any way. It was shabby treatment for a man who had deserved better. With his will he left a letter which noted that he had 'borne his hard lot as a soldier with philosophy and self-denial', but it had 'cost me all my poetic feeling for soldiering'.[10] In the seven years which elapsed before he died from cancer, embittered and old before his time, he refused to put on military uniform again.

The blow to Francis Joseph and the prestige of the house of Habsburg occasioned by defeat in Italy in 1859 had been severe, but this was much worse. The dynasty's power in Germany had been completely eclipsed by upstart Prussia. A large outdoor summer carnival in Vienna had been planned for the day on which news of the battle reached the city; it still went ahead, attended by 2,000 apparently unconcerned revellers eating, drinking and dancing in the city's Prater pleasure grounds.[11] Nevertheless, reaction varied between bitterness and shoulder-shrugging. There were some calls for the Emperor to abdicate, and the next time he appeared in public muted cheers were tempered with boos. It was rumoured that his wife might temporarily replace him as Regent, though how an Empress given to travelling far beyond the empire's borders whenever it suited her could be relied on to assume the regency was never explained. A few even demanded the overthrow of the dynasty itself. From Bavaria his mother-in-law, evidently unsettled by the gossip, telegraphed to ask whether the Emperor would stay in Vienna, or whether he had to flee.[12]

Peace was signed in Prague on 23 August. Francis Joseph ceded Venetia to Italy, the last Habsburg dominion in the Italian peninsula gone, while most of Schleswig, Holstein, Hanover, Hesse-Cassel, Nassau and the city of Frankfurt, were absorbed into Prussia, which henceforth assumed leadership of the new North German Confederation of states. The humiliation was not total, for a Southern German Union was formed at the same time, linked militarily and commercially to its northern neighbour, and with no special links to Austria, but consisting of independent sovereign states. No territorial losses were suffered by the empire, apart from Venetia which Austria had surrendered just before the war. Nevertheless, it was a blow for Francis Joseph, who wrote to Sophie that the double-dealing of Austria's enemies had been to blame for the disaster. He and his ministers had been honest, but foolish to believe in the promises of others. The world was against them, he bewailed, and they may be friendless, 'but you must go on doing what you can, fulfilling your duty and, in the end, going down with honour'.[13] For a few crisis-ridden weeks, his letters were signed 'Your poor little one'.

That this state of gloom persisted for several weeks if not months is borne out by an audience Lord Bloomfield had with Queen Victoria in December 1866. Austria, he told her, was

in an almost hopeless condition & not apparently becoming any wiser in spite of their fearful experience. Poor Alexander Mensdorff [a cousin of the Prince Consort] had been quite against the war, but was overruled. The whole affair had been shamefully, fearfully mismanaged – they were not prepared, & yet, would go to war. The Emperor had grown 10 years older, & was terribly cast down.[14]

On the outbreak of war Elizabeth had been at Ischl, but she returned at once to Vienna. She spent much of the time with Francis Joseph, trying to comfort and cheer him, only leaving his side to visit the wounded in hospital. Her selflessness and sudden rise to the challenge impressed Archduchess Sophie, who called her 'a good angel' in her letters to Rudolf.

It had been another grave defeat for Austria and a blow to its prestige, but worse was to come. Those who foresaw an ignominious end for Maximilian and Carlota in Mexico were to be proved correct. When the new Emperor and Empress landed at Vera Cruz in May 1864, there were no crowds to welcome them. Both worked unstintingly in their new surroundings, Maximilian travelling throughout the country while Carlota acted as his regent and transacted governmental business in his absence. Only gradually did they realise how much they had been misled. French troops were not in control, and resentment at a Habsburg archduke being foisted on the Mexican people ran high. When the American civil war ended, pressure on Napoleon to recall his troops and financial support intensified. Personal relations between Maximilian and Carlota were deteriorating under the strain, but the latter still stood loyally by her husband after France had withdrawn its interests.

She returned to Europe in desperation to beg Napoleon for help, but despite her accusations of treachery and double-dealing, he insisted he could do no more. From Paris she went to Rome to ask the Pope for help; he could offer nothing but sympathy. Years of tension had left their mark on her; her attendants noticed with unease her increasing moods of paranoia and outbursts of irrational temper, and her brother Philippe, Count of Flanders, was shocked at her haggard appearance. Soon she suffered a complete mental collapse, and it became apparent that she was descending irrevocably into madness. Still only twenty-six years of age and robust physically if not mentally, she was to endure a twilight existence until 1927, believing herself a reigning Empress and demanding gifts to be sent to England where she believed her husband was imprisoned. Meanwhile, in Mexico Maximilian's situation became steadily more untenable. The remaining French military presence left in February 1867 and he bravely placed himself at the head of imperialist troops, trying to ward off the Juaristas. In May his men deserted him and transferred their allegiance to General Juarez.

Austria's defeat and loss of prestige after Königgrätz precipitated a move which had been urged on the Emperor for some time by several, the Empress above all – rapprochement with Hungary. Her fascination with the country had deepened over the years. She was fluent in the language, which she had originally studied in order to make herself understood by Rudolf's nurse, and she had appointed a Hungarian, Ida Ferenczy, as a lady-in-waiting in order to help her learn it better. When the war was over the Emperor asked her to spend some time in Budapest, ostensibly to visit hospitals there, but really to speak to some of the leading politicians and prepare the way for a new climate of understanding.

While there she had important meetings with two Magyar politicians. Ferenc Deak was a prominent Magyar lawyer and country squire, and Count Julius Andrassy an aristocrat who had been involved in the revolution of 1848, gone into exile after its failure, and been hanged in absentia in 1851 for his misdeeds, only to return six years later after an amnesty. They both impressed on her the need for the Emperor to give their country internal autonomy, lest more revolutionary or radical elements might take over. At the same time she wrote to her husband regularly, telling him that she personally had been given a cordial reception, but that the mood of the people could be markedly hostile. Some young men of military age had sworn they would rather flee their homes for the woods than to serve again as Habsburg cannon fodder. Under Baron Ferdinand Beust, the prime minister of Saxony who had already won respect for his conciliatory powers between the defeated and victorious states in Germany, work on a new constitution began almost at once.

On her return to Vienna Elizabeth urged the Emperor to come to Hungary with her, and to make Andrassy minister for foreign affairs. He told her that her suggestions required consideration. Torn between concern for her husband and impatience at her failure to precipitate him into action, she returned to Budapest determined not to give way. After her repeated urging, the Emperor came to see Andrassy and Deak, but still could not make up his mind, telling her that 'it would be contrary to my duty to accept your exclusively Hungarian point of view'.[15] Preoccupied with the peace settlement as well as with Hungarian aspirations, a fortnight later he wrote to her that he was 'very depressed and find my courage leaving me the nearer we get to the peace and the internal difficulties against which we have to struggle become more apparent. Only my sense of duty keeps me going.'[16]

At length he was convinced that any settlement with Hungary would not necessarily weaken the dynasty. It was said that the crucial point in negotiations arose when he asked Deak what his demands were, and Deak assured him that they remained the same as they had been before the war with Prussia. Relieved at not being expected to make further concessions, the Emperor was satisfied.[17] An equally pleased Elizabeth returned to Vienna later that summer, knowing her mission was fulfilled.

On 30 October 1866 Francis Joseph appointed Beust the monarchy's new foreign minister. As a long-standing adversary of Bismarck, the original intention was for him to prepare for an eventual Austrian counter-offensive against Prussia, by helping to build an anti-Prussian front based on the south German kingdoms and any other state which stood in fear of Berlin, though in the end Bismarck got in first by courting their sympathies. Nevertheless, with Hungary on the agenda, work had to be done. On 18 February

1867 Andrassy was entrusted with the formation of a Hungarian government, whose members came to Vienna with their programme.

During May the official compromise, or *Ausgleich*, was agreed. The Austrian empire, with Hungary as a subservient state, became the Dual Monarchy of Austria-Hungary, and would henceforth be known as 'the Austro-Hungarian empire' or 'the Austro-Hungarian monarchy', ruled by 'the Emperor of Austria and Apostolic King of Hungary'. 'The lands of St Stephen', namely Hungary, Transylvania and Croatia-Slavonia, were united as a kingdom with internal autonomy, thereby placing a large number of Slavs under direct Magyar rule, and the rest of the Habsburg lands were left as a loose federation nominally governed by a parliament in Vienna. Both partners in the monarchy shared an army, a navy, and finance ministry, with the Emperor as their supreme commander. Only foreign affairs, defence and the joint budget remained common to Budapest and Vienna. German was still the official language of army and government offices, but military orders could be given in either tongue. The Vienna parliament was one of three in the Austro-Hungarian monarchy; another sat in Budapest, and the third comprised the Delegations, twenty members of the Upper House and forty members from the Lower House of each parliament, sitting separately in the Austrian and Hungarian capitals. There were three joint ministers, for foreign affairs, defence and finance, who did not sit in either parliament but reported to both Delegations. There were three armies: a combined army, and an Austrian and a Hungarian militia.

Over them all presided His Apostolic Majesty the King-Emperor, who was also Commander-in-Chief of the joint army. Should the Delegations not agree on something, the point at issue was referred to him and his decision was accepted as binding. The only restrictions on Hungarian self-rule were the rights which the Emperor retained to appoint and dismiss his own Hungarian prime minister, and to convoke, suspend or dissolve the Hungarian parliament. The *Ausgleich* was ratified on 29 May 1867, with the coronation arranged for 8 June.

What should have been a happy time was overshadowed by the uncertain reports of news from Mexico, where Maximilian had been captured and was held prisoner, with the likelihood of being sentenced to death for crimes against the Mexican people. Among those who sent pleas to General Juarez for clemency were King William of Prussia, General Garibaldi, and Andrew Johnson, president of the United States, while Francis Joseph, hoping to encourage Juarez to put his prisoner on board a ship for Europe, reinstated his full rights as an Austrian archduke. The press reported that should the Emperor hear of his brother's execution, the coronation in Hungary would not be postponed, but all accompanying celebrations would be cancelled.

A further pathetic family tragedy that week resulted in a few days of court mourning. Mathilde, the eighteen-year-old daughter of the Emperor's cousin Archduke Albrecht, accidentally set fire to herself. She had a cigarette in her hand when she saw her father approaching, and knowing how he disapproved of women who smoked, she hid it behind her back and set her dress alight. Within a few hours, she was dying from her burns.

By the time the Emperor was informed, the coronation was only two days away, and it was too late to alter the programme. Not even rumours of a conspiracy of terrorist explosions which would claim the lives of the sovereigns, ministers and spectators, or letters containing death threats against Deak, the Hungarian architect of the new age, would deflect them from their programme, though security precautions were increased. Though proud of her role in bringing the festivities about, Elizabeth quailed at the thought of all the fêtes she would be obliged to attend. 'It becomes a fearful burden', she wrote to her mother,

> to dress up first thing in the morning in a Court train and crown and hold Courts and receive presentations all the time – and then this appalling heat! . . . The Coronation takes place on Saturday at seven o'clock in the morning; the days before and after it are crammed with tiring ceremonies; the balls and the theatre will be the worst of all, for at present it is no cooler even at night.[18]

On the eve of the coronation there was a full rehearsal at the Church of St Matthew, for which Elizabeth tried on the magnificent costume of white and silver brocade scattered with jewels, patterned with lilac-blossom, and worn with a black velvet bodice, created by Worth in Paris at a cost of 5,000 francs. The Emperor was so captivated by her appearance that he kissed her spontaneously on the brow.

At 7 a.m. next day the procession moved off from the royal palace. The Magyar nobility, in their picturesque magnates' costumes, and riding on noble horses with trappings gleaming with gold, assembled not only to do honour to the kingdom, but also to display their own pomp and power. Francis Joseph was attired in the uniform of a Hungarian marshal and riding on horseback, while Elizabeth looked a picture in the national costume with a diamond crown on her head, driving in the state coach drawn by eight horses. The Life Guards were equally resplendent, with leopard-skins floating from their shoulders and riding grey horses.

At the ceremony itself Elizabeth was deeply moved as Andrassy, representing the Palatine, with the assistance of the Prince Primate, placed the Crown of St Stephen on the sovereign's head in the cathedral and laid the Mantle of St Stephen upon his shoulders. When, according to ancient custom, the same crown was held over Elizabeth's head to crown her Queen of Hungary, she forgot all her weariness and dislike of ceremonies and thrilled with the consciousness of the moment. As the *Te Deum* thundered forth, she and her husband laid the thick gold coins bearing their own effigy upon the golden plate; her eyes again filled with tears. They left the church together, to a roar of cheering from the crowd. The Emperor mounted his horse and rode off towards Coronation Hill and the platform where he was to take the oath, followed by a glittering procession in which rode the princes of the Church, clad in their finest robes, with coronets and mitres. While the minister of finance scattered gold and silver coins among the people, Elizabeth changed from her coronation robes into a simple white tulle dress, and took the steamer over to the Lloydpalais on the other side of the Danube. Here she watched the procession and the ceremony which followed from a flower-decked window. She could hardly suppress a smile when two unfortunate bishops, who had never been on horseback in their lives, suddenly parted company with their mounts as salvoes of musket fire were heard and cannon thundered out a salute.

She looked anxiously at the Emperor, whose splendid horse was also restive, but was held in check by its skilful rider. At the climax of the ceremony he raised his finger in taking the oath, then galloped

84

up Coronation Hill on his white charger and pointed the sword of Stephen towards all four points of the compass, in a symbolic resolution to protect Hungary from its enemies on every border. Not till the state banquet was over were the exhausted Emperor and Empress at last able to retire to their private apartments.

On the fifth day of the festivities the Emperor and Empress were each presented with a coronation offering of 5,000 gold ducats in a splendid silver casket. It was anticipated that they would use the money for the good of the country in some way, but nobody had expected it to be set apart for the widows, orphans and disabled men belonging to the *honveds* who had fought against Austria. All Hungary was convinced that this suggestion must have been made by Elizabeth.

What she most enjoyed were the natural products presented to them as offerings. A long procession of young men and maidens, dressed in the national costume, brought them glorious flowers, fruits of incredible size, a model in confectionery of the Coronation Hill with the Emperor on it, a Crown of St Stephen made of the finest pastry, enormous richly decorated hams, and a cream-coloured foal for the Crown Prince, its mane and tail plaited with tricolour ribbons in the colours of the Reich.

Despite the apprehension that had preceded them, the six exhausting days of festivities had gone off without accident. Elizabeth had captured the imagination of all who had seen her. Everybody agreed with Deak when he said that their lovely sovereign was a perfect emblem of graciousness and reconciliation. Even the Archduchess Sophie's ladies-in-waiting admitted as much, though their praises had something of a sting in the tail. One, Helene Fürstenberg, noted afterwards that 'Her Majesty looked quite supernaturally lovely during the solemn act, as moved and absorbed as a bride. I rather felt, too, as if, in *one* respect, she did interpret it in this sense.'[19]

For the Magyars, the *Ausgleich* was a resounding victory, much as it was resented by Vienna and by minority groups, such as the Slavs and Serbs, within the Dual Monarchy's borders. For Francis Joseph, it was a concession bordering on personal humiliation for Habsburg pride, which he accepted with praiseworthy grace.

FIVE

'Incredibly Devoted to his Duties'

After the coronation at Budapest, the King-Emperor and Queen-Empress went to Ischl for a holiday with Gisela and Rudolf. On 27 June they learnt that Nené's husband Maximilian, Prince of Thurn and Taxis, had died suddenly the previous day at the age of thirty-six. Ironically she had been the only one of the Wittelsbach sisters to make a genuinely happy marriage. They left to attend the funeral at Regensburg, then accompany the heartbroken widow and her four small children to Possenhofen.

Even worse news was on the way. After surrendering to government forces in Mexico, Maximilian had been tried by court martial and sentenced to death for treason. Two officers who had remained loyal to him to the end shared his fate in front of a firing squad outside Queretaro on 19 June 1867. Just before the shots rang out, Maximilian announced in Spanish that he forgave everyone, asked for forgiveness himself, and said that in giving his life he sincerely hoped peace would come to Mexico.

Only a fortnight earlier Francis Joseph had been assured by Napoleon that Maximilian's life was in no danger, as he was convinced that Mexican rebels would never dare put a Habsburg archduke to death. Full of remorse at not having forbidden his brother to go in the first place, he hurried to Vienna in order to tell their parents. Archduchess Sophie was completely broken by her favourite son's death, weeping bitterly as she declared that savages had murdered him as if he was a common criminal. To humiliate the Habsburgs even further, Juarez refused to release the body until November, and the state funeral in Vienna could not be held until February 1868.

At this point King William of Prussia and Tsar Alexander II were among crowned heads visiting the Great Exhibition in Paris. Francis Joseph had also been invited by Napoleon to attend, but the fate of his brother now ruled out a visit to Paris. In view of this, the French Emperor asked for permission to come to Salzburg and offer his condolences in person. Francis Joseph initially rejected this request from 'the arch-scoundrel of Villafranca'[1] – as if Austrian humiliation at Solferino in 1859 had rankled more deeply than the fate of his brother.

After being advised by Count Beust that Austria needed France as an ally in western Europe, he reluctantly agreed to a meeting in Salzburg in August. Both sovereigns and their consorts came face to face on 18 August, Francis Joseph's thirty-seventh birthday, amiably rather than cordially. Salzburg was illuminated with beacons on the surrounding mountains, and a banquet was held in a neighbouring castle. Beust claimed that Austria and France were 'linked together but not bound together', and suggested Francis Joseph should go to Paris in October, during the last weeks of the exhibition. Elizabeth was unwell, and thought she might be expecting another child. She stayed behind, and Francis Joseph was accompanied by his two surviving brothers. Charles Ludwig was no longer a widower; in 1862 he had married Princess Maria Annunziata of Naples, and they had two young sons, Francis Ferdinand and Otto.

This journey to France was the first time Francis Joseph had crossed the Austro-Hungarian frontiers, apart from his visits to other German princes and the tsars. To his surprise, he proclaimed himself 'struck all of a heap' by the place, as he 'had never thought it would be so overwhelmingly beautiful',[2] and clearly enjoyed himself. He was amused by the spectacle of Empress Eugenie keeping King Ludwig of Bavaria at arm's length while he was trying to steal a kiss from her, and paid several visits to the opera and theatre, though sometimes he struggled to stay awake throughout performances.

The *Ausgleich* brought Francis Joseph and Elizabeth closer again, if only for a while. His Habsburg pride might have made it hard for him to find accommodation with Hungary, but he could see that she was justifiably proud of her role, and that she seemed to have found a genuine purpose in the official life of the empire. It may have gone some way towards consoling him for the fact that she was obviously far happier in Budapest than in Vienna. At court dinners in the

Magyar capital she was animated, behaving like a different person altogether, finding that the art of fluent conversation came naturally to her. It was in stark contrast with her listless, wooden performances at Vienna where she would avoid receptions and other court functions whenever possible, and when she could not, restricted herself to asking guests 'Do you ride?' and 'Have you any children?'

By late autumn her pregnancy was confirmed, and she decided that the baby would be born in Hungary. Her success in and love for the country was deeply resented by some of the Viennese aristocracy who found her attitude divisive if not downright treacherous. They resented her appointing so many Hungarians to her household, and at least one lady at court said that it would serve the Empress right if she had a miscarriage. In February 1868 she moved to the palace in Buda, awaiting the birth of what she hoped might be a boy whom they could name Stephen, after the patron saint of Hungary.

That the child was yet another daughter, born on 22 April 1868 and named Valerie, did nothing to dampen their spirits. The proud father wrote to Rudolf, who was fascinated by the arrival of a little sister, that his little sister was 'a beauty, with great, dark blue eyes, a nose which is still a bit too fat, a very tiny mouth, enormously fat cheeks and such thick dark hair that it could be dressed already'.[3]

This child, Elizabeth decided, would be hers and hers alone, and her love for her rapidly grew into obsession. Her obvious preference for the baby led to Valerie being nicknamed 'the one and only one' (*die Einzige*) at court.[4] Elizabeth had as good as lost Gisela to her mother-in-law, while Rudolf had been handed over to a cruel military tutor who turned him into a nervous, highly strung child. Archduchess Sophie had chosen the best tutors and professors available to teach him, but the military tutor had been chosen by the Emperor. Count Leopold Gondrecourt was a savage bully with no understanding of a child's temperament. His way of making the small Crown Prince into a brave man was to fire pistols in his bedroom, or shut him up behind the gates of the wild game reserve, and shout that a wild boar was coming after him. It was no wonder that he grew up a physical coward, the very opposite of his parents.

One dark winter morning the Empress woke up to the sound of shouting outside. She looked out of the window to see Gondrecourt drilling her son and barking out orders in the snow. From then, the tutor was on dangerous ground. Early the following year, Elizabeth wrote to her husband to tell him that either Gondrecourt went or she would. She knew that her husband was so used to deferential requests that, on the rare occasions he was presented with a firm demand, he was so surprised that he would probably give in at once. Furthermore, she stipulated, she should be given unlimited powers regarding the children, the choice of those by whom they were surrounded, their place of residence, and the entire control of their upbringing.[5] At first he hesitated to countermand his mother's arrangements, but Elizabeth was unyielding. In view of her regular prolonged absences from Austria, perhaps she was exceeding her brief, and by then it was too late to undo the mental damage inflicted on her son by Gondrecourt. Nevertheless, he was dismissed and there was a relaxation in Rudolf's regime. The more liberal new tutor, Colonel Joseph Latour von Thurnberg, proved a better choice.

By the time of Valerie's birth the Emperor was thirty-seven, and had long since slipped comfortably into the daily routine from which he would never deviate for the rest of his life. Each night he slept in an ordinary military field-bed with a camelskin cover, rising soon after 4 a.m. all the year round. His valet slept in a bed beyond the curtained doorway. Pitchers of cold water and a small old-fashioned wooden washstand with basin were considered sufficient for the Emperor's ablutions, despite the washstand's sharp edges on which he often bruised himself. As soon as he woke, another valet who had been keeping watch while his master slept, would be on hand with a sponge and towels, ready to help wash and massage him while in a standing position. Once the bath attendant's duties were done for the morning, he was allowed to go to bed himself. Not surprisingly, he decided that if he must be on duty at such an unearthly hour, there was only one way to overcome the early rising difficulty, and that was to stop going to bed at all. He therefore became a regular patron at the neighbouring inn. Copious amounts of alcohol kept him cheerfully awake as well as alleviating his boredom, but on more than one occasion he reported for duty while hardly able to stand. At first the Emperor was amused, telling the others that they ought to keep an eye on the man as 'he couldn't stand much'. After the third time, when the man grabbed Francis Joseph's arms for support and they both nearly ended up in the washstand, he was relieved of his duties. Yet for all his faults he had been a faithful servant, and the Emperor asked that he should not be dismissed, merely given another post which did not involve him having to stay up so late.

Each day at home Francis Joseph dressed in the army uniform of a lieutenant. Breakfast sometimes comprised only a glass of milk, sometimes coffee (replaced by tea in later years), rolls and butter, with ham except on fast days. Then, in the words of historian Frederic Morton, he spent much of the morning following the routine laid down by his ancestors throughout many generations before him as he 'ruled and overruled with utter confidence, with axiomatic competence, and without the slightest inspiration'.[6] This involved spending two or three hours reading state papers, including proposals, petitions, budgets and ambassadorial letters placed in front of him by his principal secretary and military staff until 7 or 7.30 a.m. A large timetable was pinned to his desk, and the programme for every day was noted down, often to the last precise minute. In addition to official receptions and audiences, it included birthdays, anniversaries, bereavements, and visits of family members. Next came daily conferences with the chiefs of the cabinet and other officials, the chiefs of his military cabinet coming first. These finished at 10 a.m., to be followed by receptions of ministers and native and foreign dignitaries, which generally lasted well into the afternoon. Between breakfast and lunch he had nothing to eat, except perhaps a few biscuits. At midday came lunch, served on a silver tray and placed before him on the writing desk while he continued working. This might consist of beef stew, a couple of sausages, or a faintly flavoured hash, washed down with Bavarian, Seidel or Virginia beer.

He was always content with what was set in front of him, and never made any suggestion to the cooks as to how a dish could be served or prepared differently, or ever requested any particular dish which he had eaten elsewhere. The kitchen quarters were close to the living rooms, around which the smell of cooking, especially onions and garlic, invariably lingered. They were some distance from his study, and all the dishes had to be carried in two large tin cases. The chief cook put the finishing touches to the food in an anteroom adjoining the study, where there was a small brick oven and a spirit stove.

Only after the receptions did the Emperor take a proper break, to dine with family or guests, between 5 and 7 p.m. Formal banquets were appropriately lavish, but ordinary family meals – served with imperial ceremony – were more frugal, usually consisting of soup, entrée, beef or game, and a sweet. The servants always set the table without a sound, but Francis Joseph knew instinctively what stage the preparations had reached, and he would often come in to inspect the table before the meal was ready. He also had a habit of looking at his reflection on the blades of the knives in front of him. Though the cellars boasted a suitably magnificent collection of wines from different countries, he was content to leave these for others to enjoy, and normally only drank Austrian wine, supplied by a monastery of Scottish monks.[7]

One morning at breakfast the Emperor had just broken a bread roll and was about to raise it to his mouth, when he found a cockroach baked in it. The bread for his table was delivered by a baker well known to the court, and the household could not decide whether this was a genuine accident or some kind of demonstration against the monarchy. As a punishment, court patronage was briefly withdrawn from the baker, until he came to the valet and begged him to intercede with his master. Having made his point, Francis Joseph readily admitted that the baker was not to blame, and he was instantly restored to favour.[8]

Another unfortunate mishap occurred at a midday meal when an octogenarian valet who was close to retirement stumbled with a heavily laden tray, upsetting a soup tureen and a dish of dumplings in front of his master. 'I beg a thousand pardons!' he apologised. 'I lay myself at Your Majesty's feet!' The Emperor answered good-naturedly that there was 'enough at my feet already with the dumplings'.[9]

After dinner he would generally return to his desk for another hour or two before going to bed at around 8 or 9 p.m., unless prevented from doing so by special functions such as court banquets, balls, or visits to theatres and concerts. With advancing years, he found such breaks in his routine increasingly irksome. There was a standard rule that nothing, no matter how urgent, could be submitted to His Majesty after 8 p.m., as it would mean disturbing his routine or perhaps even waking him. Some of the court officials would complain that it was impossible to get anything important dealt with late at night, and that it would make matters much easier if he started and finished work later. But the Emperor would not be moved; he would deal with business in his own good time. As his aides-de-camp, secretaries and servants soon realised, he had a phenomenal memory for names, facts and figures – so it would not do to complain too much.

For his private correspondence large sheets of paper folded double were supplied, bearing the crest of the Private Chancellery. The Emperor was always careful to avoid waste, and if he did not use the second half of the page he would always cut off the clean part with a paper knife and put it aside, to write various orders and requests. He took great pains with his handwriting, which was remarkably neat and tidy. As his eyesight deteriorated, he took to wearing horn spectacles at his desk, and carried a pair of tortoiseshell pince-nez glasses with him for reading when away from his study.

Any decisions he made were always given in writing. He found that written communications gave him more elbow-room, and that his own train of thought was not hampered, as might well happen when other people were present to interrupt or distract him. Moreover, he trusted the written word more than the spoken, and he generally asked that any oral communications should be supplemented by simultaneous reports in writing. In important matters, he told an aide-de-camp, written communications were the safest and quickest method. 'If you really know what you want it is easy to put it down on paper; but not before! Most men are afraid of it.'[10]

These ways of working remained more or less unchanged throughout the years. No modern inventions such as typewriters or telephones intruded into his study. As so much of his time was spent in reading official documents and papers, it is hardly surprising that he never read a book.

As a ruler, his contemporaries considered Francis Joseph, while not clever, to be conscientious and thorough in his duties. His was a mind attuned to routine and rules, with an inborn distrust of experiment and improvisation which became more marked with age, and a deep respect for methodical paperwork. He required everything to be on file, and most of the documents which reached his desk were marked with some comment or correction, not least spelling mistakes, in his neat handwriting, before being passed to the relevant government department. Most could have been dealt with just as efficiently by his staff, but out of a sense of duty he made an effort to see as many of them himself as possible. Countess Marie Festetics, one of the Empress's ladies-in-waiting, commented that he possessed intelligence and quick understanding. 'Yet he gives his imagination no time to develop. Thus he sometimes acts abruptly, overworked as he is and incredibly devoted to his duties.'[11]

Balls at the Hofburg were magnificent occasions, with army officers in uniform, the nobility in their robes, and the women in their finest dresses and jewellery. The assembled company gathered on the first floor in the grand Rittersaal, decorated in white and gold, with palms and exotic flowers, lit by hundreds of candles in crystal chandeliers. At 8.30 p.m. the Grand Master of Ceremonies advanced to the end of the room and struck the floor three times with his staff of office. The doors were thrown open, the men stood to attention and the ladies curtseyed as the Emperor and Empress made their entrance. They were followed by a procession of archdukes and archduchesses and their suites, then the grand stewards of the court with their ladies, gentlemen of the bedchamber, ladies-in-waiting and chamberlains.

A description of one typical ball, held in 1880, describes Francis Joseph, 'tall with the slim figure of a fine horseman' attired in the white tunic and scarlet trousers of a field-marshal, advancing slowly down the room 'with the impersonal aloofness of a general inspecting his troops on parade',[12] with an air of distinction which immediately set him apart from everyone else. The Empress, whose presence at these functions could not be taken for granted, was beside him on this occasion, moving so lightly that she seemed to float rather than walk across the floor. Tall and slight, she wore a dress of mauve shot with silver that showed off her slender figure, her chestnut hair looped under a coronet of diamonds and emeralds with matching gems at her throat, on her bodice and round her waist. After escorting her to a dais at the far end of the room, her husband walked round good-naturedly exchanging a few words with their guests, while senior ladies from the diplomatic corps and the aristocracy were presented to her.

Once these pleasantries were concluded, the band began to play. Like everything else that evening, its programme had been timed precisely down to the last detail, with seven minutes allowed for a waltz, five minutes for a polka and twenty minutes for a quadrille. The ball always ended promptly at midnight. While dancing was in progress the Emperor walked round watching the guests. During the earlier years young ladies engaged to be married were presented to him, so when they saw him making a round of the salon they would form their own separate group. When they were pointed out to him, he would come and offer them his congratulations.

Where physical comfort was concerned, the balls left something to be desired. While the imperial family were fortunate enough to have chairs on the dais, everyone else had to compete for only two small marble seats. For most guests, that meant standing up all evening. Members of the imperial suites were able to sit down for supper, served in a separate room at small tables each presided over by an archduke. However, time-honoured protocol ensured that the same people generally sat next to each other. Those who could get near enough to the buffet might have wondered afterwards whether it was worth the effort. There were complaints about '10,000 dried up patties which for years they have had the effrontery to serve at the Hofball',[13] and the soup which was said to be made from a 300-year-old recipe. Some of the more jaundiced might have been forgiven for wondering whether the soup itself was the same age as well. Those who were lucky (or unlucky) enough to be allowed to sample any refreshments had to do so in the face of an unpleasant smell. As the Emperor insisted on all officers being dressed in accordance with army regulations, officers wore their full uniform with shako or parade headgear, swords buckled on, and their field or riding boots. The stench of boot polish was overpowering, and everyone complained of the excessive heat.

Francis Joseph also found the balls unbearably hot and boring, but he was as much a prisoner of Habsburg protocol as everyone else and would not think of making any changes. It might be tedious, but it was a chance for the dynasty to display its unity before the world, and in the name of family solidarity all archdukes and archduchesses were required to participate. If he had to take his place in the ritual, so must everyone else. Only one or two younger members, notably the Emperor's distant cousin Archduke Johann Salvator, refused to have anything to do with what they regarded as a ridiculous farce. Others, including the Empress and Crown Prince Rudolf, felt much the same, but knew better than to defy the Emperor's authority by absenting themselves.

The furniture in each of the Emperor's dwellings was extremely austere. In the Schönbrunn Palace, the imperial bedroom contained two twin beds of jacaranda wood, and for decoration there were wall coverings and curtains of blue Lyonnaise silk that had been hung in 1853, the year of his marriage, and were never replaced during his reign. The palace was said to include 1,441 rooms and 139 kitchens, but no bathroom. Such a facility, then still a very recent invention, was considered a luxury rather than a necessity.[14] Neither the Hofburg nor the villa at Ischl, his summer residence, had a bathroom either. At Ischl the bedroom was so small that there was no space for cupboards, and a small chest of drawers was used to store linen. The study was similarly inadequate for anything larger than a woefully impractical writing table, and whenever deeds and official documents of great size needed the imperial signature, his servants had to find room for a larger one into which extra leaves could be fitted as necessary. He often seemed oblivious to comfort, and when it was suggested he choose another bedroom at Ischl as his existing one became stiflingly hot in summer, he declined as he always wanted to keep the best apartments for other members of the family.

While he was never a tyrant towards his family, the Emperor believed that rules were made for their own good, and as head of the house of Habsburg he insisted on absolute obedience from them. All the archdukes, even his brothers, needed to obtain his express permission before going abroad; and they could not marry without his consent. Anyone who dared to transgress his wishes or commands could expect a sharp reprimand.

When the cares of state permitted, Emperor Francis Joseph's favourite relaxation was shooting. At Ischl he donned leather shorts, green jacket, thick woollen socks, mountaineering boots and Tyrolean hat, and with his hunting rifle and cartridge belts, he would stalk the mountain slopes for sport. While some of his contemporaries preferred the *battue*, at the end of which large numbers of victims would be brought back, he favoured what he saw as the more dignified pursuit of stalking. In the autumn he hunted at Gödöllö or Mürzsteg, a lodge in Styria, or at Lainz, rode in the Prater, or took solitary walks around the parks at Laxenburg. It was some consolation for the lack of family life while Elizabeth was away.

In 1869 Count Beust persuaded the Emperor to attend the opening ceremonies of the Suez Canal, an invitation extended to him by Khedive Ismail of Egypt when the Emperor had entertained him at Laxenburg in the first week of June. Beust urged him to emphasise Austria's interest in the Near East, not just by going to Egypt, but also by paying a courtesy call on the Sultan in Constantinople, a gesture no Christian monarch had yet made. An itinerary for the 'Imperial Tour in the East' grew longer, until it included a river trip through the Iron Gates to the lower Danube, a visit to Athens and a journey to Jerusalem – all activities which had not yet been undertaken by a Habsburg.

At first Elizabeth decided that she did not want to accompany her husband, as she thought the programme of ceremonial public appearances would be too much for her, and she said that little Valerie could not be separated from her mother for so long. Gossips thought that she had made her mind up after learning that Empress Eugenie would be formally opening the Suez Canal, instead of the ailing Emperor Napoleon, for she could not face a second round in the so-called beauty contest with her alleged rival. Both Empresses were said to be the most beautiful women of their time in Europe. As Elizabeth was preparing to say goodbye to Francis Joseph at Gödöllö, a castle in Hungary that had been presented to her as a summer residence, she tried to change her mind, but by then it was too late to alter the plans to include her as well.

The travels to a distant new part of the world clearly benefited Francis Joseph. He sent Elizabeth twelve letters, with entries written daily, reading like a travel diary of 20,000 words. Though the senior army officer in him made a careful note of the number of gun salutes or the bearing of the battalions, cavalry and field artillery of the Sultan's army on parade, he was clearly impressed with the sheer beauty of many of the scenes which he encountered. Reaching Turkish soil on 27 October, landing at Ruschuk to the standard welcoming ceremony, he was impressed by being 'in the midst of Turkish life, in the World of the East' with its sense of adventure and an extraordinary change of scene. How, he wrote to Elizabeth, he wished she was there with him to share everything, from the palaces; the glorious sunsets; the cypresses; the fleets of boats; the hurly-burly of people in every colour of costume, and above all descriptions of the Sultan's stables, his thirty-year-old favourite grey and his 800 mounts.

A few days later the imperial yacht *Greif*, followed by two other Austrian ships carrying Francis Joseph's suite and accompanying ministers, including Beust and Andrassy, sailed for the Sea of Marmora, the Dardanelles and ultimately Piraeus. On reaching the Holy Land Francis Joseph was once again entranced by his surroundings, in a party guarded by several hundred Ottoman soldiers, moving slowly forward in a caravan of camels, with Bedouin horsemen on greys as outriders. As he saw Jerusalem for the first time, he sank to his knees in prayer. He visited the holy shrines in the city and at Bethlehem, went to Jericho and the Dead Sea, stopped at the River Jordan, and, loaded with relics and holy water bottles, set off back to the coast, bivouacking in tents, their canvas embroidered with gold and silk designs. On 15 November the three Austrian vessels moored off Port Said, ready for the canal's official opening ceremonies to begin the next day.

Eugenie had already been in Egypt for a month, and Francis Joseph informed Elizabeth that she had grown quite stout and was much less beautiful than before. Even so, the opening ceremonies were her great personal triumph. The construction of the Suez Canal had been masterminded by her cousin, Ferdinand de Lesseps, and the scheme was sponsored by the French imperial establishment. The French yacht headed the procession of ships down the canal, with Francis Joseph following aboard *Greif*; then came a line of nearly forty other vessels. Overnight the flotilla anchored in the Bitter Lakes before completing the second stage of the journey to Suez. At Ismailia there was a grand ball, attended by several thousand people, with Eugenie in a bright red dress entering the ballroom on the arm of a very attentive Francis Joseph.

At Cairo the Emperor saw 410 mosques, a gala night at the new 'Italian Theatre' opera house beside the Nile, and climbed the pyramid of Cheops, the highest at Ghiza, which took him seventeen minutes. The Bedouins, he noted, were very agile, strong and self-assured. 'As they mostly only wear a shirt, when they are climbing they leave a lot exposed, and that must be the reason why English women so happily and frequently like to scale the pyramids.'[15] From there they returned to Alexandria and then to Trieste, where Francis Joseph was to see Elizabeth again. She had planned to visit her pregnant sister Marie, former Queen of the Two Sicilies now exiled in Rome, while he returned to Vienna. His travels had been a display of friendship and support towards France, and a useful gift to those in the war ministry who still hankered after a war of revenge against Bismarck's Prussia.

At around this time there were unofficial meetings between French staff officers and Austrian representatives, and in February 1870 Baron Franz Kuhn, Austro-Hungarian war minister, informed the French military attaché in Vienna that, if France and the Dual Monarchy should ever declare war on Prussia, he could guarantee full mobilisation of an army of 600,000 men within six weeks. In March Archduke Albrecht, in his capacity as titular inspector-general of the army, visited Paris and unfolded a strategic plan to the French minister of war. It included a proposal for France to keep the Prussian force engaged for weeks and to mount an offensive in the general direction of Nuremberg, whereupon the Austrians and perhaps an Italian force would cross into Saxony, raise the south German states and join the French in a march on Berlin to destroy Prussia.

France was more ready to take the field than either of her allies, and claimed she could mobilise in a fortnight as opposed to the six weeks required by Austria and Italy. The Archduke then proposed that the three powers should begin mobilisation simultaneously, but that Austria, instead of declaring war before it was ready, should feign neutrality while concentrating two army corps at Pilsen and Olmutz. A formal agreement between France and Austria was concluded on 13 June 1870, and that same day Albrecht drafted the plan of campaign, a general scheme of joint action between the two powers, and a detailed plan of campaign for the distribution and employment of the French army. But the French were not convinced by Albrecht's master-plan, not least because of the six-week delay. They suspected the Austrians would wait and see which side looked more assured of victory. Still, it would hardly suit France for its ally to be crushed while in the act of mobilising.

In June a French general visited Austria, and gathered that Francis Joseph was disinclined to risk another war. Twice in the past the Emperor had allowed his ministers and generals to talk him into disastrous wars. At the same time, he could see that Albrecht and Kuhn disagreed with each other. The former was ready to declare war, while Kuhn was convinced that the army was ill-prepared for the challenge. Later he began to urge that Austria-Hungary could not stand aside from the inevitable forthcoming struggle, and Albrecht circulated a critical anonymous pamphlet, maintaining that the army was short of modern weapons, and the parsimony of the war ministry meant that it was ill-equipped for any mobile campaign in the field. At this point, the Emperor decided to ask General Frederick von Beck, chief of the military chancellery, to report back to him on the readiness of his troops for war. Beck agreed with Albrecht rather than Kuhn; but before these arguments could be resolved, the Emperor and all his ministers were shaken by the sudden deterioration in Franco-Prussian relations over the so-called Hohenzollern candidature for the Spanish throne.

On 15 July Richard Metternich, Austrian ambassador in Paris and son of the late chancellor, learnt that war between France and Germany was imminent. Francis Joseph would not have questions of peace or war decided for him in Paris, and he summoned a council of ministers for 18 July, the day before hostilities broke out between the two nations.

Presiding over the council himself, the Emperor spoke at some length. Beust confirmed that Austria-Hungary retained a free hand and that the French had taken no notice of Austrian pleas not to allow the Hohenzollern candidature to be transformed into a German national issue. Andrassy was among those who considered Russia a more dangerous threat to the monarchy than Prussia, as he thought that Pan-Slav hotheads were in the ascendancy at St Petersburg. If Austria-Hungary was committed to a campaign in southern Germany, the Russians would seize any opportunity to stir up the southern Slavs and press forward with plans to dominate the Balkans and the lower Danube. Kuhn, who had circulated a memorandum in advance of the conference favouring immediate intervention, spoke passionately on the need for Austria to prevent the permanent siting of Prussian garrisons along the River Inn. Archduke Albrecht wanted immediate mobilisation but when, later in the day, he took the chair at a second ministerial conference, there was a strong feeling in favour of neutrality.

As a gesture of reassurance towards Andrassy, Francis Joseph ordered defensive measures to be taken along the monarchy's frontier with the Russian empire. The Duc de Grammont formally asked Austria for military help, assuring Beust that peace would be signed in Berlin, and the memories of 1866 thus effaced. Never again, he said, would such a chance occur. Beust replied that they would contribute in every way possible to the success of French arms, and that Austrian neutrality was 'only a means towards the true end of our policy; the sole means of completing our armaments without exposing ourselves to a premature attack on the part of Prussia or Russia'.[16] Beust's caution, and the warning voice of Andrassy, who saw how vulnerable Hungary was from a geographical point of view, ensured that the Dual Monarchy was unwilling to risk a Russo-German onslaught.

Like his ministers, the Emperor understood that the crisis had nothing to do with Austria-Hungary. Though he had more sympathy for France than for the over-mighty Prussia, he knew that neutrality for the Austro-Hungarian empire was the right course of action. There was something to be said for Beust's plan to enter, or at least consider entering, the war on the side of the French once they had won the decisive victory in battle over Prussia that everyone expected them to, and then exploit any ensuing peace settlement in order to restore the Habsburg protectorate over south Germany as a bulwark against France and Prussia at the same time. Francis Joseph remained at Schönbrunn, presiding over five ministerial conferences in twelve days after the German invasion of France had begun. He was convinced that entering the war prematurely would result in disaster, so tentative preparations that had been made for an imminent campaign were stopped. The Emperor believed that Beust was right in saying that they would surely gain more in influence and prestige by playing a waiting game and perhaps doing no more than being ready to offer their services in mediation. One week after the declaration of war Francis Joseph wrote personally to Emperor Napoleon, offering his good wishes but no more.

Events soon justified their caution. France was decisively defeated at Sedan in September, Napoleon and Eugenie abdicated, and a French republic was proclaimed. In January 1871 the birth of a German empire under Prussian leadership, with King William taking the title of German Emperor (rather than Emperor of Germany, in order not to provoke the other kings of German territories) seemed to have put an end to the Habsburg voice in German affairs, as well as to any Austrian hopes of seeking revenge on Prussia after 1866.

Francis Joseph was obliged to congratulate the Prussian ambassador in Vienna, General Hans Lothar von Schweinitz, on his sovereign's success, but made it plain that he did so with some reluctance. The ambassador recalled later that the Emperor said he was unable to rejoice at the event, 'neither would you expect me to do so'.[17] The future German chancellor, Prince Bülow, never a reliable source, quoted Schweinitz as saying that the occasion was one of the most painful interviews of his life, as the Emperor could initially not bring himself to speak a single word. In the end he asked curtly whether 'his' regiment in the Prussian army, Emperor Francis's Second Regiment of Guards, had sustained heavy losses, and then dismissed the ambassador.[18]

As one of those who most distrusted Prussia, Beust was required to resign his post in the interests of Austro-German friendship after peace was declared, and he was replaced as Austro-Prussian minister by Andrassy. Cynics deemed it a fitting appointment, now that Vienna was reduced to 'being the capital of the Balkans'.[19]

In April 1872 Archduchess Gisela was betrothed to Prince Leopold of Bavaria, her second cousin twice over. The Emperor consented to this marriage, he wrote to his mother, as there were so few Catholic princes that 'we had to try to secure the only one to whom we might give Gisela with any confidence'.[20] Though Archduchess Sophie was very fond of her granddaughter and of her husband-to-be, she noted in her journal that the marriage was 'no match'. Not quite sixteen, Gisela was a plain but even-tempered girl, quite unlike the mother who had never given the impression of caring much about her. As she was still so young – though exactly the same age as her mother had been at the time of her betrothal – it was agreed that the wedding would not take place for another year. Courtiers suggested that the Empress wanted the ceremony to be postponed in order to delay as long as possible the day when she would become a grandmother.

The family joy at this announcement was soon overshadowed by the death of the matriarch to whom the empire had owed so much. Archduchess Sophie had never really been the same since Max's ignominious death. Loss of Austrian prestige and the supremacy of Hohenzollern Prussia had also grieved her deeply, and put an end to any hopes she might still have entertained of a greater Austria dominating the German-speaking peoples from the North Sea to the Adriatic. In May 1872 she caught a chill which rapidly worsened, and she took to her bed knowing she would not recover. When she fell into a coma Francis Joseph placed Maria Theresa's cross and rosary, brought from the imperial treasury, in her hands, and Elizabeth barely left her bedside for four or five days. Perhaps she was belatedly making amends for maligning the woman whose intentions had always been of the best.

After the Archduchess, who had been Empress in all but name, breathed her last on the morning of 28 May, aged sixty-seven, Francis Joseph broke down and sobbed like a child, while Elizabeth was close to fainting and had to be carried from the room.

Nearly thirty years later, when talking with an aide-de-camp about the family life of the German Emperor William II, Francis Joseph remarked with sadness on the latter's difficult relationship with his mother, the widowed Empress Frederick, who had just passed away. 'Is there anything dearer on earth than one's mother?' he asked. 'Whatever differences may separate us the mother is always the mother, and when we lose her we bury a good part of ourselves in her grave.'[21] Ironically it was the German Crown Princess (the future Empress Frederick) who sounded a critical note when hearing about the Archduchess's last illness. While expressing sympathy for the dying woman, she commented to Queen Victoria with some asperity that the Emperor's mother had 'done Germany and the good cause of progress and liberty more harm than anyone. Neither Austria nor Prussia have any cause to be grateful to her.' Even her own son, she remarked, had suffered as a result of her intrigues.[22] Yet in Vienna the citizens mourned her almost as deeply as did her family, remarking sadly that they had lost their real Empress.

In September 1872 Francis Joseph visited Berlin, and Tsar Alexander II proposed at the last minute that he too should come. It was the first time that the Austrian, Prussian and Russian sovereigns had met since the inconclusive Warsaw conference twelve years earlier, and they were never to meet again. The meeting was presented as a demonstration against 'the revolution', as if to try and show some kind of solidarity between them, as well as conceal the fact that they had not agreed on anything. There was still a degree of mutual antipathy between all three rulers. Much the youngest of the triumvirate, Francis Joseph neither liked nor trusted the Tsar, while he found the 'arrogance, vanity and sanctimoniousness' of Emperor William hard to tolerate.

On 20 April 1873 Gisela and Leopold were married at the Augustinerkirche, the parish church of the Hofburg. The bride was all but outshone by her radiantly youthful-looking mother, but the shy, uncomplicated Gisela probably never minded the lack of attention paid to her. Festivities for the occasion included a gala performance of *A Midsummer Night's Dream*, and a grand ball given by the city of Vienna at the concert hall of the Musikverein. After the wedding Elizabeth seemed dry-eyed, but Rudolf broke down and wept, while even Francis Joseph had tears in his eyes.

Meanwhile, preparations were being made for a Universal Exhibition in Vienna, a successor to similar ventures in London and Paris during the preceding decades. Among those who had come to attend the opening on 1 May were the Prince of Wales, his brother Prince Arthur, the German Crown Prince and Princess Frederick William, and the Crown Princes of Saxony and Denmark. In accordance with Andrassy's plans for a rapprochement with Germany, the Crown Prince and Princess were to be treated with particular honours, and allowed to proceed to the exhibition buildings in procession immediately following the Emperor and Empress. As their carriages were preparing to assemble on the first morning, Elizabeth failed to appear, and Francis Joseph was pacing up and down in his apartments in frustration. To add to his woes, a message was sent to Count Grünne that the Crown Prince and Princess's procession was already on its way. Furious that they would get there first and he would be unable to receive his guests, the Emperor threatened to punish those responsible, until the Empress suddenly appeared, took him by the arm, and led him out to their carriage.

At the inaugural ceremony Charles Ludwig, protector of the exhibition, delivered a formal speech of welcome to the Emperor, saluting 'his gracious participation' that 'fitly terminates a work which draws up on Austria the eyes of the world, and secures to our Fatherland the recognition of prominent participation in the promotion of the welfare of mankind by instruction and labour'.[23] The Emperor then officially declared it open to the public. Beside him, Elizabeth and Rudolf on a large dais surrounded with flowers sat the other imperial and royal guests. Several crowned heads followed during the next few weeks, among them King Leopold II of Belgium, Tsar Alexander II of Russia, Shah Nasr-ed-Din of Persia, King George of the Hellenes, and King Victor Emmanuel of Italy.

Some were more welcome or better-mannered than others. The Tsar was aloof and unsmiling throughout, except for one brief moment when engaged in conversation with Elizabeth, his general attitude suggesting that he had still not forgotten Austrian ingratitude during the Crimean war, while the Hohenzollern presence required Francis Joseph to don the uniform of the Prussian Guard Grenadier Regiment of which he was Commander-in-Chief, muttering that after Königgrätz he felt like an enemy to himself.

However, he proved the most accommodating of hosts, and Elizabeth likewise steeled herself to make an effort much of the time. The German Crown Princess, who had written to Queen Victoria before leaving Berlin that she dreaded Vienna 'so much' and 'would give anything to get out of it',[24] found that 'nothing can be kinder than the Emperor and Empress are to their guests and to us in particular'.[25] Accompanying his parents was their eldest son, fourteen-year-old Prince William, who later described the Emperor somewhat flatteringly as 'full of youth and vigour' with 'the figure of a subaltern'. He recalled that when he was presented to the Emperor, 'his eyes rested upon me with fatherly tenderness'.[26]

The exhibition was dogged by misfortune. A few days after its opening, Vienna was stricken with an epidemic of cholera that claimed over 2,000 victims. When the newspapers tried to suppress the news, people worked themselves up into a panic and many fled from the city to avoid any risk of infection. Taxi drivers went on strike and, worst of all, the Vienna stock exchange collapsed, a hundred traders on the Bourse went bankrupt, and there was a rush to sell stocks and shares. Among discredited speculators were a leading member of the Emperor's military chancellery, a former minister of home affairs, and Archduke Ludwig Victor, who had used part of his mother's legacy to chance his luck.

Elizabeth soon complained that the festivities were exhausting her, and wished that all members of visiting royalty 'would all come together for one nightmare week',[27] while even her husband found the summer a strain. He complained that he was tired out, 'and should like to grant myself sick-leave for a time'.[28] To make matters worse the summer and autumn weather was poor, and the 7 million visitors fell far short of the 20 million expected. By the time it closed on 2 November it showed a deficit of 15 million gulden.

The need to entertain fellow crowned heads on their state visits, and frequent ministerial councils, meant that Francis Joseph could only leave his capital for a short holiday with Elizabeth at Ischl in August. She fell ill with gastric fever in September on the eve of the King of Italy's visit and spent ten days in bed. Any suspicions that she might have been malingering in order to avoid meeting the man whose united Italy had been achieved at the cost of her sister and brother-in-law, ex-King and Queen of the Two Sicilies, were dispelled when she was too unwell to attend a grand horse show in the Prater. Countess Festetics noted bitterly that she had been constantly on duty throughout the exhibition, 'and now she has had to go to bed for ten days and miss the horse show, the only social event she really enjoys. But everyone thinks they have the right to criticise her.'[29] In October the family escaped to Gödöllö, though even there the Empress's recuperation proved slow.

However, she was sufficiently well to return to Vienna for her husband's silver jubilee celebrations. The city streets were decorated with bunting and discreetly illuminated, as on the evening of 1 December the Emperor and Rudolf drove around the Ringstrasse in an open carriage, the Empress following in a closed one. Next day, the anniversary of his accession, he and his generals exchanged compliments at a ceremony in the Hofburg, Rudolf in uniform standing beside his father while Archduke Albrecht offered those of the other officers. In the evening Francis Joseph and Elizabeth attended a gala performance of *The Taming of the Shrew* at the Stadttheater. Though the Emperor was not particularly interested in literature, after the performance he summoned Laube, the producer, to the imperial box to tell him that the performance had given him much pleasure. Nobody could foresee that the actress playing Kate, a grocer's daughter from Baden named Katherine Schratt whom he saw for the first time that night, would soon become a central figure in his life.

On the day after the celebrations, Elizabeth returned to Gödöllö. Her swift disappearance prompted at least one newspaper to remark that 'that strange woman the Empress' preferred to stay anywhere rather than Vienna. When a deputation of journalists called upon the Emperor soon afterwards to congratulate him on the anniversary, in his address of thanks he could not resist saying that he hoped in future the press would not concern itself with the private and family life of the Empress.[30]

SIX

'He Stands Alone on his Promontory'

The new year of 1874 was barely under way before Francis Joseph and Elizabeth became grandparents. Gisela gave birth on 8 January to a baby girl whom she named Elizabeth after her own mother. 'Only 44 and already a grandfather!' commented the Emperor, though he was seven months short of his birthday. Elizabeth immediately left to be with her daughter, and stayed with her for a fortnight. She wrote to Rudolf that his little niece was 'unusually ugly, but very lively – not a thing to choose between her and Gisela'.[1]

In February Francis Joseph visited Russia as a gesture of reassurance to Tsar Alexander II, who mistrusted Austria-Hungary's Balkan policies. One of his first acts was to lay a wreath on the tomb of Tsar Nicholas I and stand at the vault in silent prayer. Next Alexander took him into his father's apartments, still maintained as they had been at the time of his death. At last the bitterness of nearly twenty years could be laid to rest. Imperial solidarity was sealed, as both rulers knew that mutual support would be invaluable over the years and crises ahead. During his visit Francis Joseph took part in political discussions with Gorchakov, the chancellor, as well as lavish entertainments and banquets in St Petersburg, where he met some of the Tsar's English and Danish relatives by marriage.

Elizabeth did not accompany her husband. Uncharacteristically she stayed at the Hofburg, as he had asked her to remain there until he returned. She was becoming increasingly restless and had taken to exploring Vienna in disguise. While he was away she embarked on one of her most bizarre escapades. In disguise at a masked ball during the carnival season, she struck up a friendship with a civil servant called Fritz Pascher. She questioned him closely on how people in Vienna felt about the court, the Emperor and Empress, receiving very guarded answers. He realised who he was speaking to, but rather naively the Empress assumed that he would not recognise her. For some weeks after the ball she sent him letters signed 'Gabrielle' via her sister Marie, former Queen of the Two Sicilies, who had leased a house in London and sent these letters on to Pascher. Fortunately Pascher was the soul of discretion, and kept the letters secret until shortly before his death almost sixty years later. The Emperor never found out about them.

Valerie was a sickly child, and in her early years suffered from bronchial weakness. While often protective towards her favourite youngest child, Elizabeth was keen to see her grow up properly, ready to take part in normal rough-and-tumble with those of her own age. When she was about six, Countess Sandra Vorontzov-Dashkov, a playmate of Tsarevich Alexander's children in Russia, was staying with her family in Vienna for a time, and Elizabeth invited her to Schönbrunn to play with Valerie, who was a year older than Sandra. During a game of tag in the palace gardens Valerie tried to catch Sandra, fell over and her nose started bleeding. A lady-in-waiting scolded the little countess, saying that she 'should be more careful when playing with an august personage'. At that moment the Empress emerged from a clump of trees, and said that it was not her fault, but her daughter's – she did not know how to play tag.[2]

Soon after Valerie's sixth birthday in April 1874, the Empress told her husband that their daughter needed a holiday with plenty of sea air, and fine weather without too much heat. At the time Beust was ambassador in London, and she asked him to find somewhere suitable for a summer visit. In August 'Countess von Hohenembs', the Empress's incognito, and Valerie arrived at Steephill Castle, Ventnor, on the Isle of Wight, for a short holiday. The location proved perfect in every sense except one, for within hours of her arrival Queen Victoria had called. The last thing Elizabeth wanted was an invitation to dine with the Widow of Windsor at Osborne, and twice she declined on the grounds that she was indisposed. Nevertheless, she tactlessly accepted an invitation to visit the Duke and Duchess of Teck at White Lodge, near Richmond, during which she saw something of London.

Francis Joseph was on manoeuvres at home, and she wrote to him regularly of her delight in England, pressing him to take a fortnight off and come to join her, so he could visit London and enjoy a little hunting in the countryside himself. Despite her persuasion, and the fact that he had no pressing commitments for a few weeks, he never came. Any tentative ideas he might have had about joining her that summer were the nearest he ever came to visiting England. She later returned to hunt at Althorp, the Northamptonshire estates of Earl Spencer, riding with a recklessness which amazed if not alarmed those closest to her.

In June 1875 the empire said farewell to *der Praguer Majestas*, when ex-Emperor Ferdinand passed away at the age of eighty-two. He left his nephew a considerable fortune, as his financial advisers had been prudent enough to avoid the stock market, leaving him unaffected by the crash of 1873. His widow remained at Prague for the last nine years of her life.

Though the frugal habits of a lifetime were too ingrained for him to change, the Emperor was now probably the wealthiest sovereign in Europe. Characteristically, he wanted to share this newly acquired windfall. He tripled the annual allowance of 100,000 florins which had been assigned to the Empress on their marriage, and presented her with a capital sum of 2 million florins, much of which was invested for her in the event of his predeceasing her. In future years he would show considerable indulgence in buying the finest thoroughbreds for her to ride to hounds, as well as financing the construction and furnishing of various new residences which she asked for during her years of wandering throughout Europe. He also humoured her in what seemed like one of her more eccentric requests, though in fact it was a charitable inspiration. She had always been sympathetic to the plight of the mentally ill, despite the assertions of those at court who put it down to a sense of misplaced curiosity. More than once she had said she would like a new lunatic asylum to be built. Now her wish could be granted by the husband who was always ready to give her what she wanted, even if he found it difficult to understand why.

Throughout his reign, Francis Joseph made various visits to his provinces. Their purpose was ostensibly for him to learn more about the different regions of his realm, but in fact they were more a chance for him and his court to display the majesty of empire to his subjects. A large court entourage went with him each time, but he remained largely shielded from reality, and though these journeys helped to convey the image of an Emperor being above party and national politics, they kept him isolated and at a distance from those over whom he ruled. As was generally the case with heads of state, senior members of royal and imperial families, and senior politicians in other countries, a retinue and a carefully devised programme ensured that by and large only the right people, places and things were seen, and that there should be as little opportunity as possible for anything to go wrong. A fateful visit to Sarajevo undertaken almost four decades later by the man who would otherwise have succeeded Francis Joseph as Emperor would serve as a salutary reminder of how the smallest error in an itinerary could have tragic repercussions.

In March 1875 General Rodić, governor of Dalmatia, formally invited Francis Joseph to make a visit to the province. After his meeting with King Victor Emmanuel in Venice, he was to spend a month visiting every important town on the coast and several of the offshore islands. Close to the Dalmatian border were the Ottoman provinces of Bosnia and Herzegovina, which acknowledged the sovereignty of the Sultan and were predominantly Islamic in culture, though the people were mainly Slavs. For four centuries they had formed the north-western frontier of the Ottoman empire, isolated from the Mediterranean world yet keeping their distance from Constantinople so indifferent to the reforms of the Sultans. Their economic potential was limited, but in 1854 the war ministry in Vienna had prepared detailed plans for their seizure, and Radetzky had urged the Emperor two years later to put them into operation. The Austrian generals wanted to protect Dalmatia by securing a land route to safeguard garrisons in the area in case of a blockade by sea from the other powers. In 1869 General Beck urged annexation of the provinces in order to prevent them from falling into the hands of the two Southern Slav principalities, Serbia and Montenegro, should the Ottoman empire collapse. Otherwise they might become Russian puppets, easily manipulated in Great Power politics to serve Russian interests.

Francis Joseph was reluctant to tackle the problem by bringing more Slavs into the Dual Monarchy, as it would disturb the delicate balance between the German-Austrians and Hungarians. Nevertheless, he was keen to see something of the southern outposts of his empire in person. On 10 April 1875 he landed from the warship *Miramare* at Zadar, to be received by the civil and military dignitaries of his Dalmatian lands. He enjoyed his sightseeing, and the welcoming parties, with small children presenting bouquets of flowers beneath triumphal arches in the towns and villages where he stopped. Nearly every day he wrote to Elizabeth of his movements, though he made no mention of any political implications.

By 28 April, when he reached Dubrovnik, the Emperor must have sensed a degree of political tension. Franciscans in Dubrovnik were in close contact with those in Herzegovina, and made no secret of their hopes that if Austria-Hungary absorbed the twin provinces, the Emperor would protect the Christian religion and put an end to an allegedly corrupt system of government. Reports reached the Sultan of Francis Joseph's triumphal progress and alarmed him so much that he sent his governor in Bosnia to meet the Emperor. The governor, Dervish Pasha, was granted an audience, but it was a strictly formal occasion and neither man had much to say to the other.

More fruitful were Francis Joseph's visits by land and sea to the Gulf of Cattaro. He received several deputations, and on 3 May had a meeting with Prince Nicholas of Montenegro. They had already come face to face at the Vienna World Exhibition, where Nicholas had been a guest, and Francis Joseph reported back that Nicholas was very well disposed towards Austria. In mid-May he arrived back in Vienna, impressed by what he had seen along the Adriatic coast, and understood the advantages of securing the new provinces, which would be some compensation for the loss of his Italian possessions. General Anton Mollinary, army commander in Zagreb, was warned to stand by and be ready to command an army of occupation if the provinces should suddenly appear to be slipping from the Sultan's grasp.

A month after the Emperor's return, one of the dignitaries who had come to meet him during his Balkan visit was murdered. Revolts broke out in the provinces, with Herzegovinian clansmen raiding Muslim villages and attacking Muslim caravans. Mollinary was ready with his army, but no order for occupation came from Vienna. The internal bloodshed died down, only to erupt with even greater savagery in Bulgaria the following spring. In Constantinople a palace revolution deposed the Sultan, Turkish liberals demanded the granting of a constitution, and Serbia and Montenegro jointly declared war on the Ottoman empire.

If the war was to remain localised, it seemed vital that the League of the Three Emperors should coordinate policy. Francis Joseph sent Archduke Albrecht to Berlin for talks with Emperor William I and Bismarck, while Tsar Alexander II and his chancellor, Gorchakov, also went to Berlin. Then, at Gorchakov's request, Francis Joseph asked the Tsar to meet him and Andrassy in Bohemia during his journey home from Berlin. They met on 8 July at Bohmisch-Leipa, with the Tsarevich accompanying his father. Francis Joseph and his foreign minister noted with relief that their Russian opposite numbers did not want a Russo-Turkish war.

The Reichstadt Agreement later that day guaranteed that if the Ottoman armies defeated the Serbs and Montenegrins, Austria-Hungary and Russia would ensure that no changes would be made in the existing territorial boundaries. If Serbia and Montenegro were to force the Sultan to sue for peace, the Ottomans would be virtually expelled from Europe. Francis Joseph believed that this agreement would help him to acquire the provinces in due course without the risk of conflict with Russia, and a friendly meeting with Emperor William at Salzburg in August reinforced the amicable arrangements between the Emperors.

Contrary to general expectations, the resistance of Serbia and Montenegro soon began to crumble. By October the Russians were considering intervening in the Balkans to save their Orthodox brethren from Ottoman retribution, and ministers at St Petersburg ordered the Turks to agree to an armistice with Serbia. By the end of 1876, it was apparent that Tsar Alexander II was paying less attention to the Reichstadt Agreement than to the voices of Pan-Slavs around him who cared little for the well-being of Austria-Hungary. Though Francis Joseph and Andrassy still believed that the Tsar sought a peaceful solution to the Eastern question, they feared that a Russo-Turkish war was imminent. It came as little surprise when, on 24 April 1877, Russia declared war on the Ottoman Empire.

Francis Joseph had little sympathy with the Russian cause. On 15 January 1878 he presided over a conference of ministers in

Vienna. The Russian army was already in Sofia and advancing towards Constantinople, where troops would probably arrive by the end of the month. Andrassy thought some token military demonstration should be made in order to assert the prestige of the Dual Monarchy, but Archduke Albrecht was averse to any anti-Russian move. Declaring war on Russia was an impossibility, as to risk a protracted conflict would be to court almost certain state bankruptcy. Even short campaigns in the Balkans would impose too much of a financial burden on the treasury, let alone challenging a power with such a long shared frontier as the Russian empire.

On 3 March a Russo-Turkish peace treaty was signed at San Stefano. It proved unacceptable to the other nations, and ran counter to the terms of the Reichstadt Agreement and all exchanges between Alexander II and Francis Joseph. In particular the creation of a large Russian satellite state of Bulgaria encroaching on the western Balkans, with no territorial compensation offered to the Dual Monarchy, was clearly unsatisfactory to the other nations. A settlement of the Eastern question acceptable to Europe as a whole was the only solution, and a general conference was arranged to take place at Berlin that summer.

Francis Joseph was temporarily distracted by the final illness and death of his father, Archduke Francis Charles, who died at Vienna on 8 March. Though the court was still in mourning, he gave a courteous welcome to General Nikolai Ignatiev, Russian ambassador in Constantinople, whom the Tsar had sent to Vienna on 27 March to try and reconcile the Austrians to a Russian military presence in Bulgaria and assure them that St Petersburg would raise no objection to any action taken by the government in Vienna to secure the provinces. There were long talks between Ignatiev and Andrassy, but the former was not trusted, and after returning to St Petersburg he tried to intrigue against Andrassy, hoping that a more pro-Russian minister might be installed instead. Francis Joseph was angered by his behaviour, denouncing him as a 'notorious father of lies'.

The Congress of Berlin, bringing together Europe's greatest statesmen, met in June and July 1878. A revised treaty was drawn up at the end, by which it was agreed that the new principality of Bulgaria would be reduced to one-third of the size proposed at San Stefano, while Austria-Hungary was given its long-coveted mandate to occupy and administer Bosnia and Herzegovina, in order to bring to an end the state of civil war between the Christians and Muslims of both territories. Rudolf, and many others, saw the gain of these territories as some compensation for the loss of Lombardy and Venetia earlier in the reign.

Andrassy did not have things all his own way. The Ottoman delegates would not allow troops from the Dual Monarchy to enter the provinces, and only when Andrassy pledged that the Sultan's sovereign rights would not be impaired and that an occupation would merely be regarded as a temporary necessity, did they agree to sign the treaty. In March 1879 the Hungarian and Austrian governments approved the treaty, and in April a formal agreement concerning the occupation and administration of Bosnia and Herzegovina was concluded with the Ottoman government and that of the Dual Monarchy.

Feeling that his life's work was as good as done, Andrassy offered his resignation as foreign minister, which the Emperor declined to accept immediately. Instead he asked Andrassy to remain in office during the summer, in order to give his successor, Baron Heinrich Haymerle, sufficient time to learn about his role.

The end of the decade coincided with the coming of age of Emperor Francis Joseph's son and heir. After the disastrous start with Gondrecourt, Crown Prince Rudolf had been fortunate in having as a tutor General Latour, who appreciated the importance of providing mental stimulation for his charge. Rudolf was fascinated by scientific subjects, particularly ornithology, and at the age of twenty he went on a short expedition to observe animal and bird life in the forests of the Danube in southern Hungary, later providing source for a book which he wrote and published, *Funfzehn Tage auf der Donau* (*Fifteen Days on the Danube*), with the zoologist Alfred Brehm acting as consultant. He had also accompanied his mother on one of her visits to England, and won the approval of Queen Victoria and the Prince of Wales. The latter had thought highly of Rudolf ever since a visit to Vienna early in 1869, though he had remarked that the Crown Prince was 'treated almost as a boy by his Parents'.[3] As Rudolf was only ten years old at the time, this hardly seems surprising.

Though he would never have considered himself an intellectual, Francis Joseph was proud of his son, and supported him against criticism at court of those who feared he was turning into something unorthodox. Archduke Albrecht, Inspector-General of the army since 1867, was a diehard conservative to whom modern concepts of liberalism and democracy were anathema, and thought the young heir to the throne showed signs of becoming a dangerous subversive.

On 24 April 1879 Francis Joseph and Elizabeth celebrated their silver wedding anniversary, and the family gathered in Vienna for four days of festivities. A procession through the city had to be postponed because of heavy rain. On the day of the anniversary itself there was a service of thanksgiving in the Votivkirche. The previous evening Archduke Charles Ludwig, now twice-widowed and married for a third time to Princess Maria Theresa of Portugal, had been host at a reception in which he arranged for a series of historical tableaux to be staged before his brother and sister-in-law, with each figure from the past played by an archduke or archduchess. Most of the decorations and costumes had been borrowed from the city's museums or the imperial treasury. In the first scene the Crown Prince, representing his thirteenth-century ancestor Rudolf I, wore the real crown of the Holy Roman Empire. He reappeared a little later as Charles V, and then as Charles of Lorraine, the victor over the Turks.

In twenty-five years together, Francis Joseph and Elizabeth had come to terms with what had become a largely one-sided marriage. It was apparent that he was still devoted to her and resigned to the fact that he could never totally possess this temperamental wife with her antipathy to court life and obsession with travel, while he toiled at home, writing fondly to her whenever they were apart in a study below her portrait, counting the days until they would be reunited. While outwardly she seemed devoted to him, it was a curiously selfish, egotistical devotion. She apparently took it as read that he would always be at home waiting for her, while he meekly granted her licence to wander around Europe like the free spirit she had been brought up to be, taking advantage of the fact that he would refuse her nothing. The wags said that it was customary to celebrate a silver wedding after twenty-five years of *ménage* (housekeeping), but not after twenty-five years of *manège* (riding school). This quip was repeated to Elizabeth, who saw the funny side.[4]

The last few years had proved to them and to the outside world that in temperament and interests the Emperor and Empress had little if anything in common. The Emperor was stolid and unimaginative, did not trust new ideas and recoiled from new fashions. His self-control often gave others the misleading impression that he was insensitive, at least in public. As his letters to those nearest to him demonstrated, this was far from the case, but even to them he had difficulty in expressing himself. Most of his letters to Elizabeth were dry-as-dust records about the state of the weather, the health of their relations, what he had shot and whom he had sat next to at dinner.

Her poetical dream world, her love of literature, was something which he could not share or enter into with any enthusiasm. When he was persuaded to see a performance at the Burgtheater of her favourite Shakespeare play, *A Midsummer Night's Dream*, he remarked afterwards that he found it 'indescribably stupid'. He tolerated her interest in new ideas and fashion – which were alien if not distasteful to him – in the same way as he accepted her foibles, such as her dieting and obsession with slimming, her large dogs, and her extraordinary passion for riding. He reluctantly put up with her eccentricities such as her finding a small black boy to play with their youngest daughter, or her curious choice of birthday presents, which included not only a lunatic asylum but also on other occasions a tiger and a medallion.

When his wife was or appeared to be ill Francis Joseph's concern for her was evident, but lacking in understanding. Like many other people who enjoyed excellent health, illness was beyond him, and he was one of those people who believed that people were either living or dead, with nothing in between the two. But he bore with more patience than any of his courtiers her frequent refusals to make the ceremonial appearances which her position demanded, and her failure to understand the responsibilities incumbent on her as an Empress. She was aware that he knew her habits, her likes and dislikes, her moods, her depressions, her sudden change from tears to gaiety, and he had to be prepared to accept her as she was. He had learnt to endure his loneliness during her many absences and to be grateful for the times when she was with him. Maybe it was her elusiveness, the fact that he could never wholly possess nor understand her, which bound him to her with such deep and enduring love.

Elizabeth reciprocated this love after her own fashion. Some courtiers and guests, who only saw her in passing, found her impossibly cold and withdrawn, with a face that may have been beautiful but which had all the expression of a fashion photograph. While her wanderings throughout Europe and her increasing reluctance to participate in court and state functions suggested the ultimate in selfishness, she became tenderly concerned for her husband and showed a fondness towards him which was more like that of a mother than a wife. Yet she was incapable of making a sustained effort. At times of crisis she would be by his side, but to put up with life in surroundings which she found uncomfortable for more than a few months of even weeks at a time was an impossibility. Withdrawing into herself and seeking refuge in travel to more congenial places became her way of life.

Nevertheless, Francis Joseph was pleased by the public response to their wedding anniversary, which he called the 'lasting family celebration for all the peoples of my empire',[5] though Elizabeth found the festivities exhausting. She was more concerned with the business of finding a suitable bride for their son, who would soon be twenty-one. In Lisbon and Madrid, he gave some thought to a Spanish infanta, and at Dresden a princess of Saxony, though neither really seemed suitable for various reasons. By July he was back with his regiment near Prague, and on his father's birthday promotions list he was confirmed as commanding officer of the regiment. On 28 August he led his men on parade before their Emperor, and afterwards told Bombelles, who had succeeded Latour as head of the Crown Prince's official household, that he belonged to the army 'heart and soul'.

In his adolescent years Rudolf wrote essays for his tutor which read like professions of romantic liberalism. Yet he was not in revolt against his father and the structure of the monarchy. Francis Joseph was worldly enough to realise that his son might express views contrary to his own, and doubtless assumed that his radicalism would diminish with age and experience.

Rudolf's progressive outlook could be explained by several factors. Firstly, there were the Austrian military defeats at Solferino and Königgrätz, and the measured if reluctant retreat from old-fashioned autocracy as personified in the *Ausgleich* during his formative years. Secondly, the coming to power of German Liberals in Austria resulted in a period of economic prosperity, and a loosening of the grip of the Church on government. Thirdly, Rudolf had received a much more modern education than his father. It was natural that he would think for himself and become increasingly dissatisfied with life in a court and dynasty which seemed rooted in unbending tradition.

Rudolf respected his father, much as he disagreed with his political views. But he rebelled against the status quo, and was impatient to try and change the world around him, and felt that his father was losing touch with reality, though it was not his own fault. He regarded the more reactionary elements in the empire as its enemies, leading it to disaster. He had some interesting criticisms to make of the trappings of imperial power in general, and his father's remote position in particular.

Writing in 1881, he observed that the Emperor had no friends, as his nature did not allow it. 'He stands alone on his promontory; he discusses the official business of everyone with his servants, but a real conversation is carefully avoided. Therefore he knows little of the thinking and feeling of the populace, the views of the people.' Furthermore, the Crown Prince noted, the Emperor was convinced (probably by the words of one of his more sycophantic aides or ministers) that they were enjoying one of the happiest epochs in Austrian history. 'He is told so officially, and in the newspapers he reads only the sections marked in red, and so he is kept from any purely human contact, from any non-partisan, truly thoughtful advice.'[6] Such reasoning shows a farsightedness well beyond the normal outpourings of youthful rebellion, particularly as Rudolf was in his early twenties when he wrote this. Had Francis Joseph still been the heir-in-waiting at this age, it is difficult to imagine him committing such thoughts about the sovereign to paper.

Ironically, the Crown Prince took after his mother much more than his father. There was a lot of the wayward Wittelsbach in him, his less submissive attitude towards authority and his general

Archduchess Sophie with her eldest child Archduke Francis Joseph, aged two, from an engraving after a painting by Joseph Stieler. All her ambitions were concentrated in this child, whom she saw as the eventual saviour of the Habsburg empire.

Emperor Francis Joseph, at around the time of his accession in 1848. 'Farewell my youth', was the reaction of the eighteen-year-old ruler on assuming the title.

Emperor Francis I, Archduchess Sophie and Francis Joseph as a boy, engraved after a painting by Charles Skoliksen of a military review which they attended.

The Emperor's parents, Archduchess Sophie and her husband Archduke Francis Charles, about 1860. The Archduke, 'a good fellow', should have succeeded his brother Ferdinand as Emperor, but was easily persuaded to renounce his place in the succession in favour of their eldest son.

Archduke Ferdinand Maximilian, after an engraving by Nargeot. 'Max' was briefly Governor-General of Lombardy and Venetia, before being chosen as Emperor of Mexico, a venture which ended in tragedy. *(By kind permission of Mary Evans Picture Library)*

Empress Elizabeth and her dog Shadow, about 1861. Throughout her life the Empress had a passion for dogs.

Schönbrunn Palace, Vienna, the main home of Emperor Francis Joseph and his family, from a photograph by Sue Woolmans.

The Kaiservilla, Bad Ischl, where Emperor Francis Joseph spent several weeks every summer.

Emperor Francis Joseph in the robes of the Order of the Golden Fleece.

Emperor Francis Joseph and King Edward VII at the Opera, Vienna, 1 September 1903, from a drawing by Edward Cucuel. The King tried unsuccessfully to persuade the Emperor to pay a return state visit to England the following year.

Archduke Francis Ferdinand and Sophie, who was raised from the rank of Princess to Duchess of Hohenberg in 1909. It was believed that on his accession her husband would try to have her proclaimed Empress.

Archduke Charles, who became heir to the throne on the assassination of Archduke Francis Ferdinand, paying a visit to Bukovina, shortly before his accession to the throne.

Emperor Francis Joseph on his deathbed. He died at Schönbrunn Palace on 21 November 1916, in a bedroom just one corridor away from that in which he had been born eighty-six years earlier.

restlessness, and little of the Habsburg respect for time-honoured tradition and blind obedience. As a boy he had been closer to her than his father, but as her absence from court and her wanderings increased, so did their estrangement.

It never occurred to the Emperor to take Rudolf into his confidence. He bore sole responsibility for the rule and preservation of the monarchy, and any question of giving the young man some experience or training as befitting the next Emperor did not seem to have entered his head. Rudolf was an intelligent youth, anxious to be of service to the Dual Monarchy and to do more than pursue the normal army career which archdukes were expected to follow. Little did his father appreciate that Rudolf actively hated military discipline, and looked on military appointments as nothing more than ostensibly distinguished but hollow amusements for his Habsburg cousins.

One thing the Emperor did notice was that social climbers were bound to make attempts to ingratiate themselves with the heir to the throne, but he considered it inevitable and it did not bother him unduly. However, at Gödöllö in 1879 he remarked to Countess Festetics that he found the behaviour of one particular woman tiresome. Baroness Helene Vetsera, a daughter of the Levantine banker Themistocles Baltazzi and wife of a diplomat at the Austrian embassy, had a reputation at court for being 'fast'. Her regular pursuit of the Crown Prince and sending him presents did not pass unnoticed.

Any wayward behaviour on Rudolf's part, within reason, was only to be expected. Neither of his parents were in a position to criticise. Francis Joseph was involved at this time in a relationship with Anna Nahowski, the young wife of a railway official. Emperor and subject had met by chance on a morning walk in the Schönbrunn parkland, and for some years they enjoyed a discreet affair. With Elizabeth wandering throughout Europe, be it Bavaria, Greece, England or Ireland, the Emperor needed feminine company. Herr Nahowski was content with the situation and with the generous gifts to his wife. Thanks to discretion, and the payment of ready money in order to keep the liaison hushed up, their secret remained safe for over a century.[7]

Although Elizabeth stopped short of conducting passionate affairs, she was not above mild flirtations with good-looking skilled horsemen at home and abroad. Her friendship with Captain William 'Bay' Middleton, an experienced rider who had piloted her on her sporting visit to England, had provoked a good deal of ribald gossip at the time, although he was engaged to be married and there was nothing serious between them, beyond a mutual respect for each other's skill in the hunting field. Yet Elizabeth had the all-too-common possessive streak of royalty, resenting any wish by favoured male or female courtiers to marry and try to lead their own lives.

It would have been surprising if Rudolf had not wished to play the field. There was soon gossip about his activities and liaisons, and his parents and ministers were united in thinking it time he settled down to married life. In 1880 Count Bohuslav Chotek, Austrian minister in Brussels, approached King Leopold II with a view to arranging a meeting between his younger daughter Princess Stephanie and the Crown Prince. Stephanie's mother Queen Marie-Henriette, daughter of Archduke Joseph, Palatine of Hungary, was a Habsburg princess by birth. Rudolf travelled dutifully to Brussels in March 1880 to meet Stephanie, who had been told by her father that he and her mother wished her to become the future Empress of Austria and Queen of Hungary. A tall, plump and somewhat plain girl of fifteen, she knew where her duty lay. They met on 5 March and he proposed to her. Two days later he telegraphed the family to announce that she had accepted him.

His old tutor Latour was pleased, but Elizabeth, at Claridge's Hotel in London, turned white when she received her telegram, telling Countess Festetics that she hoped it would not become a calamity. She disliked King Leopold and Queen Marie-Henriette, and felt Stephanie, with her shallow education and frivolous nature, was quite unsuitable for her son. Moreover, the dynastic precedent of Stephanie's aunt, the hapless former Empress of Mexico, was hardly promising. 'Hasn't Charlotte been experience enough for us?'[8] was her reaction.

On her way back to Vienna Elizabeth spent four hours with Rudolf and Stephanie, and though the meeting did nothing to assuage her fears, her son was convinced that he was doing the right thing. Their wedding was planned for the summer, until it was revealed that Stephanie was still so physically immature that she had not even begun to menstruate. Elizabeth insisted that no ceremony could take place while the bride was still 'an unformed child', and it was rearranged for 10 May 1881.

Stephanie arrived in Vienna four days before the wedding, which took place at the Augustinerkirche at the Hofburg. Like his parents before him, the groom and his bride spent their honeymoon at Laxenburg. Her memoirs, written and partly ghost-written many years later, recalled an inhospitable setting with unseasonal snow falling as they reached the palace, the smell of mould indoors, no flowers in vases or any similar homely touches to welcome them on their arrival, and no dressing table or bathroom, but only a wash handstand on a three-legged framework. It was an unpromising start to their marriage. All the same, they gave every initial appearance of settling down contentedly as husband and wife, with Rudolf devoted to his young bride, while she was happy to accompany him on official visits and sometimes on hunting expeditions and shoots. Her own home life had been cheerless, and all the evidence suggests that she was prepared to make a success of their life together. He appreciated her readiness to learn, and was encouraged by the interest she showed in politics as they discussed the issues of the day together.

In June 1881 there was a renewal of the Three Emperors' Alliance; Haymerle, now foreign minister, secured from Germany and Russia virtual recognition of Austro-Hungarian supremacy over the western Balkans, including the eventual annexation of Bosnia and Herzegovina. In return Francis Joseph pledged the monarchy's benevolent neutrality should either of his partners be at war with a fourth power, other than Turkey. Haymerle died suddenly in October 1881 and was succeeded by Count Gustav Kálnoky, ambassador to St Petersburg. Rudolf had admired Haymerle but did not extend this admiration to his successor.

Shortly after this Rudolf was introduced to the journalist Moritz Szeps, editor-in-chief of the radical *Neues Wiener Tageblatt*. He was in regular correspondence with Szeps, who replaced Latour as the main recipient of his political observations. For a time Rudolf contributed anonymous articles himself. He had to go to elaborate lengths to keep these contacts secret, as he knew that the authorities kept him under surveillance, on the pretext of protecting him from would-be assassins.

Thanks to the private intelligence connections of Archduke Albrecht and Beck, Francis Joseph was aware of these contacts, and thoroughly disapproved of them. To him, journalism as a profession was the lowest of the low, its practitioners nothing but trouble-makers and subversives. He prevailed on his chancellor Count Taaffe to invoke the Press Law, which empowered the confiscation of publications containing what might be deemed any offensive articles. Most German journals, especially *Neues Wiener Tageblatt*, were openly critical of the government, and in 1880 there were 635 cases of confiscation.[9] Nevertheless, the Emperor was still prepared to treat his son with indulgence. As long as Rudolf was a good and faithful husband, and showed promise as a regimental officer, he was prepared to take a little youthful waywardness in his stride. The young man would surely grow up in time.

For the first two years of their marriage, Rudolf and Stephanie gave every appearance of settling down together satisfactorily at Hradčany Palace, Prague. Notwithstanding their differences in temperament and background, they had achieved a mutual understanding. Stephanie showed greater willingness to take part in court functions than Rudolf, a factor which won the Emperor's approval. In the spring of 1883, Stephanie became pregnant, and a delighted Rudolf travelled to Vienna to tell his father in person. Whenever military duties took him away from home, his letters to Stephanie referred to their unborn child as Vaclav (Wenceslas), the patron saint of Bohemia. Maybe this was a subconscious wish to name the infant thus if it was a boy, but this was not to be the case.

On 2 September 1883 at Laxenburg Stephanie gave birth to a daughter. When told after her long and painful labour that she had not given her husband a son and heir she sobbed bitterly, but he reassured her that little girls were 'nice and affectionate'. Two days later he wrote to Latour that the young mother 'looks as blooming as ever, as though nothing had happened, and the little one is a strapping girl weighing seven pounds, completely healthy and strongly developed'.[10] She was named Elizabeth after her grandmother, and among the family she was known by the Magyar diminutive of 'Erszi'. Rudolf was delighted with the baby and became a doting father, though he naturally hoped and expected that a son would follow. Yet Stephanie thought that he 'was absolutely stricken, as he had set his heart upon an heir to the throne'.[11]

In the autumn of 1881 Francis Joseph had agreed to have a small villa built in a secluded part of the Lainzer Tiergarten park for Elizabeth, intended as a family lodge free from court ceremonial, with life similar to that at Gödöllö, her favourite royal residence. He would pay for it from his personal funds and present it to her as a gift. Plans by the architect, Karl von Hasenauer, were ready for approval in December 1881, and it was estimated that it would be ready for occupation in another four or five years. Now aged forty-four, the Empress was losing interest in riding, and suffering from sciatica. She sold her stud, and never returned to the hunting fields of England or Ireland. Instead she yielded to an ever-increasing urge to exercise, in particular with her gymnastic routines in the morning, later supplemented with fencing lessons. Gradually she started undertaking long walks, sometimes covering a distance of twenty miles or more, spending up to eight or nine hours per day on foot. She took hardly any nourishment, drinking a glass of milk or orange juice instead of a proper meal.

To the Emperor's alarm, she became increasingly pale and thin. Her parents, by now in their mid-seventies, became concerned about the change in her attitude to people, and her obsessions. In particular she seemed to have developed an attachment to her cousin King Ludwig II of Bavaria, whose behaviour had become ever more erratic, his personal extravagance untenable. She had been more ready to forgive him for having jilted her sister Sophie than the rest of the family.

On 24 May 1886 Elizabeth took her husband and youngest daughter to pay a visit to her new hideaway, which she had decided to name the Hermes Villa, though it was another year before she would be able to take up residence there. The Emperor tactfully admired its decoration, though he remarked ruefully that he would 'always be afraid of spoiling things'.[12] Valerie found the whole atmosphere excessive, confiding to her journal her dismay at 'these marble reliefs, these luxurious carpets, these fireplaces of chased bronze, these innumerable angels and Cupids, the carvings in every hole and corner, this mannered rococo style! How I wish we were back at home again.'[13]

At first Elizabeth was delighted with this creation, like a child with a new toy. But barely two years after her first visit, she lost interest and told the Emperor that instead she wanted to have a small palace dedicated to Achilles built for her on Corfu. In the Reichsrat, opposition deputies were beginning to ask questions about the enormous sums being spent on these buildings for their Empress. Francis Joseph admitted sadly that it would do him no good with the Viennese,[14] but he could refuse her nothing, and in due course she had her Achilleion.

SEVEN

'One Cannot Possibly Think of Anything Else'

Francis Joseph's lonely existence had been enlivened for some time at Schönbrunn by the company of Anna Nahowski. In 1883 when she gave birth to a daughter named Helene, he gave Anna the sum of 100,000 gulden. Yet though their relationship was to last until the end of the decade, he found the 29-year gap in their ages difficult to bridge, and the fact that they had hardly any interests in common proved an additional barrier. Fortunately the Emperor was about to find a far more congenial companion, one who would be able to lighten the many dark times during his remaining thirty years of life.

On a visit to the Burgtheater in 1884 he met and was presented to the actress Katherine Schratt, whom he had seen in *The Taming of the Shrew*. In 1879 she had married Nicholas Kiss von Itebbe, retired from the stage and given birth to a son. Her husband was a notorious spendthrift, and in 1882 he fled from his creditors, leaving her and their child at the mercy of the bailiffs. Now a single parent, she had little choice but to resume her theatrical career, playing in New York for a time, and with assistance from friends she was soon able to return to Vienna. Not long after this, she was introduced to the Emperor, and it was noticed that they were often deep in conversation. In the summer of 1885 she accepted a seasonal engagement at Ischl, where he generally celebrated his birthday. On 17 August that year he was accompanied by the Crown Prince and Princess, Prince Leopold of Bavaria and Archduchess Valerie, to the Kurhaustheater for a birthday evening's entertainment, to see Katherine in *Der Verschwender* (*The Spendthrift*).

Nine days later she appeared before the Emperor and Tsar Alexander III in a one-act comedy presented by the Burgtheater company at a command performance in Kremsier during the Austro-Russian summit conference in the Moravian archbishop's summer palace there. At the Tsar's suggestion, all the leading actresses joined the emperors and empresses for supper that evening. Having drunk well if not too wisely, the Tsar had been ogling Katherine ever since they had been introduced, paying her unsubtle compliments, and after they had eaten he insisted on taking her for a stroll through the illuminated gardens late that night. One did not refuse such an imperial command lightly, if at all, and next morning Francis Joseph angrily told Elizabeth that their Romanov guest's behaviour had been unpardonable.[1] Greatly amused by her husband's reaction, Elizabeth wondered if there might have been a hint of jealousy that the wily Tsar (who, unlike his late father, was normally the most faithful of husbands) had provoked such an outburst.

The liaison met with Elizabeth's total approval. Although often increasingly self-absorbed, she felt guilty at leaving her husband alone so much, and felt that encouraging him in this relationship was the least she could do to make amends. In the elegant phraseology of Rebecca West, if she did not actively introduce the actress into her husband's life, she certainly encouraged this friendship with a woman whom he had only met in passing, much as a woman might put flowers into a room she felt to be dreary. She commissioned a portrait of Katherine from the court painter Heinrich von Angeli, to present to her husband. In 1886 Katherine was at Angeli's studio when she was astonished to see the Empress bringing her husband to inspect progress on the portrait. While Elizabeth took an interest in Angeli's other portraits, Emperor and actress chatted happily together. Two days later, he wrote Katherine what would be the first of more than 500 letters over the next thirty years.

Meanwhile, Europe was threatened with war once again. Emperor and Tsar were keen to preserve good relations and reaffirm their belief in the League of the Three Emperors, but Elizabeth and Rudolf did not trust the Tsar's offers of friendship. Shortly before the Kremsier meeting Francis Joseph had received Prince Alexander of Battenberg, sovereign Prince of Bulgaria, who proclaimed the union of the two Bulgarias, linking the predominantly Bulgarian Ottoman province of Eastern Rumelia with his principality. Neighbouring Serbia, alarmed by the shift of power in the Balkans, invaded Bulgaria, only to be defeated by Alexander at the battle of Slivnitza. In this crisis Francis Joseph and Kálnoky both strove to keep the peace, holding Austria-Hungary to a common policy of mediation agreed by its partners in the League of the Three Emperors. However, Andrassy, contemplating a return to public life, advised the Emperor in a long memorandum to consider the imposition of a settlement of Balkan frontiers agreeable to political and commercial interests in Vienna and Budapest.

Neither Francis Joseph nor General Beck were prepared to risk a war in which they could not count on unqualified German support. Diplomatic pressure had to be brought to bear on halting the Bulgarians after Slivnitza, and a series of ambassadorial conferences in Constantinople patched up the Balkan frontiers the following spring.

Tragedy was about to strike the Wittelsbachs. In June 1886 King Ludwig II of Bavaria was compelled to abdicate his throne on the grounds of his increasingly abnormal behaviour and paranoia, and placed under what amounted to house arrest. On the evening of 13 June his body and that of Dr Gudden, his physician who had tried to restrain him, were found by the Starnbergersee. Though their last movements had never been clearly pieced together, it was apparent that the deposed monarch had been involved in a struggle and both men had drowned as a result. Elizabeth was distraught by the news, and for several days she locked herself in her room weeping, convinced that the Bavarian authorities had been guilty of complicity in his murder. On the evening after they had received the news, Valerie was horrified to find her mother lying prone on the floor of the room, and the girl's terrified screams somehow brought her to her senses again.

Even so, Elizabeth's hysterical reaction to her cousin's suicide seemed so out of proportion that her children seriously began to question her sanity. For a while Rudolf, who had been close to Ludwig himself, only had to enter the same room as his mother for her to burst into tears. The level-headed Gisela, now almost thirty years of age, would have liked to help, but ironically it was her father-in-law, the Regent of Bavaria, who had signed Ludwig's arrest warrant. Elizabeth had had an irrational antipathy to her daughter ever since the latter's childhood, when she had been blamed for passing on the infection that had brought about her sister Sophie's early death. This latest connection, unfortunate though it was, did nothing to reconcile mother and daughter. Elizabeth was in no fit state to attend the funeral, and Rudolf went to represent her.

Depending on one's point of view, Francis Joseph was either the least imaginative of his family, or the one whose personality was most deeply rooted in simple common sense and who therefore had no time for playing psychological games. He was the only member who would not admit or even believe that his wife was abnormal or mentally disturbed. Possibly fearful for their jobs, his physicians did not attempt to convince him otherwise, and the only cure they could suggest was to continue sending her to one watering place after another for the benefit of her nerves.

That summer Francis Joseph was preoccupied with another Balkan crisis. In August 1886 the Russians kidnapped Prince Alexander of Bulgaria, whom they regarded as too headstrong and independently minded. Tsar Alexander III, it was feared, planned to nominate a puppet ruler himself, with the intention of ensuring Pan-Slav control throughout the Balkans. Francis Joseph agreed with Kálnoky that the scheme was unthinkable for Austria-Hungary, and for a time there was the threat of war. Bismarck made it clear that Germany would give no military assistance, and only the recall of General Kaulbars, the Tsar's aide-de-camp, from Sofia to St Petersburg, averted such a crisis.

It was a gloomy Christmas at the Hofburg that year. Elizabeth was suffering from sciatica, and Francis Joseph was filled with foreboding as to Russia's intentions.

In the spring of 1888 Vienna's Ringstrasse was completed, and on the anniversary of the birth of Maria Theresa the Emperor was to unveil a vast monument to his great-great-grandmother in a square between museums just built to house the empire's finest collections of natural history and art. The ceremony on 13 May was intended to be a salute from the dynasty to the woman whose courage had saved the Habsburg crown. The result was a brilliant dynastic parade in Vienna, with sixty-six archdukes and archduchesses joining Francis Joseph and Elizabeth for the ceremony at which the regiments appeared with their bands, and Viennese choirs sang a *Te Deum*. Francis Joseph was delighted with the day's proceedings, while Elizabeth, who so hated public displays and being part of them, was deeply moved by the ceremony. Yet she was alarmed by the appearance of Rudolf, who was pale, with dull listless eyes and clearly out of sorts.

Yet the day was in a sense the climax of Francis Joseph's reign, or the calm before the storm.

Francis Joseph was proud of Rudolf, his range of interests and the way in which he discharged his duties. The Crown Prince was a good public speaker, and had made an excellent speech at the opening of Vienna's electrical exhibitions in August 1883. He also encouraged the publication of a twenty-four volume encyclopaedic survey of the Habsburg realm, to which he made substantial contributions. The work was not finished until after the turn of the twentieth century, but the Emperor was honoured to be presented with the first completed volume of the project.

Rudolf still regarded himself as a professional soldier, and recognised the army's role in binding the different provinces of the monarchy together. But Emperor and Crown Prince differed in their aims. Francis Joseph placed increasing importance on the traditional role of his officers in bringing a splendour to distant towns scattered across the empire, while Rudolf was ever searching for new ideas in the old regiments, looking for greater efficiency, and planning ideas such as backing a preventative war during the Bulgarian crises. Francis Joseph thought him too immature to be entrusted with high military responsibility. So did Archduke Albrecht, who regarded the heir as a dangerous liberal. He and prime minister Eduard Taaffe were alarmed by his links with radical journalists. In spring 1888 Rudolf expected to receive the command of the Second Army Corps, with headquarters in Vienna. Instead he was made Inspector-General of Infantry, a somewhat inferior post created for him, with ill-defined duties carefully monitored by Archduke Albrecht. He suspected, and complained to friends, that he was under surveillance from the Emperor's inner circle of military advisers.

By this time Rudolf's health was deteriorating. Early in 1886 he fell seriously ill, probably with a venereal infection, and was confined to bed for several weeks. Towards the end of the year persistent bronchitis and rheumatic pains left him increasingly weak, and the Emperor suggested he should spend a month in convalescence on the island of Lacroma, off Dubrovnik. He declined to do so, but from that time onwards he was a very sick man, heavily dependent on morphia, and drinking too much. Since his fall from a tree in childhood he had been susceptible to severe blinding headaches, and now they became more frequent. He was capable of great charm, and when representing his father at Queen Victoria's golden jubilee celebrations in June 1887, he had bewitched both the Queen and the Prince of Wales, who had become a close friend. But ill-health and self-indulgence were slowly destroying him, and a severe eye complaint made it difficult for him to enjoy shooting, which had been one of his passions.

His marriage had not been a success. Stephanie's difficult pregnancy in 1883, and a venereal infection (thought to be gonorrhoea, rather than syphilis)[2] caught from Rudolf had made her chances of conceiving again most unlikely. By spring 1887 she had noticed a great change for the worse in him. Not only was his physical health deteriorating sharply, but he was increasingly restless and could not settle down to anything. His love of sport had become obsessive, and 'he could not bear to spend an evening in circles that did not share his interest in these matters'.[3] She had always fulfilled her duties as Crown Princess conscientiously, accompanying him on his various representative missions. Although she was certainly the more faithful partner, on one visit outside the empire she had had a brief dalliance with a Polish count. Rudolf could hardly complain, as he was seeking his pleasures elsewhere, and never made any effort to conceal his infidelities from her. He had still kept his bachelor quarters in the Hofburg in order to entertain mistresses, and she was never allowed to pass through the door. To friends, she once claimed that he had at least thirty illegitimate children.[4]

As Rudolf's strength ebbed, he neglected his intellectual interests and plunged into more military routine work. By late 1888 it was rumoured that he was seeking an annulment of his marriage, and that he had quarrelled with his father over the matter. It was also said that Rudolf had suggested a suicide pact to Stephanie, that she was terrified and went to the Emperor for help, only to be told gently that she was giving way to idle fancies, that her husband was overworking, and that it was her duty as a wife to keep him at home more. In spite of all this, a mutual tolerance, and love for their daughter, kept them together.

Stephanie's concern about Rudolf's failing health did not seem to be shared by his parents. There was an apparent conspiracy of silence among Elizabeth's entourage, to shield her from hearing about his infidelities and over-reliance on morphine and alcohol. Had she spent more time in Vienna, or at least seen more of him, she would certainly have noticed his physical deterioration. As for Francis Joseph, he was probably too unobservant, or perhaps too proud, to admit that anything could be seriously wrong with his son. In the same way that he refused to face the possibility that his neurotic wife was mentally unbalanced, he likewise turned a blind eye to his son's pitiful condition. Ill-health, whether physical, mental or both, was simply beyond his limited experience. He had lived nearly sixty years without illness or psychological problems, and like many other people with a robust constitution, he probably found it impossible to acknowledge such afflictions in others, least of all his two closest relations.

By this time Francis Joseph's youngest child, Valerie, was on the threshold of adult life. For a couple of years Elizabeth had spent longer in Vienna than usual, as a series of balls were held in the Hofburg to which the young Archduchess's closest friends and young men attached to the court were invited. While her mother made an effort to put herself out for their guests, her remote manner tended to intimidate them. On the other hand Francis Joseph, who genuinely enjoyed the company of younger people, was at his most charming.

In April 1888 Valerie celebrated her twentieth birthday. By this time she had begun to form a close attachment with her childhood friend Archduke Francis Salvator, from the Tuscan branch of the Habsburgs. While Elizabeth was inconsolable at the thought of losing her favourite child, she could see the advantages of a marriage which would keep her in Austria and still, hopefully, under her mother's control to a certain extent. Rudolf disapproved of Salvator, thinking him not good enough for his sister. He was not alone, for the Emperor agreed with him that it would be far better for Valerie to seek a husband from another foreign house instead of marrying a kinsman of limited means. That winter the Crown Princes of Saxony and Portugal planned to visit Vienna, mainly in order to ask the Emperor for the hand of his youngest daughter. Yet if Valerie's father or brother dared to suggest the virtues of a marriage to one man or the other, Elizabeth would burst into tears and complain about their cruelty to Valerie, or about how lonely and unhappy she would be after her daughter had gone. It was clearly tactless to say the least for her to suggest that her life would be worthless after a perfectly normal family event, namely the marriage of a child.

Although they clearly differed in outlook, father and son were still close. Francis Joseph may have found it difficult to understand his heir, and been bemused by his unpredictability, but they were united by their common love of sport, and still frequently went stalking together.

Even so, one potentially serious incident should have warned him of impending trouble. In January 1888 father and son were at a shoot in Mürzsteg, and the drive was almost over when Rudolf saw another herd of deer. Though he was close to the Emperor, he fired suddenly, if not indiscriminately, and a beater raised his arm to protect the Emperor. This action, which shattered the man's forearm and ended his career as a royal huntsman, probably saved the sovereign from serious injury if not death. What was probably a thoughtless and dangerous action on Rudolf's part could easily have been construed as a clumsy attempt to assassinate his father, who was fearful of stories being spread that the Crown Prince was trying to kill him. Some said that Rudolf was banned from subsequent imperial shooting parties, but the more likely outcome was that his father spoke to him severely and exacted an undertaking that nothing of the sort must ever happen again.

On 9 March 1888 the German Emperor William I passed away, aged ninety. Francis Joseph could not mourn for the man who had been little more than a mouthpiece for Chancellor Bismarck, and he was interested in what changes there might be under his son and successor Frederick III. However, the latter was mortally ill with cancer of the larynx, and only reigned for ninety-nine days before dying. During the short reign Francis Joseph met Queen Victoria briefly at Frankfurt as she came to pay what she knew would be her last visit to the stricken sovereign in Berlin, her beloved son-in-law. Over lunch, the Emperor told her of his pleasure 'at the good relations existing between our 2 countries, which he hoped would continue, as in case of war, we could act together'. Russia, he told her, 'was incomprehensible, & he thought Bismarck much too weak & yielding to Russia, which was a great mistake'.[5]

The third of Germany's emperors that year was the hotheaded William II. Francis Joseph hoped that the traditional Austro-German friendship would be maintained under his rule, though Rudolf personally disliked the new ruler, who was only five months his junior. The Crown Prince had been on the best of terms with the liberal Frederick and his far-sighted consort Victoria. When they were eclipsed by their son William he was deeply dismayed, as he found him an unctuous hypocrite and suspected that he was hostile towards Austria.

Rudolf's friendship with the Prince of Wales and his dislike of the new Emperor, the British heir's nephew, was to have unfortunate repercussions in what has gone down in royal history as the 'Vienna incident'. That summer, Francis Joseph invited the Prince of Wales to attend autumn manoeuvres of the Austrian army, in his capacity as honorary colonel of the Austrian 12th Hussars. The Prince knew that William would be paying an official visit to Vienna at about the same time, and wrote to express his pleasure at the likelihood of their meeting on that occasion. Despite receiving no acknowledgement, he went to Vienna as planned, arriving early on 10 September. After breakfast he donned his colonel's red and gold uniform, and prepared to receive the Austrian Emperor and Crown Prince. They asked how he would like to be entertained, and drew up a programme which would involve his absence from Vienna on 3 October. After he had approved it in principle, he was told casually by the Emperor that William II was due in the city on that date. The Prince of Wales suggested that he would return to Vienna on that day, and stay throughout his nephew's visit. That evening he dined with Francis Joseph, and on the next day he planned to entertain the ambassador Sir Augustus Paget and his wife to luncheon. Paget arrived early in some embarrassment and asked to see the Prince's senior equerry at once. Count Kálnoky had had to tell Paget that the German Emperor wanted no royal guests except himself in Vienna during his visit. Genuinely astonished and hurt, the Prince of Wales told Paget that he had wished to avoid provoking ill-natured gossip by staying away from the capital while his nephew was there. Nevertheless, within twenty-four hours it was being said throughout Vienna that Emperor William had threatened to cancel his visit unless the heir to the British throne was asked to leave.

Rudolf, who was as angry as the Prince of Wales, told him bitterly that German agents had spread rumours that the Prince wanted to interfere with forthcoming conversations between Francis Joseph and William II, and to embroil both with Tsar Alexander, so as to make mischief which could only benefit France and England. His presence in Vienna was therefore not required. Kálnoky had no intention of displeasing Austria's most powerful personal ally, and decided that the private family quarrels of uncle and nephew would have to take place outside the Austro-Hungarian empire. The Prince of Wales had no alternative but to withdraw to Bucharest at the beginning of October, and stay with the King and Queen of Roumania. Meanwhile, he had to be entertained in Vienna, so he and Rudolf applied themselves to a round of hunting by day, receptions and parties by night. Rudolf was astonished at his friend's stamina, telling Stephanie that 'nothing seems to tire the old boy'. Nevertheless, both heirs appreciated each other's company, whereas Rudolf said he would only invite William 'to get rid of him by an elegant hunting misadventure'.[6] Perhaps he recalled the fate of an earlier William II, King of England, who had perished in such a manner.

Francis Joseph also found his British guest's energy a little too much. He wrote to Katherine Schratt about a shoot at Gödöllö and army manoeuvres in Croatia attended by the Prince. By trotting and galloping, he said, he went to some pains to shake off the Prince of Wales, but with no luck. 'The fat man was always with me and held out quite unbelievably, only he got very stiff and tore his red Hussar trousers and, as he was wearing nothing underneath, that must have been very uncomfortable for him.'[7] Nevertheless, 'Wales' was clearly a more welcome guest than Emperor William, who left a bad impression behind in Vienna. Francis Joseph found his general ebullience tiresome, and William also had the effrontery after an Austrian military review to criticise in conversation with Francis Joseph and Elizabeth the efficiency and turnout of the infantry. Elizabeth found his attitude so infuriating that she pleaded a headache and walked out. After William's return to Berlin he sent a letter, drafted by Bismarck, suggesting that the Crown Prince should be replaced as inspector-general by a professional soldier.

On 14 October Francis Joseph and the Prince of Wales went to the gala opening of the new Burgtheater, where the Prince noticed the attractive seventeen-year-old Marie Vetsera in the audience. He pointed her out to Rudolf, who had never met her though he had been pursued by the flighty Helene, her mother. A meeting was soon to follow, thanks to Countess Marie Larisch, the daughter of Elizabeth's eldest brother who had renounced his rights in order to marry the actress Henriette Mendel, created Baroness von Wallersee on their wedding. In her earlier years Marie Wallersee had thrown herself shamelessly at Rudolf, and to try and keep her in order Elizabeth had helped to arrange a marriage between her and the good-natured if uninspiring Lieutenant George von Larisch von Moennich. Marie had sought revenge by indulging in spiteful gossip about the imperial family, and became the confidante of Countess Vetsera and her family. On 5 November Marie Larisch led Marie Vetsera to Rudolf's apartments at the Hofburg and formally introduced them.

Francis Joseph had other family preoccupations that winter. Valerie was about to become betrothed, and he knew that it would sadden Elizabeth to be deprived of the constant companionship of her favourite child. Though she told Valerie that she was determined never to become a possessive mother or mother-in-law like Archduchess Sophie had been, she found it hard to let go. Only the previous December she had told her youngest daughter that she was the only person she really loved, and 'if you leave me, my life is at an end. But one can only love like this once in one's life.' She could never forget how Sophie, her mother-in-law, had taken the place of a mother towards the other children,

> but from the very first moment I said to myself that things must be different with you. You had got to remain my own, my ownest child, my treasure, over whom none but myself must be allowed any right, and the whole of that capacity for loving which had hitherto been imprisoned in my heart I have poured out on you.[8]

Elizabeth was also worried about her father's health. Max had been ailing ever since a stroke during the summer, and he passed away on 15 November. The court at Vienna went into mourning, but Elizabeth did not attend the funeral.

On 1 December the Emperor and Empress quietly celebrated the fortieth anniversary of his accession. Two weeks earlier Rudolf had suffered a bad fall from his horse, but insisted on keeping news of the accident secret. Just before Christmas, Crown Princess Stephanie broke convention by insisting on coming to see her father-in-law privately in order to draw his attention to her husband's increasingly erratic behaviour and worsening health. She asked if it was possible to give him a complete change, such as sending him on a goodwill voyage around the world, primarily for his own good. The Emperor was still apparently unaware that anything was the matter with his son, telling her that the Crown Prince was 'rather pale, gets about too much, expects too much of himself', and 'ought to stay at home with you more than he does'.[9]

It was a cheerless Christmas again at the Hofburg that year. Gifts were exchanged on the afternoon of Christmas Eve, Elizabeth's fifty-first birthday, and Rudolf presented his mother with eleven autograph letters by her favourite poet Heinrich Heine. That evening the family also celebrated Valerie's betrothal to Francis Salvator. Resigned but still depressed at the prospect of losing her daughter, Elizabeth had arranged to go to Munich on 26 December to see her widowed mother, taking Valerie for what might be their last family visit before the latter's wedding. Francis Joseph was denied the pleasure of Katherine Schratt, who was in quarantine as her son had just caught measles. She was not even allowed to write to the Emperor, only to send him telegrams. In his loneliness, he paid what was to be his last purely social call on Anna Nahowski.

By the second week in January 1889 he had the family with him once again. Elizabeth and Valerie were back from Munich, and he spent some days hunting at Mürzsteg with Rudolf, who appeared in better spirits. As regards matters of state, his main preoccupations at this time were reports from Hungary on army legislation, and celebrations, a reception and a state dinner, at the end of the month for the thirtieth birthday of Emperor William, hosted by the German ambassador, Prince Reuss. The first of these could be dealt with easily by Kálmán Tisza, his Hungarian prime minister. The second was the more irritating, as he confessed privately that it would please him little.

As Rudolf held honorary rank in the 2nd Prussian Lancers, courtesy would require him to appear at the reception at the embassy in his German uniform. On 16 January the twelfth issue of a new weekly journal, *Schwarzgeld*, which had Rudolf's backing and which was strongly anti-German in its tone, carried a front-page article headed 'Ten Commandments of an Austrian'. The feature was strongly critical of Prussia, and newspaper articles elsewhere in the press suggested that the Crown Prince of Austria-Hungary favoured a reversal of alliances, with the Dual Monarchy abandoning Germany and Italy in favour of France and Russia.

On the morning of 26 January, the Emperor summoned his son to an audience. There was no record as to what was said by father and son, but according to at least one court dignitary shouting was heard. Maybe the Emperor urged Rudolf to cut his connections with journalists, maybe the Crown Prince urged a change of policy, maybe his private life was questioned. It has been suggested that Marie Vetsera was expecting his child, and that he felt unable to put an end to the affair. He might have confided as much to his father, who would have been angry but surely understanding, in view of his relationship with Anna Nahowski. Be that as it may, Rudolf seemed in a black mood when he left the Hofburg. Yet the following evening he was at the reception, suitably attired as a Prussian Lancer and complaining privately that he found the uniform personally distasteful. Lady Paget noticed that when the Emperor arrived, Rudolf bent low over his father's hand, almost touching it with his lips.[10] It was the last meeting between father and son.

Others, taking as their source the memoirs of Frau Zuckerkandl, a daughter of the journalist Moritz Szeps (who was not there at the time), insisted that there were dramatic scenes, with the Emperor turning his back on his son, and Crown Princess Stephanie and Mary Vetsera glaring at each other. Lady Paget saw no such thing. All these people, particularly the Emperor, were far too conscious of their dignity to consider causing anything resembling a scene in public. Later Francis Joseph said something to the ambassador's wife about the year that had just closed, to which she answered that she did not regret the year 1888: 'it was a very bad year, but I fear 1889 will be worse'.[11] The Emperor, whom she thought always seemed so shy and embarrassed on these occasions, looked at her aghast at this odd way of wishing him a happy new year.

Rudolf spent the night with Mitzi Caspar, another of his mistresses. He had told his servants that he would be leaving the Hofburg for his hunting lodge at Mayerling before noon on 28 January. On the evening of 29 January Francis Joseph was concerned when Rudolf failed to show up for a family dinner party, until Stephanie told him she had received a telegram to say that he was suffering from a feverish cold and sent his apologies. The tale was confirmed by her brother-in-law and his closest male friend Prince Philip of Coburg, who had just arrived from Mayerling and said that the Crown Prince had been too unwell to go shooting that morning with him and Count Joseph Hoyos, the court chamberlain.

On the morning of 30 January the Emperor was at his desk, working on a sheaf of papers with recommendations for a forthcoming visit to Budapest. After that he looked forward to spending some time in the company of Katherine Schratt, and with Elizabeth as well. The Empress was having her Greek lesson, the Crown Princess practising her singing.

At about 10.30 a.m. a thoroughly distressed Count Hoyos arrived in a cab, sought the Emperor's adjutant and told him that a few hours earlier he and Prince Philip had found the bodies of the Crown Prince and Marie Vetsera in a locked room at Mayerling. She had been shot in the left temple; as she was right-handed, she could not have fired the bullet herself, and she must have died several hours before her imperial lover who lay on the floor, his skull shattered, with bone and brain fragments strewn everywhere, the gun by his hand. Neither of them wanted to break such dreadful news directly to His Majesty. Philip was so devastated by the discovery that he was temporarily incapable of doing anything, and Hoyos was left to undertake the grim task.

Driving along the icy roads to Baden, he arrived as the Trieste–Vienna express train was coming towards the platform. It did not generally stop at Baden, so in order to convince the stationmaster of the urgency of his tidings, he had to tell him that the Crown Prince was dead. The distraught Hoyos added that the heir had been shot, a fact he would later deny. The stationmaster, a local employee of the Südbahn railway, of which the Rothschild bank was the principal shareholder, was so amazed at being one of the first to know that he promptly telegraphed the news to the bank, so the

Rothschilds and their connections in foreign embassies knew before the imperial family at the Hofburg.

Ironically in view of the fact that the Emperor and his entourage had always insisted that his wife should be spared emotional shocks as far as possible, it was to the Empress that they broke the news and asked her to tell her husband. Totally self-absorbed and preoccupied with Valerie's romance during the last few months, she had hardly been aware of Rudolf's deterioration and probably knew nothing of the existence of Marie Vetsera. Nevertheless, she could rise to the occasion in times of crisis, and she steeled herself to tell her husband that their son lay dead at Mayerling, apparently poisoned by one of his mistresses. Soon afterwards a very worried Countess Helene Vetsera came to the Hofburg, seeking news of her missing daughter. Coldly, Elizabeth told her that her daughter was dead, adding that her own son was dead too. As she swept away, she warned the Countess to remember that Rudolf died of a heart attack.

Early in the afternoon Francis Joseph told his immediate aides that his daughter-in-law, the Crown Princess, must be informed. Next, his people should know of their Crown Prince's death. After consulting his ministers, they decided to tell the press that he had succumbed to a stroke. This was duly reported in a special edition of the official *Wiener Zeitung*. Shortly after midday the regimental bands, theatres, music halls and other places of public entertainment were ordered to stop playing or close their doors, as there was grave news concerning their Crown Prince. Telegrams were despatched that same day to other European sovereigns, including the German Emperor William, Queen Victoria of England, and Dowager Queen Maria Cristina of Spain, saying that he had died suddenly, 'probably from heart failure'.

At that time the court still believed that Rudolf had been poisoned, and as a good Roman Catholic, Francis Joseph was reluctant to lie to the Holy Father. The telegram informing His Holiness Pope Leo XIII was despatched a day later. It merely informed him 'with most profound grief' of the sudden death of his son, expressing an assurance 'that you will participate sincerely in my grief over this terrible loss'.[12] No mention was made of the cause of death. A reply from the Pope assured the Emperor of his sympathy, and informed him that he had said a Requiem Mass for the late Crown Prince that morning.

Few members of the public believed that their Crown Prince, the scion of such a healthy family, could have perished from a stroke or heart attack at such an early age. Two days later, it was admitted that he had committed suicide. Yet there was gossip that he had been a victim of political murder. Rumours flew that a group of Hungarian separatists had killed him for going back on his word and betraying them; he had taken his life after attempting a coup d'état in Hungary; or a cuckolded husband had sought the ultimate revenge. On the day after the news broke, Queen Victoria was told by her prime minister, Lord Salisbury, that he had learnt from Paget 'that there is a general impression that the Crown Prince did not die a natural death. The popular belief is that His Imperial Highness was assassinated.'[13]

Another story was that the Emperor had had an affair with Baroness Vetsera, that Marie was his illegitimate daughter, and that when the young couple found out that they were half-brother and half-sister, they were so ashamed at having had an incestuous affair that there was no alternative to a suicide pact. Another suggested that Rudolf had been so deeply involved in treason that Count Taaffe, informed that he and his mistress had gone to Mayerling, had arranged for agents to stage an assassination which would look like suicide. Within three or four days a Munich newspaper printed the full story of Marie Vetsera having died with the Crown Prince, and before the authorities could act, copies were on sale in Vienna.

The Emperor had been misinformed. Hoyos had not seen the Crown Prince's revolver, but only an empty glass which he had assumed contained cyanide. Not until receiving the report from his physician, Dr Hermann Widerhofer, did Francis Joseph realise that his son had shot his mistress, and then himself. The full horror and shame was too much for him, and he collapsed with grief.[14] At length he regained his composure, and after consulting Count Taaffe, they agreed on the need to secure papal permission for a full Christian burial, despite the stigma of suicide. The presence of the young Baroness Vetsera must be concealed from press and public, and they should ascertain if any of the Crown Prince's friends had any responsibility for the tragedy.

On the day after his death, Rudolf's body was laid out on a bed in the Hofburg to be prepared for burial. Francis Joseph ordered his adjutant to put white officer's gloves on the Crown Prince's hands, put his own gloves on, girded himself with his sword, walked to his son's bedroom, and stood silently throughout a fifteen-minute vigil. In accordance with custom and regulation, he was saying his last farewell to a brother officer.[15] Stephanie brought their daughter Erszi to say goodbye to him and to lay her own small wreath of white roses. The tearful, distressed girl of five clung to the skirts of her attendant, saying over and over again that 'that is not my father' and begging to be taken away.[16]

An autopsy conducted by Dr Widerhofer on 2 February produced the verdict that the Crown Prince had died as a result of the shattering of his skull and the anterior parts of the brain, produced by a shot fired against the right temple at close range. There was no doubt that he had fired the shot himself and that death was instantaneous. A detailed examination of the head and brain revealed signs of abnormal mental conditions 'and therefore justify the assumption that the deed was committed in a state of mental confusion'.[17] This was enough to obtain permission from the Pope to approve the full rites of Christian burial, but it added to Elizabeth's fears that she had brought into the family the strain of insanity which haunted the Wittelsbachs. 'The Emperor should never have married me,' she told the court physician, Dr Kerzl, 'I have inherited the taint of madness!'[18] Sometimes she too feared that the balance of her own mind might be disturbed.

Any possibility of a state funeral in the circumstances was out of the question, and the Emperor requested that no crowned heads should attend. Emperor William had expressed his intention to come, presumably more out of solidarity with the Emperor and as a manifestation of the strength of the Austro-German alliance, than out of any feelings for a dead Crown Prince with whom he had had so little in common and whose feelings of contempt had always been reciprocated. Yet Francis Joseph had asked him in a telegram not to come: 'you may judge how deeply crushed my family is if we have to address this request even to you'.[19]

The Emperor tried unsuccessfully to dissuade King Leopold and Queen Marie-Henriette of the Belgians, Rudolf's parents-in-law, from attending as well, even though as family they had more right to be invited than any others. Francis Joseph had written to the Queen that Stephanie 'instructs me to ask you urgently not to realise your intention of coming here just yet but only after a little while, when it will be the greatest possible comfort to her'.[20] Such a wish probably came less from the widowed Crown Princess than from her father-in-law, who was afraid that Stephanie would tell her parents the whole story of what she had had to endure at the hands of her profligate husband throughout their miserable marriage. He and Elizabeth made it clear that they held her partly responsible for the tragedy, through her inability to provide their son with a happy home. Never, perhaps, did the Emperor and Empress demonstrate their lamentable failure as parents more starkly than in their clear lack of understanding on this occasion. Even a more determined character than Stephanie would have found it difficult to make a faithful clean-living husband out of Crown Prince Rudolf.

It was ironic that the only sovereign who had to be there for family reasons was the one that Francis Joseph liked the least, for he regarded the avaricious Coburg monarch with distaste, considering his commercial, peddler-like traits 'incompatible with the dignity of a sovereign'.[21] Leopold had never cared much for his daughters, and was too honest to make any pretence of appearing affected by the tragedy. He had more pressing matters on his mind, and his first act on arriving in Vienna was to make an appointment with a financier regarding his notorious ventures in the Congo.

Neither Elizabeth, Stephanie nor Valerie attended the funeral on 5 February. It was left to Francis Joseph and Gisela to lead those among Rudolf's closest relations to say farewell in person on that cold winter afternoon, as the coffin was borne in solemn procession on a hearse drawn by six Lippizaner greys from the Hofburg chapel, where Rudolf had lain in state, his shattered head partly reconstructed with false hair, wax and rouge, to the Capuchin church. At the service Francis Joseph stood perfectly calm, looking around himself with quick movements of the head. After the chanting of the Requiem Mass, he stepped out from his place, walked up to his son's coffin, and knelt beside it, remaining for a moment in prayer with clasped hands. Not a sound was to be heard until he rose from his knees and walked back calmly to his place. Afterwards, he told his wife and Katherine that he bore up well, and it was only in the crypt that he could 'endure it no longer'.[22] Seven members of the family, among them Rudolf's paternal uncles Charles Ludwig and Ludwig Victor, his brother-in-law Leopold of Bavaria, his future brother-in-law Francis Salvator, Philip of Saxe-Coburg, and Francis Ferdinand, had been chosen to accompany him to the vault where his son was laid to rest among his ancestors, where they saw the desolate father break down and weep bitterly.

No such dignity had attended the burial of Marie Vetsera. Her body was thrown into a disused storeroom until her uncle Alexander Baltazzi was summoned by the police to come and identify her. She would probably have been buried in an unhallowed grave had it not been for the timely intervention of Katherine Schratt, the one person in touch with both the Emperor's entourage and the Baltazzis. Astonished and angered by the way Count Taaffe and the police were treating the Vetseras, she suggested tactfully to the court officials that if the family were denied a Christian burial for the girl, the imperial court would suffer even more once the news came out, as it surely would. Thus it was that two days after her murder by the heir to the throne, Alexander and Marie's brother-in-law Count George Stockau were allowed to undertake the grim duty of escorting her body from Mayerling to a shrine at Heiligenkreuz. Under cover of darkness on a stormy night the corpse was dressed and lifted into a closed carriage to travel between the men, a stick placed along her spine, held by scarves knotted over her forehead and chest, in order to stop her head from lolling forward. There, the Abbot was waiting to provide a Christian funeral for the girl.

Rudolf had left messages for his wife, mother, sister and several friends, including Mitzi Caspar, and Baron Maurice Hirsch. All, apart from the note for his mother, were thought to have been written at Vienna on or before the morning of 28 January. The one written to the Empress was assumed to have originated at Mayerling, as it referred to the death of Marie Vetsera, acknowledging that 'I have no right to go on living; I have killed!' It also asked forgiveness from his father, admitting that 'I know very well that I was not worthy to be his son'.[23] Finally, he asked her to carry out Marie's greatest wish, for both of them to be buried together in a little church at Alland. No farewell letter to his father was ever found, and it was evident that none had been written.

The stricken Emperor sought to put pained memories aside after the funeral, resuming his daily routine at his desk, trying to bury himself in work while telling Katherine Schratt of his worries for the Empress's health. He tried to find consolation in talking to members of Rudolf's household, trying through them to make some sense of events. As he admitted to Katherine, 'one cannot possibly think of anything else, and talking at least brings a certain relief'.[24]

On 6 February he issued a proclamation to his people. Overwhelmed with grief, he said, he bowed humbly

before the inscrutable decree of Divine Providence, appealing with my people to the Almighty to give me strength so that I may not falter in the conscientious performance of my duties as Ruler, but may keep before my eyes that course, my steadfast adherence to which is still assured for the future, of bravely and confidently persevering in unremitting care for the common weal and the maintenance of the blessings of peace. It has been a consolation for me, in these days of bitter woe, to know that I was upheld by the heartfelt sympathy ever secured to me by my peoples, and of which I have received from all sides the most touching and manifold tokens. It is with profound gratitude that I feel how the bond of mutual love and faithfulness, uniting me and my House with all the peoples of the Monarchy, only gains in strength and security in times of such great affliction.[25]

Within a fortnight he was exchanging theatre gossip with Katherine Schratt once more, in an attempt to distract himself and try and get back to the old routine. Some of those around him could see that he was still haunted by the tragedy, however, and they thought that the heart had gone out of him. Count Joseph Hübner, who had served under him for almost forty years, thought that after his son's death the Emperor was a completely different person, and that when not talking, he acted like a person 'who had been knocked on the head'.[26] Others, notably Captain Middleton, the Empress's riding partner in England, and Dr Widerhofer, who had conducted the post-mortem, thought that he got over the shock relatively quickly – thanks largely to the evidence of Rudolf's mental derangement, and the indications that pointed to symptoms of advanced paralysis which would probably have proved fatal within a year. 'God's ways are inscrutable,' the Emperor told Widerhofer. 'Perhaps He has sent me this trial to spare me a yet harder one!'[27] On the other hand, the doctor may have told a little white lie in order to soften the blow for the grieving father.

Francis Joseph told his adjutant Count Eduard Paar how grateful he was for the Empress's support. 'If it hadn't been for my wife, who kept me going with her superhuman strength of mind even though she was stricken with grief herself, I should have gone under altogether.'[28] He was reported to have told associates that his son died like a coward, though when writing to other sovereigns he referred to Rudolf as 'the best of sons and the loyalest of subjects'.[29]

When Countess Larisch's role in the tragedy and the part she had played as a go-between between Rudolf and Marie Vetsera were revealed from her letters, she became *persona non grata* at court. She sought revenge in two subsequent books, a volume of highly inaccurate recollections and a spiteful memoir of the Empress Elizabeth. One of the Countess's five children, a boy who was aged only two at the time of these events, took his own life as a young man when he learnt of his mother's part in them.

Within three weeks of the tragedy, a decision was made to demolish the lodge at Mayerling, and as an act of atonement a chapel was to be built on the site, with a convent of Carmelite nuns. On All Souls Day, 2 November, the Emperor went there to hear Mass in the new chapel, and see the cloisters and communal buildings. He commissioned the Viennese artist Joseph Kastner to paint an ornate fresco above the high altar, which was erected on the site of the room where Rudolf and Marie had died.

For Emperor Francis Joseph as head of the family without a direct male heir, the immediate problem was the imperial succession. Habsburg family convention forbade the succession of an archduchess, and next in line was the Emperor's eldest surviving brother. Charles Ludwig was a pleasant if ineffectual, unambitious man of fifty-five, thrice married and twice widowed. He took an active interest in arts, crafts and industries in the empire, and was sometimes seen attending exhibitions and conferences in an honorary capacity, as well as presenting annual prizes for pictures and works of sculpture at the academies. Apart from such representative duties he had taken little part in public life, never attempted to exert any political influence, and had never expected to succeed to the throne. As he was only three years younger than his brother, who had always been in the best of health, his reign – if he ever did succeed – would not be a long one. Nobody saw him as a future emperor. He was best known as a somewhat unworldly prince, given to quoting the Bible at length and making the sign of the cross every time he greeted people.

It was commonly believed that, given the chance, Charles Ludwig would renounce his place in the succession in favour of his elder son, Francis Ferdinand. A few days after Rudolf's funeral, one newspaper claimed prematurely that he had done so, and that Francis Ferdinand had been received in special audience by the Emperor who told him that he would henceforth be considered the successor to the throne. It was also said that the young Archduke had mentioned to the Emperor his father's wish to step aside, only to be answered with a frosty 'Why don't you wait until I am no longer around?'[30] A close friend of Rudolf, but unlike him a strong supporter of close ties with Berlin, Francis Ferdinand was also firmly opposed to the idea of war with Russia, and longed to see the *Dreikaiserbund* restored. He hated the Magyars, and felt their separatist ambitions posed a threat to the stability of the Dual Monarchy. Some also saw in him a fanatical, even hysterical, anti-clericalism and deep-seated loathing of the kingdom of Italy. As a grandson of Ferdinand II, King of the Two Sicilies, and as one who had inherited the title and fortune of the last Duke of Modena, this prejudice had some justification.

Yet there were grave doubts that Francis Ferdinand would live for more than a few years. He had inherited from his mother Marie Annunziata of Naples, a sickly princess who had died in 1871 at the age of twenty-eight, the weak lungs which had caused her death from consumption. He was frequently sent abroad during the winter on medical advice, and doctors feared that with his tubercular lapses, and without his uncle's constitution, his days were numbered. However, some saw in him the hopes of the Habsburg dynasty for another generation. It was rumoured that forces at court would try and bring about a marriage between him and Stephanie, who were the same age. Some said that the Empress had other ideas for him, namely one of her Bavarian nieces, and had warned him to 'marry for love, or else you will have ugly children'.[31] Much to the Emperor's displeasure, his nephew would indeed marry for love.

A fundamental lack of self-confidence, possibly connected to his ill-health and the feeling that people were ready to write him off, made Francis Ferdinand suspicious, hypersensitive and unwilling to trust people. With those whom he knew and liked, he was almost invariably seen at his most forthcoming. With his passion for hunting, or wholesale slaughter as some would say, and a reputation for being bad-tempered, intolerant and prejudiced, he looked none too promising either. He had refused to marry Prince Maria Josepha of Saxony, a plain and bigoted German prude, who then found herself married to Francis Ferdinand's younger brother Otto instead. The latter found consolation for his unhappy married life in perpetual debauchery which soon undermined his health. However, as a major serving with an infantry regiment in Prague, Francis Ferdinand was a dedicated and conscientious soldier. Despite his shortcomings, he revealed a strength of character which suggested he would make a perfectly adequate if not particularly popular successor to Francis Joseph.

This was more than could be said for the Emperor's youngest brother. Ludwig Victor, the mischievous adolescent who had always shown more interest in gossip than women, had never matured. Now in his late forties, he was known as 'the Archduke of the Bath' after an unseemly incident in the public baths. With his penchant for cross-dressing and roaming the city streets in search of handsome young boys, he was regarded as a joke at best and a disgrace at worst. Yet at least he had not openly rebelled against the good name of the family, like his outspoken cousin Johann Salvator, who had renounced his title and position, and assumed the name of Johann Orth. To the old guard, such a move was desertion, and Archduke Albrecht took this to heart just as much as the Emperor. It was a bleak time for them all – 'two unheard-of ignominies in a single year on the hitherto immaculate honour of our House'.[32]

EIGHT

'Nothing at All is to Be Spared Me'

For Emperor Francis Joseph, the last decade of the nineteenth century brought little peace or satisfaction. It was as if the mainspring of his life had gone, to be replaced by an empty ritual in the name of service to his empire, combined with an unspoken yet fierce determination to stay at the helm and carry on as long as possible in order to stave off the day when his inheritance would be in the hands of the unassuming, little-known Charles Ludwig and his unsatisfactory sons. The heir was dismissed by the sharp-tongued Marie Larisch as 'a fat old man with brutish instincts',[1] although where the imperial family were concerned she was hardly an unbiased witness.

Any hopes for a new understanding between Francis Joseph and Elizabeth after the tragedy of Rudolf were short-lived. During their rare times together in Vienna or occasionally Budapest, she alternated between listless apathy, acute melancholia and tears. To those who knew them well, he still seemed very much in love with her, while it was as if she had been wounded too often and was trying to keep her distance from him by wandering aimlessly around Europe. Her persistent melancholy irritated him, and he confided to the German ambassador that she spoke of death so often that he became quite depressed.[2] He was becoming increasingly deaf, and in what may have been a subconscious wish to annoy him, she spoke more quietly than ever. Valerie urged her mother to raise her voice a little in conversation with her father, only to be told that she could not shout.

Shortly after Mayerling, Lady Paget compared the husband and wife in a brutally frank description, praising the devotion to industry of one and the self-absorption of the other. The Emperor, she noted, had been 'overcome' at first, but with his unerring sense of duty,

148

he has not only worked as usual, but he has constantly been seeing people, giving dinners and appearing to be interested and pleased with everything. The Empress on the contrary bore up very well at first, but she has been getting constantly worse. Having led a life of unalloyed selfishness, worshipping her own health and beauty as the sole objects in life, she has nothing but herself to fall back on.

Elizabeth would never show herself again, the ambassador's wife believed, and she 'has become a ghost during her own life'.[3]

In the months following her brother's death, Valerie spent much of her time with one parent or the other, and she was distressed to see how much they apparently got on each other's nerves. Though she had always been her mother's favourite child, she resented the maternal possessiveness that made her feel guilty about being with her betrothed, Francis Salvator, particularly as he was serving in the army and could only see her when he was on leave. Her sympathies were overwhelmingly with her father, who had sacrificed so much in the name of imperial duty and received so little thanks from his ungrateful wife. When Valerie was alone with her mother or father, child and parent enjoyed each other's company. But her father had so few interests by now, apart from what she referred to bluntly as 'his unfortunate relationship with the Schratt woman'.[4] He had become ponderous and narrow-minded, and both he and Elizabeth became worked up over the most trivial matters.

The very mention of Valerie's marriage made the Empress burst into tears and bewail the desolation she would feel once her youngest child had flown the nest. Fortunately for Valerie herself, the ceremony could not be postponed indefinitely because of mourning for Rudolf. It took place on 30 July 1890 at Ischl. Over 100 members of the family, Habsburgs, Wittelsbachs, Bourbons and Salvators of the Tuscan branch, crowded into the hotels and villas of the small town which was already packed with summer visitors. Flags and banners fluttered from every house, and the square in front of the church boasted a beribboned maypole. Dressed in white, Elizabeth made an effort to appear cheerful throughout the ceremony. Francis Joseph was glad to see their daughter so radiantly happy, but his wife broke down and afterwards, when mother and daughter were alone and she was helping the bride change into her travelling clothes, she asked what was to become of her now. At the age of fifteen, she told Valerie, she had made a promise, the meaning of which she did not understand, and for ever afterwards 'one is imprisoned by that oath'.[5]

Though very much in love with her husband, and relieved to be escaping from a home of sadness, Valerie was desperately worried about her mother, and begged her uncle Charles Theodore to try and keep an eye on her, especially as the Emperor seemed too bowed down by burdens of state for him to fulfil the role adequately any longer. Almost immediately after the wedding Elizabeth announced that she was about to go on her travels again. Though Gisela had never been very close to her mother, she too was alarmed, and warned Valerie before a visit to the waterfalls at Gastein to make sure their mother did not try to throw herself in.

As Elizabeth still had her life of travel, Francis Joseph was the greater loser. With the marriage of their youngest child, he now had no real family life left. For the next quarter of a century he lived alone in his large palaces, surrounded by obsequious courtiers and servants. Occasional visits from his daughters and their families, and the intermittent company of his melancholy wife, were all he had to look forward to. He loved small children, was devoted to his granddaughter 'Erszi', who lived with Stephanie at Laxenburg, and was determined that the little girl should suffer as little as possible despite the tragic death of her father.

Though Stephanie had been so sympathetic to Rudolf, and desperate to help him in his last weeks of life, she had suffered too much from his infidelities and boorish behaviour to mourn his death too deeply. Yet the loss of her position as Crown Princess was a grave humiliation, especially as her father King Leopold was notorious for his ill-treatment of his wife and daughters, and had told her that there was no question of a return to her old home in Belgium. At court she now had to take second place to Archduchess Maria Theresa, wife of Charles Ludwig. She felt unwelcome in the empire, for her father-in-law, normally the most fair-minded of men, gave the impression that he held her partly responsible for her husband's suicide, and the mere sight of their daughter-in-law reduced the Empress to floods of tears. Elizabeth never tried to conceal her detestation of Stephanie, who was guilty of nothing more than having the misfortune to marry a totally unsuitable husband, and she was coolly indifferent to the granddaughter who bore her name.

From 1890 onwards foreign ambassadors complained increasingly about the dullness of the Viennese court. The long period of mourning and the Empress's extended absences made it a lifeless place, especially as she would never allow any of the archduchesses to deputise for her, and the Emperor found balls and other functions an unpleasant ritual. Yet he remained as considerate as ever. One evening he returned to his room after a court ball, very hot, tired and in need of a cool drink. Finding not even so much as a bottle of mineral water, he had to make do with tepid tap water. When he told Katherine Schratt a day or so later, she asked him why he had not rung for his valet to bring a bottle of champagne, as the ball was still in progress. He replied that he did not wish to disturb anyone at that time of night.

Political woes pursued the Emperor, not least in Hungary, where a defence bill was provoking furious debates in the Reichsrat and threatened to unleash unrest in the capital. It reminded him painfully of Rudolf's subversive activities and pro-Hungarian sympathies, especially as he had been a close political friend and outspoken supporter of Count Stefan Károlyi, leader of the opposition. The resulting parliamentary upheavals culminated in the resignation of Kálmán Tisza. During his fifteen years in office as prime minister the Emperor had learnt to trust and respect the man, and he now feared that the era of strong Hungarian leadership was at an end. He appointed Count Gyula Szapáry to succeed Tisza, but the new prime minister did not have much parliamentary support, and he was to be the first of six incumbents of the post during the next fifteen years.

In Vienna trade unionists were urged by Victor Adler, a Jewish intellectual and prominent Austrian socialist leader, to observe May Day as the workers' festival of unity. Adler urged trade unionists to hold meetings of what he called a popular character open to the public on the morning of 1 May 1890, and be free to enjoy 'Nature's springtime' in the afternoon. This summons alarmed the Emperor, who dreaded a repetition of 1848, and he called meetings of the ministers in Vienna, insisting that Taaffe must be ready to take action to check the spread of dangerous beliefs. The police were prepared for mass violence, shops were closed, women and children were urged to stay indoors, and Adler was summarily interned. Late that evening the warden released him, telling him that everything had gone off peacefully and the demonstration was 'magnificent'.

Such an outcome was some consolation for the Emperor, who had a certain liking for Adler (which was reciprocated), yet felt that socialism if unchecked could lead to anarchy. It would have been surprising if an Emperor born and raised in Europe before the year of revolutions had become a wholehearted democrat in his advancing years. Though very much set in his ways, to an extent Francis Joseph appreciated the wisdom of moving steadily with the times, and readily welcomed proposals to extend the vote to more of his subjects in the empire. Though a natural conservative, he would have nothing to do with anti-Semitism, telling Taaffe that the Jews were brave and patriotic men, always ready to risk their lives for Emperor and fatherland.[6] While he did share something of his class and his generation's suspicion of Jews, and occasionally expressed impatience with them, he was dismayed by the increasing support for the reactionary mayor of Vienna, Karl Lueger, and his anti-Semitic Christian Socialist Party.

On assuming office in 1879, Taaffe had stated that he did not belong to any party and was not a party minister. He had been appointed by the crown, and the will of the Emperor would always be decisive for him. His brief was to remain loyal above all to the sovereign, while presiding over and ensuring the smooth running of a parliamentary system. This, he had realised, was best achieved by playing off the different linguistic groupings against one another, in the interests of the dynasty, or as he himself put it, 'to keep the races in a balanced state of mild dissatisfaction'. As long as each group felt that none of the others was getting a better deal, and as long as none had any major grievances, then the government would survive and his position was safe. His political balance rested mainly on reconciliation between the Czechs and the Germans, first in Bohemia and Moravia, then later in Cisleithania. The growth of unrest and militancy among the Czechs and in other provinces persuaded Emil Steinbach, Taaffe's minister of finance, to put forward a proposal to broaden the franchise in elections for the lower house of the Reichsrat. Intensive nationalism, he argued, was a middle-class phenomenon, and if working classes were given the vote, nationalistic antagonism which threatened the structure of the monarchy would be contained. Taaffe was won over and, to the ministers' surprise, so was Francis Joseph himself. In the countryside and smaller towns, he had always enjoyed loyal support from the less sophisticated of his subjects, and he welcomed any proposal to extend the franchise. Steinbach was asked to prepare a suffrage bill which would have given the vote to almost every literate male in the empire over the age of twenty-five. This had to be done in secret, in order to prevent a political crisis, and he needed to preserve the electoral system by which the proportion of deputies was stacked in favour of the large landowners and businessmen.

The draft proposals proved unpopular, with almost every parliamentary group except the Young Czechs opposed. Taaffe, who had recently celebrated his sixtieth birthday, was weary after more than a decade in office. In November 1893 Francis Joseph dismissed him and appointed as his successor Prince Alfred Windischgrätz, grandson of the general who had helped to save the monarchy in 1848. The new prime minister was told that the Steinbach proposals must not be dropped, but instead referred to a parliamentary committee for close scrutiny. Yet disagreements continued, the government was split, Windischgrätz resigned in July 1895, and the new prime minister Count Erich Kielmansegg only held office for a few weeks before being succeeded in September by the well-respected former governor of Galicia, Count Casimir von Badeni.

Regarded by many as a 'strong man', and even by his admirers as a Polish Bismarck, Badeni was seen by the Emperor as perhaps the one man able to call the fractious Reichsrat to heel. Three major problems confronted the Emperor and his head of government: reform of the suffrage, appeasement of the Young Czechs, and renewal of the *Ausgleich* with Hungary, which was due for re-negotiation. The bill extending voting rights was passed, and after an election held in March 1897 representatives of twenty-five parties took their seats in parliament. As the Young Czechs had made a strong showing Badeni felt he needed to keep them on board, so in April two Language Ordinances were issued, substantially extending concessions granted to the Czechs in the previous decade. Within four years, every civil servant in Bohemia would be required to speak and write Czech as well as German. This was bitterly resented by the German Austrians, who thought it absurd to force Czech, to them 'a mere dialect', on Germans, especially as the proposition had not been presented for debate to the deputies first. Throughout Austria there were demonstrations and counter-demonstrations, and violence spread to the chamber of the Austrian parliament where nationalist leaders shouted and stamped their feet for hours on end, desks were banged and inkpots hurled at the Speaker. The police were called in and in June 1897 Francis Joseph issued a decree which closed the Reichsrat down.

When it reconvened in the autumn, violence resumed, with delegates organising an 'Obstruction Concert', bringing in musical instruments, metal lids, and anything to make enough noise to drown out any speakers. On 28 November 1897 demonstrations in Vienna demanded Badeni's resignation. Military guards and police patrolled the streets in order to contain the increasingly restive students and demonstrators, but they admitted they could no longer maintain law and order without resorting to extreme force. Fearing a repeat of the worst excesses of 1848, the Emperor dismissed Badeni. At first he refused to concede changes in the law; not for another two years did he accept that the Language Ordinances were not only unpopular but impracticable, and allow them to be withdrawn.

This marked the end of effective parliamentary government in the Austro-Hungarian empire. The Reichsrat continued to exist, but representatives on all sides had learnt that it was possible to obstruct any measures with which they disagreed. The government could literally be talked to a standstill. Francis Joseph could say that he had tried to reign as a constitutional monarch, and found the exercise futile. From now on he would rule as an absolute monarch within a legal structure of constitutionalism. For the rest of his life, if parliamentary consensus could not be reached, he resorted to Article 14 of the Constitution of 1861, which empowered him to rule by 'imperial emergency decree'. With a parliament which often found itself unable to agree, Article 14 would be regularly needed during the next few years.

According to one parliamentarian, Joseph Redlich, the man who would later become one of the Emperor's first biographers, 'the constitutional principle had been smashed', and while nobody could see it at the time, 'from this moment the Habsburg realm was doomed'.[7]

Throughout these years Elizabeth's wanderlust continued unabated. After Valerie's wedding she travelled to Corfu, Switzerland, the French Riviera, the Azores and North Africa. When told that Tasmania was an attractive place, she made plans to set out on a world cruise in a chartered sailing ship. Her family and household were relieved when she had second thoughts, realising that such a voyage would now be beyond her physical strength.[8] In January 1892 she lost her mother, who succumbed to pneumonia at the age of eighty-four. Valerie was approaching her first confinement and on the next day she gave birth to the first of ten children, a daughter, whom she named Elizabeth after her mother.

Elizabeth repeatedly urged the Emperor to join her on a vacation, and put court life to one side for a while. In March 1893 husband and wife spent a fortnight in Switzerland, staying in a hotel at Territet, near Montreux, enjoying some walks together to the Castle of Chillon, up the mountain foothills behind the lake. Yet Francis Joseph did not really find the experience much of a holiday. Within twenty-four hours the hotel had seen through his incognito and proudly flew the black and gold imperial standard from its flagpole, and the following day he had to spend a whole morning in the hotel dealing with official papers a courier had brought him from Vienna. He left alone, with Elizabeth still planning to travel for a few more months.

At least in Vienna Francis Joseph still had the companionship of Katherine Schratt. Her common sense and sympathy had helped to steady Elizabeth's nerves after Mayerling and had also given Francis Joseph himself much comfort. In March 1889 he had added a codicil to his will by which he would leave her a legacy of half a million florins, in recognition of 'the deepest and purest of friendships'. With the Emperor's support and approval, she bought a villa at Hietzing overlooking the botanical gardens of Schönbrunn. It was close enough for him to come to breakfast, after which they would enjoy a leisurely stroll together in the gardens. One of their favourite walks was to the private zoo, where they would feed the bears with scraps left over from breakfast. While they walked, the coachmen would wait discreetly round the corner, but the imperial carriage was always recognised, and a loyal crowd would gather to see their Emperor. When an over-conscientious police officer gave orders for the throng of people to be sent away, Francis Joseph countermanded his instructions, saying there was no reason why they should not greet their sovereign when he was paying a friendly visit to the neighbourhood.[9]

Elizabeth remained supportive of the relationship between Katherine and her husband, and there was rarely any malicious gossip. The shy, straitlaced and unworldly Valerie resented the way in which people were continually speculating about her father and Katherine, even if it was merely well-intentioned curiosity, and could never understand why her mother encouraged the friendship so much, or why she always referred to Katherine as 'the friend'. Although she knew her father had been lonely for years, to her it seemed utterly at odds with his wedding vows to take such pleasure in and have no shame over such a close relationship with a married woman. It was even more incomprehensible to Valerie that her mother should be such a willing accessory. Francis Salvator agreed with his wife, and perhaps only strengthened her views on the matter, saying bluntly that 'the Emperor should not be talked about'.[10] Elizabeth sometimes talked of Frau Schratt with great affection, and on other occasions bewailed the fact that she herself was coming between her husband and 'the friend', so that she felt ridiculous, envied Rudolf, and wondered what point there was in still living. It irritated Valerie that her mother was so much to blame for what she called 'Papa's unfortunate entanglement' by being away so often, by her continuing to treat the actress as a close friend, and even calling her her adopted sister.

Deeply in love with her husband, Valerie could see that her father was not merely infatuated with the actress, but very much emotionally attached to her. The general view of Viennese society, according to Lady Paget, was that Frau Schratt was rather stupid, but with a naive way of blurting out the truth, thus suggesting that she had a way of telling the Emperor the things that nobody else would. Lady Paget also heard a rumour that she was supposed to be a daughter of Francis Joseph, and whatever the truth or lack of it, their relationship was completely platonic.[11] This most self-effacing of crowned heads knew how tiresome he could be to his nearest and dearest. In some of his letters to Katherine he would apologise for being such a bore, and tell her how marvellous she was to put up with him. It did not stop him from becoming more and more possessive of her, jealous of the zest for life she clearly still enjoyed, and resentful of what he considered her extraordinary craving for publicity.

There were additional difficulties that ruffled their friendship. He was uneasy at her friendship with Prince Ferdinand of Coburg, who had been chosen as sovereign Prince of Bulgaria in 1887, a few months after Alexander von Battenberg's enforced abdication. At the same time he was also annoyed by her efforts to secure a more rewarding post in the diplomatic service for her husband, who in 1892 was at last transferred from the consulate in Tunis to that in Barcelona. Even less welcome was her insistence on making a balloon flight over Vienna in June 1890, which was highly publicised by the press. He thought the flight a foolhardy mission, and was even less pleased to find out that her companion was Alexander Baltazzi, brother of Helene Vetsera. After the Mayerling tragedy it would not do for any of the Vetsera family to have such a close connection with the Emperor, or someone near to him. Katherine was suitably apologetic, pledging to keep the matter secret if ever she should take to the air again.

Despite these problems, Katherine found her illustrious friend and his consort ever supportive. In June 1892 Francis Joseph was aghast when her twelve-year-old son Toni received at school a poison pen letter slandering his mother. The Emperor and Katherine's banker friend Edward Palmer got together to dissuade her from taking any action which might be seen as attaching too much importance to it, lest Toni become frightened. The Vienna police chief was nonetheless alerted, but no prosecutions resulted. That summer when Francis Joseph and Elizabeth were in residence, at Ischl, Katherine and Toni were invited to tea, and Elizabeth took the boy for a walk on his own, praising his mother, telling him how valued her friendship and support were to the Emperor. Ironically, Katherine was by now the main link between husband and wife. When they did not have her or the grandchildren to talk about, they had very little to say to each other. Elizabeth clearly had no more than a reluctant interest in matters of state, while Francis Joseph found it hard to share her enthusiasm for foreign travel.

Elizabeth and Valerie both kept diaries, but Francis Joseph never did. Instead he poured out his feelings in long letters to Elizabeth and Katherine. To the former, he generally wrote on alternate days during her travels. There are nearly 500 surviving letters from husband to wife written between September 1890 and September 1898. Most of them were strictly descriptive, chronicling news of his activities, their daughters and of 'little Erszi', of whom he was far more fond than was Elizabeth herself, of visits to plays (particularly, but not exclusively, those in which Frau Schratt appeared), and also such modern inventions as the Edison phonograph, which was demonstrated to the Emperor and on which he could hear on wax cylinder the sound of a German band playing the *Radetzky March*.

Francis Joseph also wrote more than 200 letters to Katherine during the same period. These were lighter in character than those to the Empress, with a certain amount of self-effacement and occasional self-pity, admitting how anxious the Empress's exploits made him, particularly on her sea voyages, and also warning Katherine herself against hazardous ventures such as ballooning, mountaineering and excursions to the glaciers. When his elder daughter Gisela took up cycling, he was fearful of the risks involved.

From 1894 onwards husband and wife made four annual visits to the French Riviera, each lasting between one and three weeks. These brought some liveliness and colour back to what was becoming an increasingly lonely and duty-bound existence. The sheer novelty of staying in a hotel fascinated Francis Joseph, though he could not be persuaded to break the habit of a lifetime and go to bed late. But when his head of the police at Schönbrunn went to Cap Martin with a squad of detectives, the Emperor asked them not to accompany him as guards, as he said he had no fear of being assassinated abroad. It was to be an entirely private visit, and the Emperor was as amused as everyone else when they attended an army dinner and the general in command, unused to royalty, addressed him as Monsieur. Noticing the smiles of the Emperor's suite, he offered his apologies, to be assured it was perfectly all right. 'I am always surrounded by courtiers,' the monarch answered, 'but you are a soldier – a comrade!'[12]

The Emperor's recently appointed valet de chambre, Eugen Ketterl, was intrigued by his master's extraordinary sense of economy.

To save money, he ruled out use of the Viennese imperial train and they travelled to Cap Martin in two coaches and a dining car coupled to the ordinary train. On their arrival at Menton, as they were about to leave the train Ketterl asked a local councillor for some small French change for the porter who was looking after their luggage. He was told that the Emperor of Austria only paid such sums in gold, and the porter was duly rewarded handsomely for his work.[13]

On their first visit to the French Riviera Elizabeth had suggested that Frau Schratt should be invited to join them, but then changed her mind as she feared that the presence of so much other European royalty, and censorious tongues, would give rise to unsavoury innuendo. Yet by the time of their second French break, in February 1895, she no longer had any such doubts. An aide-de-camp was instructed to reserve rooms for the actress, but she chose to visit nearby Monte Carlo on her own instead. On the imperial couple's arrival in 1896, the Emperor wrote to Katherine, they dined in their suite at 7 p.m. and were soon lulled to sleep by music from the hotel lounge. Once Francis Joseph visited the gambling rooms at Monte Carlo, perhaps on Katherine's recommendation, but he was dissuaded from trying his luck at the tables by the number of onlookers present and the fear of what gossips would say afterwards. However, for once he could enjoy his food in comfort, and was persuaded to try the restaurants. A little guiltily he wrote to Katherine telling her about the different establishments they frequented, and of his fear that perhaps they were eating too much and too varied a fare. After leading such a spartan existence for so long, the idea of relaxing and enjoying himself like any other holidaymaker must have been a remarkable – and, one hopes, very pleasant – experience.

In March 1896 the Emperor met the head of a republic for the first time, when he visited the French President Felix Fauré, who was on an official tour of the Alpes Maritimes. He was interested to watch the Alpine infantry as they carried out field exercises with live ammunition. It came as some surprise to him to find that this part of the Third Republic's coastline played host during the winter to several European royals, among them the Prince of Wales, and his old friend Empress Eugenie. On 13 March 1896 Queen Victoria was at Cimiez, and received the Emperor and Empress together for the first and only time. From there Victoria wrote to her prime minister Lord Salisbury that the Emperor had been most cordial, and 'hoped our countries would always go together, and repeated several times how important it was that England and Germany should be on the best terms together, and one thing he felt sure of, *viz.* that everyone wished for peace'.[14] Francis Joseph left no impressions of their meeting, but Elizabeth had written to Valerie the previous year telling her that the Queen had taken over an entire hotel and two villas, as she was bringing a suite of seventy people, including a number of Indians; 'it must be a great pleasure to travel like a circus'.[15]

That same year also marked the thousandth anniversary of the coming of the Magyars to the Danubian plain, and Budapest was preparing to celebrate from spring until autumn. These millennial celebrations were of crucial importance to the stability of the Dual Monarchy as a whole, and would either confirm Hungary's economic self-sufficiency and cohesion, or else spark off friction between Austria and the Slav minorities. By now Elizabeth had withdrawn almost completely from public life, and lost interest even in Hungary and its politics. On her visits to the country she hardly ever went beyond the castle grounds. However, she was persuaded to return for the festivities which began on 2 May 1896, when she and Francis Joseph opened the Millennial Exposition of Hungarian achievement in the Városliget, the Budapest town park.

To take visitors from the inner city to the park, the municipal authorities had authorised construction of an underground railway only a few feet below the surface of the city's smartest boulevard, with stops at eight stations. Such an innovation was until then unknown outside London. Four days after the first trains ran, on 6 May, the Emperor travelled on the train in a specially decorated imperial carriage, though the Empress did not accompany him, as she had felt overwhelmed by the pomp and splendour of the opening of the exhibition. She was saddened by memories of earlier grand occasions, when Rudolf had been with them. They attended a thanksgiving Mass in the coronation church that same week, and in June they were together for the opening of a new wing of the royal palace in Budapest and for a solemn procession in which the Holy

Crown of St Stephen and the coronation regalia were borne across the Danube to the Parliament House and back to the Crown Room beneath the palace dome.

Later that same month, the question of the imperial succession was settled by a quirk of fate. The increasingly devout Archduke Charles Ludwig, heir to the throne, had recently made a pilgrimage to the Holy Land. In a mood of excessive religious zeal he had drunk a cup of water from the River Jordan and, soon after his return to Vienna, on 19 May 1896 he succumbed to typhoid.

Of the Emperor's three brothers, dubbed 'Austria's idiot Archdukes' by Bismarck,[16] only the youngest was left. For most of his adult life Ludwig Victor had lived at Klesheim, his castle in Salzburg. It was rumoured that he had been sent there in disgrace or in exile as a young man after having been involved in a public fight with homosexuals. While something scandalous of the kind probably did take place and relations between the brothers cooled temporarily as a result, the Emperor neither imposed penal sanctions on him nor restricted his public duties or appearances.[17] Yet this wayward brother preferred to pursue his rather eccentric mode of living at Klesheim than at court. He returned to Vienna to see the family from time to time, and they all kept in touch with him, frequently visited him and invited him to stay with them. Rudolf had valued him as a hunting companion, while Gisela and Valerie found him entertaining company. He was passionately interested in theatre and the arts, and a generous employer to the servants on his estate. Even Francis Joseph had long since come to terms with his foibles. Bisexual rather than homosexual, although probably the only Habsburg of his time to be photographed as an adult in women's dresses, he had had an affair with a dancer, Claudine Couqui, and carried a small album of her photographs around with him. Being the youngest sibling of an emperor meant a degree of personal freedom which the eldest brother must have envied many a time.

Charles Ludwig's tubercular eldest son Francis Ferdinand was now the dynasty's best hope. There was little to be said for his younger brother Otto, whose marriage had not curtailed his incessant quest for pleasure and debauchery. His public behaviour was notorious. He was said to have danced in cafes wearing nothing but a képi and a sword, and at a meal with friends he once poured a dish of spinach over a bust of the Emperor, saying this was what he thought of the head of his family.[18]

In August 1895 Francis Joseph had written firmly to Francis Ferdinand, signing himself 'in true friendship, your most affectionate uncle', to stress that the younger man had a duty to get well. The Archduke did not want to give up his military command, but as he was clearly suffering from tuberculosis, the only cure was complete rest in a mild climate. 'As soon as possible you must go to a peaceful mountain resort,' the Emperor ordered, 'stay there absolutely quietly, and then move on to a southern climate . . . where you must remain and rest for the entire winter, obeying your doctor's instructions. I know this will be extremely boring, but I hope that for my sake you will patiently persevere with it.'[19]

On 27 August 1896 the Empress was present at a gala dinner at the Hofburg in honour of Tsar Nicholas II and Empress Alexandra, who had come with the intention of promoting his foreign minister Count Goluchowski's plans for an Austro-Russian entente. At Elizabeth's orders, the table was decorated entirely with edelweiss from the mountain peaks. Though she was still dressed in mourning, to many observers she still had enough of her beauty left to put the Tsarina, thirty-four years younger, completely in the shade.

However, the dinner was an ordeal for her. Soon afterwards, Elizabeth's doctors demanded that she should retire from public life. Despite her anaemia, she still insisted on an unnecessarily punishing diet. She became giddy on her long walks, which were clearly too taxing for a woman of almost sixty years of age, and fainted when her hair was being done. Marie Festetics was saddened by her ridiculous obsession with becoming stout, warned her that she was too pale, and that she ate so little she would have a stroke or die of malnutrition. On some days she ate no more than a few oranges.

Francis Joseph never ceased to worry about his wife, though he had long since given up trying to make her see reason. 'I am only depressed by the thought of the gnawing hunger which you punish by fasting, instead of appeasing it as other sensible people do, but the case is beyond all remedy, so we will pass over it in silence.'[20] She was suffering from a facial rash, a severe blow to a woman who had always prided herself on her beauty, and a medical examination hinted at heart trouble. Shortly before husband and wife paid their last visit to Cap

Martin in March 1897, Francis Joseph warned Katherine Schratt that she would probably be shocked by the Empress's appearance. The visit was completely ruined for him by anxiety over her health, for she seemed increasingly depressed and weary of life. When he returned to Vienna he told Count Eulenburg, the German ambassador, that she was 'in such a state of nerves that our life together was seriously deranged'.[21]

After he returned to Vienna Elizabeth visited Biarritz, where she spent hours by the sea finding comfort in the sound of the roaring waves. Later she went to San Remo, and briefly contemplated having another villa built there. A visit to Switzerland, and orders from a new doctor to eat more sensibly, brought about a temporary improvement in her health. Then tragedy struck again. On 4 May 1897 fire broke out at a charity bazaar in Paris, when some curtains were set alight, the hall burst into flames, and at least 200 people were burnt to death. One of them was her youngest sister Sophie, who had married the Duc d'Alençon, and who was running one of the stalls. She had refused to leave the building until all the girls working under her had been rescued, and nobody was aware of her fate until her dentist managed to identify her from otherwise unrecognisable human remains.

Elizabeth was totally crushed by the news. Referring with bitterness to the epithet given her mother and aunts, 'the Bavarian sisters of misfortune', she said that 'the misfortune always continues, and gets ever worse'.[22] It was a prophecy which would be fulfilled in little more than a year. Frederick Barker, who had taught her Greek and become a regular member of her entourage, had been sending Francis Joseph regular reports on Elizabeth's health, and soon after her sister's tragic death told him that, at one stage, she was so weak she could hardly drag herself from one room to another.

The success of the Hungarian celebrations had seemed a fitting prelude to what should have been even more glorious festivities two years hence, for the golden jubilee of Francis Joseph's accession. Yet by the spring of 1898 it was evident that the Empress would be unable to take part. An official bulletin was issued to excuse her prolonged absence from Austria at a time of national celebrations, saying that she was suffering from anaemia, inflammation of the nerves, insomnia and a heart condition. Having travelled ceaselessly abroad between Biarritz, the Riviera and the German spas, she was now in Kissingen, where Francis Joseph and Valerie came to see her. They were both horrified by her appearance and general condition, and though she struggled to appear cheerful in front of her husband, she confessed to her daughter that she longed to die. Her greatest fear was that she might survive the Emperor.

Husband and wife were together once more for a fortnight during the summer at Ischl. Dr Widerhofer warned the Emperor that Her Majesty must either resign herself to being a complete invalid, or submit to a thorough cure at Bad Nauheim, and she was too ill to argue. On 16 July the couple parted, both fearing they might never see each other again. 'I miss you here unspeakably,' he wrote to her the next day, 'my thoughts are with you and I think sorrowfully of the endless time for which we are to be parted; your empty, dismantled rooms make me particularly sad.'[23]

Francis Joseph remained at Ischl until the end of August, then went to Schönbrunn before visiting southern Hungary to attend autumn manoeuvres along the Danube frontier with Serbia. As usual, he wrote to Elizabeth every other day. After a visit to the Hermes Villa, he told her that several times he 'looked up at your window with feelings of great sadness, and went back in thought to the days which we spent together in our dear villa'.[24] He was back in Vienna on 9 September, attending to urgent administrative matters, and planning to leave for Gödöllö the following evening. On the morning of 10 September he wrote to Katherine with joy in his heart, telling her that he had 'really good news from the Empress' who was enjoying the pure invigorating air of Switzerland.

On the previous day Elizabeth had set out from Territet for Geneva. The city had a reputation for harbouring some of the most dangerous revolutionaries in Europe, and one of her entourage, Major-General Berzeviczy, begged her to change her itinerary, or at least alert the police before proceeding there. She brushed his warnings aside, asking what anybody would want 'with an old woman like me'. To those around her it seemed that she might be getting homesick, especially after receiving her husband's last letter. How happy he would be, he had written,

if I could enjoy all that with you quietly as you wish, and see you again after such a long separation; but unfortunately I cannot think of it. Apart from the difficult political situation at home the whole of the second half of September is already booked up with jubilee festivities, dedications of churches, and visits to the Exhibition. . . .[25]

Though Elizabeth must have felt a twinge of pity for the lonely husband waiting at home for her, she was in unexpectedly high spirits after arriving at the Hotel Beau-Rivage. For once she did justice to her meal and iced champagne. Afterwards she handed the menu to Irma, Countess Sztáray, her lady-in-waiting, asking her to send it to the Emperor, underlining the *Timbale de Volaille* and the *crème glacée à l'Hongroise*, which had particularly taken her fancy. After dining she visited the aviaries, aquarium and conservatories, then rested at the hotel before going out to buy presents for her grandchildren.

On the following morning, she stayed in Geneva, intending to leave on the ferry for Territet early in the afternoon. As she and Countess Sztáray were about to reach the landing stage, a man suddenly confronted them. They stepped aside to let him pass, and to her horror the Countess saw him raise his fist and attack the Empress. She fell backwards, knocking her head on the pavement, but was soon helped to her feet. A hotel porter and cab driver had witnessed events and alerted the police. Insisting that she was frightened but not hurt, Elizabeth told everyone she was well enough to continue on her journey. After crossing the gangway, she suddenly turned white and asked the Countess to give her her arm. A male servant came to assist, and from a distance they heard the porter calling out that 'the assassin' had been apprehended.

Only then did it dawn on the Countess what had happened. With the aid of a passenger, a former nurse, on the ferry, Elizabeth was taken on to an upper deck of the ferry, which had just started. They tried to revive her with water and sugar soaked in alcohol, but she was beyond salvation. Her bodice was unbuttoned to reveal a stain on her chemise, and a small wound on the breast with a tiny clot of blood. The captain was informed, and only then did he realise her identity. He ordered the vessel to return to Geneva, and Elizabeth was taken on an improvised stretcher back to her hotel. A doctor and priest were summoned, one to confirm that there was nothing he could do, and the other to give her the last sacraments. She died without regaining consciousness.

At Schönbrunn, Francis Joseph was writing to his wife before leaving for the autumn manoeuvres, telling her that he would be driving to the station at 8.30 that evening. Lying on the desk in front of him was one of her last presents given to him during the celebrations in Budapest, two years earlier – a model of her hand cast in gold with a bracelet containing a diamond, an emerald and a ruby, the Hungarian national colours, each of the stones ringing a separate electric bell. In front of him, standing on an easel, was a very early portrait of her by Winterhalter, in the simple white gown she wore every morning while visiting her children when they were small.

At 4.30 in the afternoon Count Paar urgently requested an audience. The Emperor realised at once from his expression that he brought bad news. His Majesty, the man answered, would not be able to leave that evening, for they had just received a telegram from Countess Sztáray at Geneva, saying that the Empress had been seriously injured. Francis Joseph begged him to telegraph or telephone, get details any way he could. Just then an aide-de-camp brought a second telegram from Geneva. The Emperor, tears rolling down his cheeks, took it from him to read the news that 'Her Majesty the Empress has just passed away'.

'So nothing at all is to be spared me upon earth!'[26] Count Paar heard him cry. Struggling to control his feelings, he pulled himself together and gave orders that the manoeuvres were not to be cancelled, but Beck would lead them instead. After the men had withdrawn to leave him on his own, according to a report in the press next day, he was heard weeping bitterly, saying softly to himself that nobody would ever know how much they loved each other.

Yet there was some small consolation in the manner of Elizabeth's shocking death. When the entourage received the first telegram, some feared that she might have taken her own life. News that she had been assassinated came as something of a relief. Moreover, as the Emperor later told the German Chancellor, Prince von Bülow, at least she had 'found the death which she had always desired – sudden and painless'.[27]

The man responsible was Luigi Luccheni, an Italian builder's labourer. Aged twenty-six, he was a self-professed anarchist with a deep contempt for monarchies and aristocrats. He had come to Geneva intending to kill the Duc d'Orléans, and after failing in this self-sought mission vowed to kill the next crowned head who came his way. Hearing that the Empress of Austria was about to visit the city, his mind was made up. He willingly gave himself up to the police, was tried and sentenced to life imprisonment, and in 1910 hanged himself with a belt in his cell.

Though Elizabeth had not been seen in Vienna for a long time, reaction to the news of her assassination was swift. Black flags hung from every window, and her portrait, framed or wreathed in black crepe, adorned shop windows. People went to weep and pray in the churches or stood horrified in the streets, as newspaper editors rushed out evening editions, vendors benefited from the trade, and those who could not buy their own copies listened thunderstruck while others read out the printed details. A crowd went to a restaurant known as a regular haunt of labourers from abroad who had been employed by the city corporation to lay new gas pipes, shouting angrily that the Italians were stealing their bread – and had killed their Empress. The police had to come and quell the resulting disturbance. At an open-air concert in Trieste, angry Austrians vented their wrath by throwing glasses and chairs at the Italian musicians.

Gossips in Vienna recalled a curse said to have been pronounced against the Emperor and the Habsburg dynasty early in his reign, after the Hungarian rebellion and the execution of Count Batthyany, by his mother, calling upon Heaven and Hell to blast the Emperor's happiness and exterminate his family. Now, nearly fifty years later, a journal published an article detailing the long and sad catalogue of violent or unnatural deaths among his immediate relations. In addition to Rudolf's suicide, the Duchess of Alençon's death in a fire, and Maximilian's execution by firing squad, there had been Archduke William Francis's fatal fall from his horse, Archduke Johann's disappearance on the high seas off the coast of South America, the suicides of King Ludwig and also Ludwig, Count of Trani, husband of Empress Elizabeth's sister Mathilde, Archduchess Mathilde's fatal cigarette, and Archduke Ladislas (son of Archduke

Joseph)'s fatal gunshot wound while hunting. 'And now we learn that the Empress Elizabeth has been murdered.'[28]

With the court in mourning, all remaining golden jubilee festivities were immediately cancelled. Katherine Schratt was away on holiday at the time, but as soon as she heard the news she travelled back to Vienna, where she arrived the following morning. Francis Joseph was deeply grateful for her prompt return, writing her a short note that there was nobody else with whom he could 'speak more openly about the transfigured one'.[29]

Gisela and Valerie came to support their father. Of the two, Valerie was the more devout, and it worried her that her mother had lost consciousness before receiving the last rites. She was encouraged by a Jesuit chaplain to persuade the Emperor to go regularly to confession, dedicating himself to God once again for the sake of his wife's immortal soul. Though a Christian and a believer himself, Francis Joseph found the religious zeal of his younger daughter and her husband, and their obsession with prayer and repentance, rather a trial. Katherine Schratt told Count von Eulenburg that she had to remind His Majesty that there was little point in him going to confession when he had no sins on his conscience to confess.

Elizabeth had told Constantine Christomanos, one of her Greek teachers, that after death she wanted her body to be laid to rest in Corfu. As she must have known, any such request from an Empress of Austria was a forlorn hope. On 12 September her body was taken to the Habsburg chapel of the Capuchin church, where large silent crowds carried forget-me-nots, lilies and white roses, swathed in dark muslin. The hearse was escorted through the streets by a contingent of Austrian, Hungarian and Polish cavalry. A state funeral followed five days later, but only one other Emperor, William II, was present. It was ironic that he should have been at the side of Francis Joseph at such a time, following the remains of the woman who had never bothered to conceal her distaste for his nation and had asked her children's tutors to 'make them as little German as possible'.[30] At the end of the ceremony Francis Joseph fell to his knees and sobbed for several minutes.

'The Emperor had been of course most impatient to hear Countess Sztáray's account of the whole tragedy,' Sir Horace Rumbold, British ambassador in Vienna, wrote to Queen Victoria, but such is his thoughtfulness & consideration that when she reached the Hofburg at night in the funeral train H.M. asked of her as a favour whether, if she did not feel too weary & exhausted, she would give him a few particulars. His Majesty then arranged that she should come to Schönbrunn the next day to give him the full details. She told Countess Harrach afterwards that H.M. had been so kind & patient with her that she felt quite relieved, having naturally greatly dreaded the interview. It is such traits as these that the unselfishness & nobility of the Emperor's disposition come out so strongly.[31]

Count Paar was probably not alone in his view that 'a less brilliant wife' would have suited the Emperor better, and that it took him too long to understand her – if he ever did.[32] Just as he had rarely if ever talked about Rudolf after his death to anyone outside the immediate family, Francis Joseph likewise remained silent on the subject of Elizabeth. Staff and courtiers around him from then on would recall that her name was simply not to come up in conversation in his presence.

Yet for the rest of his life he always marked the anniversary of her murder by going down to the vaults alone, and saying a long prayer over her coffin. To his aide-de-camp, Baron Albert von Margutti, 'the memory of his dear wife still had healing force, though probably to no one but himself and his daughters'.[33] Ketterl would often find him gazing with profound sadness at his favourite portrait of her, which stood on an easel near his desk.[34]

NINE

'A Crown of Thorns'

It was inevitable that the Empress's death would bring about a change in the relationship between the Emperor and Katherine Schratt. She was intelligent enough to recognise that, now her protector was gone, the old friendship was in jeopardy. Elizabeth had had the foresight to see how vulnerable 'the friend' would be in the event of her sudden death, when she would be the target of jealousy and innuendo. She had commended Frau Schratt to her daughters and asked them to treat her kindly once she was gone. The uncomplicated Gisela and Leopold remained resolutely loyal, but Valerie and Francis Salvator had never approved of her father's close extra-marital companionship. Elizabeth's public demonstration of approval of Katherine's presence had prevented tongues from wagging, and now that she was gone, the situation was less easy for them both. Nobody else ventured to show such disrespect as one of the junior archdukes, who had the effrontery to address the Emperor to his face as 'Herr Schratt', but the balance was a delicate one.

The actress was disappointed to find she had not been mentioned in the Empress's will, an omission which the Emperor made good by presenting her with a St George's thaler, one of the jewels which Elizabeth had frequently worn. A greater blow was to follow. Elizabeth had told her that a new medal, the Elizabeth Order, would be issued to commemorate the golden jubilee, and that she, Katherine, would be one of the first recipients. When it was struck, Katherine's name was not included among the recipients. She tactfully informed Francis Joseph of the Empress's promise. He told her sadly but firmly that now the Empress was dead he could not possibly bestow such an Order on her without the risk of potentially harmful gossip. This, and other small incidents, put a strain on their friendship. Faithful to her mother's wishes, Valerie invited Katherine to visit her and Francis Salvator at their home at Wallsee, and she eagerly accepted. Francis Joseph knew that the invitation had only been extended reluctantly, and feared the visit would not be a happy one for either party. He advised Katherine to refuse. Furious with them all, she lost her temper and openly criticised the Archduchess, a misdemeanour which Francis Joseph found hard to tolerate. He answered angrily, and in her fury she left suddenly for three weeks in Monte Carlo without telling him in advance.

While they continued to correspond, it was clear that nothing could ever be the same again. On her side, Katherine began to find him something of a bore. She was also saddened to find him apparently no longer his usual supportive self in her difficulties with the theatre management. In the winter of 1899 she acquired the rights to a play from Paris which Paul Schlenther, director of the Burgtheater, refused to stage. She demanded his dismissal, but the Emperor refused to become involved. In January 1900 he went to the theatre for the first time since the Empress's death, to accompany his guest King Alexander of Serbia, at a performance of Frau Schratt's *The Spendthrift*. For once, she did not give her usual welcoming glance towards the royal box, an omission which rankled with him.

On 18 August 1900 the Emperor celebrated his seventieth birthday at Ischl. Each street in the town was hung with black and yellow flags, bonfires blazed from the mountains nearby, and deputations came to offer His Majesty their congratulations. Among gifts which poured into the Kaiservilla were some from Frau Schratt. However, ten days later Valerie noticed her father looking particularly sad. She invited him to go out that afternoon with her and the children, only to be told that he could not as he was going to see the actress for the last time; she had made up her mind to leave him, probably forever. Although she had been increasingly cool about her father's friendship, Valerie was very concerned. She had hoped and prayed for an end to it, but only when she looked into his tired face, so close to tears, did she realise just how much Frau Schratt's company had meant to him, and just what a void would be left in his life.

It was a painful meeting for both. Afterwards Francis Joseph wrote to Katherine that he hoped she would tell him everything one day 'when your nerves are better, which with God's help will happen in not too long a time, and I will again be receiving your dear, *dear* letters'.[1]

After Elizabeth's assassination, Francis Joseph generally spent Christmas at Wallsee with Valerie, Francis and their growing family. He always got involved in decorating the tree, and loved helping to distribute the presents. On the next day he went to Munich to celebrate with Gisela and Leopold, who postponed their Christmas festivities until his arrival. Both daughters were touched to see how happy he was in such an environment, and seemed so unlike the elderly careworn gentleman he appeared the rest of the time. It must have saddened them to think that he had been denied such contentment throughout his forty-four years of marriage.

Maybe, Valerie thought, it was not too late for him to find another wife. She did nothing to disguise the fact that she wanted him to marry again. If he did, perhaps he would find the peace of mind and comfortable home life he had conspicuously failed to find before; the court at Vienna might become the focus of high society once more; and he might provide the Habsburgs and the empire with another male heir. The same idea had occurred to the Austrian government, who were thought to be preparing to recommend remarriage after court mourning was over. Their first choice was said to be his sister-in-law Archduchess Maria Theresa, the widow of Charles Ludwig. At forty-two, she might still be able to bear him a son. Valerie was thought to prefer the claims of a younger candidate, one of the unmarried Orléans princesses.

Francis Joseph would probably have been aghast at the thought, had he known – although he must have been vaguely aware of such schemes. At seventy, he had no intention of taking a second wife. Though increasingly lonely, he had somehow grown used to such an existence. Much as he enjoyed having his small grandchildren around him, he lived for his work, and had long become used to the humdrum routine of everyday life as an Emperor. More than anything else he dreaded change, and refused to have any alteration made to his rooms in the Hofburg. When the royal palace in Budapest was completed, he took only a perfunctory interest in the new apartments, and insisted on staying in his old quarters in an older part of the castle. Though it must have brought back distressing memories, he still regularly visited Gödöllö, alone except for his household.

In a life which had been so marred by violent death and tragedy within his immediate family, the Emperor found comfort in the familiar routine to which he had clung so doggedly over the last few decades.

Between Emperor Francis Joseph and his heir, Archduke Francis Ferdinand, relations had been civil enough but never close. They became particularly distant after the sovereign was advised of a most unwelcome discovery. The wife of his second cousin Archduke Frederick, Duke of Teschen, the redoutable Archduchess Isabella, believed the heir was paying court to her eldest daughter. Her dismay can be imagined that summer day in 1899 after a tennis party at their castle at Bratislava, when a servant found Francis Ferdinand's gold watch, which he had left behind. Hanging from it was a locket which contained a miniature picture, not of her daughter, but of her lady-in-waiting, Countess Sophie Chotek von Chotkowa und Wognin, his occasional doubles partner on the court. Aged thirty-one, she came from a good family of Bohemian nobility, and her father was the diplomat in Brussels who had helped to negotiate the marriage between Rudolf and Stephanie. Nevertheless, she was not considered of sufficiently high rank to become the next Empress of Austria-Hungary.

Archduchess Isabella dismissed her at once, and informed the Emperor. At first he was prepared to regard it as infatuation, but his nephew insisted that he and the Countess had been passionately in love for five years, and he intended to marry her. It seemed grossly unfair to him that, if any member of the family was attracted to someone, there was always some minor blemish in their lineage that ruled out marriage. As a consequence, 'we constantly marry our relatives and the result is that of the children of these unions half are cretins or epileptics'.[2]

Here at last was a Habsburg archduke aware of the perils of inbreeding. Some scientists likewise expressed concern at the way in which the dynasty had thus imperilled its prospects of survival. Dr Galippe, author of a treatise on the science of eugenics, forecast that the Habsburgs of Austria would probably go the same way as those of Spain in the seventeenth century. Due to intermarriages with blood relations, he observed, they had developed 'a degenerate taint', and if they persisted in such a practice, it was quite possible that they would disappear altogether.[3] How many of the family also foresaw the danger? The heir to the throne might have been the only one.

Moreover, most of the eligible princesses, in Francis Ferdinand's view, were 'ugly underdeveloped ducklings' of seventeen or eighteen; he was far too old for them and simply had neither 'the time nor the inclination to attend to the education of a wife'.[4]

Francis Ferdinand's stepmother interceded with the Emperor, assuring her that the Countess had transformed her difficult, unhappy son whose existence had been such a hard one, and that she would make him an excellent wife. Nevertheless, Francis Joseph summoned his nephew for an interview, told him firmly his behaviour was regrettable because it had caused a rift with his cousins which he must now repair, and that he must break off all contact with Isabella's lady-in-waiting. Francis Ferdinand remained obdurate; he formally requested permission to marry Sophie.

The Emperor said he forbade such a marriage, but, finding his nephew immovable, icily gave him a week to think the matter over. Next, Francis Ferdinand consulted his physician, Dr Eisenmenger, on one small but nagging doubt; were any children of the marriage likely to inherit his tuberculosis? He was reassured that the disease was rarely passed on, that measures could be taken to protect his family in the unlikely event of his doing so, and that his health would clearly benefit from a happy marriage.

Faced with trying to win the Emperor's support and waiting, or the possibility that Sophie might be sent away from Austria so they would never see each other again, Francis Ferdinand decided that life without her would be intolerable. The Emperor told him he could marry the Countess, but would have to renounce his succession to the throne. That, the Archduke told him, was impossible as his place in the succession had been conferred on him by God. Confronted with stalemate, the Emperor gave his assent to the marriage, while insisting it could only be a morganatic union. On learning that it would be theoretically possible for Sophie to become Queen of Hungary when Francis Ferdinand succeeded him (ironic, in view of the Archduke's well-known antipathy to the Magyars), he decided that all possible pressure must be put on the young man to call off the marriage. If he was to marry without permission, he would have to be expelled from the Habsburg family.

As that would leave his philandering younger brother Otto as heir, it was not an alternative to be viewed lightly.

At the family dinner on New Year's Day 1900, it was noticed that Francis Joseph raised his glass silently to Charles, the twelve-year-old son of Otto, as if the old gentleman recognised the boy as his real heir. If so, it was a prescient gesture. Valerie, watching Francis Ferdinand's face carefully, thought he looked very grave.[5]

To Francis Ferdinand's dismay, nearly all the rest of the family supported the Emperor. His stepmother Maria Theresa stood by the couple, but everyone else told him that for the future Emperor to marry a lady-in-waiting would endanger the future of the dynasty. His brother Otto, whose marriage had been loveless, had no sympathy for him, and would probably have been quite content to see his elder brother likewise contract an unhappy union while taking Sophie as his mistress.

In April 1900 the position was clarified. As long as any constitutional problems resulting from a morganatic marriage could be settled, the Emperor would reluctantly give his consent. The Countess could never become an Empress, and any children the couple might have would be excluded from the succession. On 12 June all male members of the Most Serene Arch-House of Habsburg were summoned to the Hofburg for a family council, presided over by the Emperor and his Lord High Chamberlain, Prince Montenuovo. Francis Joseph told the assembled company that his successor's marriage plan was well known to everyone present, and that it contravened the family statute. Nevertheless, as the matter was so dear to his nephew's heart, he would grant his wish as far as possible. For the sake of order, and to minimise the harmful consequences of such an action for the monarchy, he needed to have the consent of all members of the Arch-House and their signatures on a clarifying appendix to the family statute. Torn between loyalty to the family and to his own future, Francis Ferdinand reluctantly signed as well.

Eleven days later, the Emperor received his nephew in a short audience at Schönbrunn. It was a painful occasion for them both. Francis Joseph was uneasy as he had been unable to prevent such an unsuitable matrimonial alliance, while Francis Ferdinand chafed at being forced to agree to a morganatic union. If the former was hoping to prevail on him to change his mind, he was unsuccessful. Francis Ferdinand said he would not be deflected from his purpose, and was accordingly asked to sign and swear to a renunciation of certain rights for his wife and any children. He was assured that Sophie would receive the title of Princess Hohenberg on their marriage.

At a further ceremony in the Hofburg on 28 June, the Emperor, fifteen senior archdukes and a select group of court officials heard the heir renounce under a solemn and binding oath all claims of his proposed wife and children for the rights of status or inheritance that would normally be accorded to 'a marriage between equals'. On 1 July the couple were married at the chapel of Reichstadt, a castle in Bohemia given to Archduchess Maria Theresa by the Emperor. Neither he nor any of the archdukes were present at the celebrations, which included a simple service performed by the village priest with two Capuchin monks, with no address. There was no reception afterwards either, merely a wedding breakfast for the immediate family, during the course of which a telegram arrived from Ischl, decreeing that the morganatic consort of the groom was to be raised to the hereditary rank of princess under the name Hohenberg and with the title Her Grace.[6] The couple spent their honeymoon at Konopischt, a fortress some thirty miles from Prague, which Francis Ferdinand had bought in 1887 and converted into a charming *pied à terre* surrounded by his speciality, rose gardens, and which would be their home.

Though he disapproved of his heir's morganatic marriage, Francis Joseph bore him and his wife no ill-will. He gave them the finest of Vienna's baroque palaces, the Upper Belvedere, as their official residence in the capital. Two months after the wedding, he officially received Sophie for the first time, and afterwards wrote to Frau Schratt that the occasion went off very well. Sophie was 'natural and modest, but appears to be no longer young'.[7]

Unlike those of the Emperor and his ill-fated son, this marriage was extremely happy. A daughter, named Sophie after her mother, was born in 1901, a son Maximilian in 1902, and a second son Ernst two years later. The petty humiliations of Habsburg protocol did little to disturb their domestic life. Francis Ferdinand was prepared to put up with such annoyances as Sophie not being allowed to attend official gala dinners at the Belvedere hosted by him for foreign royalty, and with sentries being withdrawn from the gates when he was not in residence, even though his wife and children remained behind. However, he was highly gratified when some of the foreign royalty themselves, notably the German Emperor William II, went out of their way to flatter her, showed that they saw no distinction in rank, and were prepared to treat her like an empress consort-in-waiting.

Guests who enjoyed their hospitality at home must have wondered if their host at Konopischt or the Belvedere was the same bad-tempered, intolerant Archduke of popular legend, of whose shortcomings they had heard or been warned. At one party they were much amused when he led them through the rooms in a conga, only to come face to face with Sophie's recently washed underwear hung by the maid to dry on a chandelier. Her embarrassed protests were soon drowned by the unrestrained mirth of everyone else, not least that of her husband.

Not everyone at court trusted Sophie, however. Dr Godfried Marschall, Suffragan Bishop of Vienna, was convinced that she was scheming for the Archduke 'to clear the way for her children', as if he had forgotten that the youngsters were equally his children too. He told others that she was a woman of 'unbridled ambition' who claimed to her intimate circle that Providence had 'assigned to her personally a great mission for the Habsburg Empire'.[8] It was inevitable that certain figures in the imperial hierarchy would resent her presence and what she stood for. Yet few others were prepared to speak out openly or find fault with a princess against whose character little could be said with conviction.

At the turn of the century, Francis Joseph was in his seventy-first year. Though lonely and prone to self-pity, he was not the tired, virtually senile old man of popular legend. After an audience with the Emperor in September 1900 to present his letter of recall to England at the end of his period as ambassador at Vienna, Sir Horace Rumbold wrote to Queen Victoria of his pleasure 'in reporting that the Emperor looks very well & happily preserves his spirits in the midst of all the worries, both personal & political, that beset him. His Majesty leaves Vienna tomorrow morning for the manoeuvres in Galicia which this year are on an uncommonly large scale – His Majesty is never so happy as among his troops.'[9]

Though he might find her a little too ready to know what was good for him, Francis Joseph still enjoyed the company of Valerie and her husband, and doted on the four grandsons and six grand-daughters this marriage had brought. The older one gets, he said, the more childlike one becomes, and he found himself relishing their company more and more. When the family came to stay with him in Vienna, the children would play in his study while he was there, tumbling around happily on the carpet. He gave them used envelopes and coloured pencils to draw with. When more serious matters claimed his attention, he would tell them gently that he 'must really get to work'. They obediently handed everything back to him, bid him 'Adieu, Grandpapa!' and went into another room to continue their games.[10]

Valerie's children may have been happy at Schönbrunn, but for guests and foreign diplomats her presence did little to relieve the general atmosphere of gloom. Count Eulenburg, a close confidant of Emperor William II and of Frau Schratt, dreaded invitations to dine at the palace, as he thought Emperor Francis Joseph had such a stultifying effect on his younger daughter. In her husband's company she was an agreeable host, but when her father was around, she was so overcome with shyness that she rarely opened her mouth. As the Emperor was hardly the most amusing of men, the result was an evening of utter boredom which could hardly finish too soon for host or guests.[11] Valerie would sit for hours knitting, yawning or sighing, until her father's patience was exhausted and he would remark politely that it was time for him to get back to work.

He had no such problems with his other daughter. The more outgoing Gisela was a sprightly and witty conversationalist, and her husband Leopold was the Emperor's favourite hunting companion. Gisela had inherited her father's thrifty habits. Until electric lighting was installed in the Hofburg, the chandeliers were supplied daily with fresh candles, irrespective of whether those from the previous day had even been lighted. Gisela could always be relied upon to pack up partly used or even unused candles and take them back to Munich for her own use.[12]

When Katherine Schratt renewed contact with Francis Joseph again in the spring of 1902 he was almost beside himself with joy, writing self-deprecatingly that she would find him 'aged a lot and feebler in mind', though he was more spry than he might admit. When she returned to Vienna, she resumed the old habit of entertaining him to breakfast, though it was at her wish rather than his that the time of their meal was put back an hour to 9 a.m. He continued to take an interest in her appearances on stage, though perhaps less so than formerly. When she told him that she was to accept the title role in a new play about Empress Maria Theresa, his ancestor, to be staged at the Deutsches Volkstheater in Vienna, he made it clear that he was not pleased. Another source – she did not dare mention it herself – announced that she would be wearing her own jewellery onstage, including gifts from the Emperor. Maybe he took some quiet satisfaction in the fact that the play had a short run, and did not attend a single performance.

The Emperor could still spend long hours in the saddle on his autumn manoeuvres without suffering undue strain. For his officers, these were a chance to prove the army's importance to those citizens who considered their calling a useless and expensive matter of mere playing at soldiers. For the Emperor, they constituted a vital part of the empire's role, being in effect 'a full-dress rehearsal for murderous war', a chance to judge the qualities of his army, as well as warn him and them of what might be needed in the future. In his last years his interest in the army manoeuvres diminished, for modern warfare did not interest him. He found something disconcerting about trench warfare, as 'one only sees the debacle, but never the manoeuvres', as he had been brought up in the tradition of being in the midst of his men, riding close to them in the ranks.[13]

Though his demands on these occasions might be small, Francis Joseph always insisted on the highest standards of efficiency and dress. Every officer serving under him had to be turned out properly according to military standards, and woe betide any man whose attire did not conform to the smallest detail. His servants knew that he must always have the right clothes if possible, though occasionally ways had to be found to circumvent his instructions. Soon after being appointed to the imperial household, his valet was tidying his master's linen chest, when he was asked to produce a pair of trousers for a particular uniform. The poor man rummaged through all the boxes without success, and eventually a footman suggested they should tell him that the missing garment had been eaten by moths. When told, the Emperor's expression did not change. He shook his head and said how dreadful it was that they had not even left the buttons.[14]

At a time of life when other monarchs might gladly have delegated the study of paperwork relating to foreign affairs and military matters, Francis Joseph still maintained that it was his duty and his right to study them alone, or at least be the first to see them. A British family, visiting Vienna for two weeks in 1904, were impressed to see him driving into the War Office at 10 a.m. punctually each day to the strains of the national anthem. He rode in a victoria cab, much less smart than many others they saw in the Prater, his only attendant being an adjutant beside him. Throughout the day, he worked as hard and conscientiously as any of his civil servants, until 4 p.m., when the anthem was played again as he drove back, with a similar absence of ceremony, into the Ringstrasse and back to Schönbrunn. The Emperor's daily carriage ride to and from work was one of the sights of Vienna.[15]

With the onset of old age, his insistence on good manners and the occasional intolerance of what he regarded as unseemly behaviour increased. Outbursts of temper and demonstrative gestures in his presence, loud conversation, over-hearty laughter and 'somewhat too lively stories'[16] at table, as his courtiers put it, tended to irritate him. Any offenders would be put in their place with a disapproving glance. However, funny stories had their time and place. In a tribute written and published to mark the centenary of his birth, the journalist Henry Wickham Steed would recall the Emperor laughing as loud as anyone at card parties with Jewish bankers over, of all things, Jewish jokes which they stored up to tell him for his amusement.[17] If he expected high standards of courtesy from others, he invariably practised what he preached. To his valets and servants he was always kind and polite. He never ordered, but always asked that something might be done, and thanked everyone, even those responsible for such menial favours as handing him a glass of water.[18] Despite his habitual household economies, he never wore clothes that had been mended. Anything that was discarded was stamped with the letter A (*ausgemustert*, or set aside), and auctioned at the end of the year. Even brushes, combs, sponges, old toothbrushes and remnants of soap went in the sale, with proceeds going to the servants.[19]

One of his foibles, to which he attached great importance, was a habit of only shaking hands with certain people, such as the most important political functionaries and military officers, members of the highest nobility, whether they had an official position or were too young yet to hold one, foreign diplomats and distinguished visitors, and his aides-de-camp. When he spoke to guests after court luncheons or dinners, he always extended his hand to the aristocrats but never the officers, who sometimes complained afterwards, thinking they had been snubbed or passed over for some reason. He would not change his ideas; 'he adhered to his view that for him to shake hands was an altogether exceptional mark of esteem and that he must not be too free with it'.[20]

Like most other sovereigns of the time, Francis Joseph was rather out of touch with the conditions in which his poorer subjects lived. Working-class poverty was beyond his comprehension. In his defence, Margutti noted that he made a point of not going too deeply 'into political and social questions in order to avoid the discovery of social grievances and being forced to take disagreeable action'. By the time he reached his seventies, he was rarely in close contact with the parliamentary deputies, except when he personally opened the sessions of the chambers and read the speech from the imperial throne. He had a low opinion of his parliaments, regarding them as talking shops obsessed with time-wasting trivialities. The Austrian Reichsrat, he felt, wrangled endlessly over minor issues like questions of language and national susceptibilities, and its Magyar equivalent 'never rose above its petty policy of pin-pricks towards the western half of the empire and its strivings for full Magyar independence'. Practical questions of the day, and claims of the people's welfare, it seemed to him, were largely ignored. Parliamentary procedure was therefore not to be taken seriously as it never produced any definite results. During a lunch at Gödöllö in the autumn of 1904 he remarked to Count Stephen Tisza, Hungarian prime minister, that so long as the deputies could find nothing better to do than wrangle perpetually about questions of nationality, he would have nothing to do with them.[21]

Few of those who worked with the Emperor would, or even could, find much to say against him. Though socialists and radicals might bemoan the institution of monarchy and trappings of imperial power, they all had respect for the kindly old Emperor as an individual. The most they might say was that he lacked firm personal judgement, and was likely to be swayed too easily; 'with the Emperor the last speaker is nearly always right'.[22]

They were startled when he announced to his ministers in November 1905 that he intended to introduce general suffrage in both halves of the monarchy. Though the matter had been debated in both capitals for several years, he had been precipitated into action by a pledge from Tsar Nicholas II of Russia to summon his own representative parliament, the Duma. In May 1907, Vienna's own parliament convened. The Emperor still held supreme power, and could pass any measure he chose in consultation with his ministers, despite what the deputies thought or said, through a clause in the constitution which sanctioned any emergency measure deemed necessary by the crown.

Nevertheless, ballots were no longer weighted to conserve old class values. For the electorate, it would henceforth be one man one vote, and Austria now had a parliamentary body in which all the people were represented, either through a complex of small racial blocs or through the two major parties, Catholic Christian Socials and Social Democrats.

Though Francis Joseph never considered himself a connoisseur of the arts, he often visited exhibitions, where his tastes tended to be rather conservative. Works by modern artists were generally criticised as daubs. According to Ketterl, he 'did not like to see canvases that looked like snapshots, as for instance, the strained postures of galloping horses; he objected to anything forced, always wishing a character of peace and quietness to be preserved'.[23] Music never interested him, and there was no piano or harmonium in his private apartments. None of the family had been particularly musical. Elizabeth had inherited a love of folk song from her father, Rudolf had taken after her in his taste for Hungarian gipsy music, and she had been fascinated by mechanical organs and enjoyed the music of Wagner, but neither had showed any interest in learning the piano or organ.

From time to time Francis Joseph entertained the other sovereigns of Europe. A regular visitor to Austria was the much-travelled King

Edward VII of England, who had succeeded his mother Queen Victoria in January 1901. King and Emperor had little in common, and differed in outlook in many ways. Yet both, it was said, desired the peace of Europe – King Edward because he loved peace, Emperor Francis Joseph because he was afraid of war. During the Boer war of 1899–1902, the latter had been almost unique on the European mainland in expressing sympathy for the British point of view. At a court ball, he had declared in the presence of foreign diplomats, that with regard to the war he was completely English. King Edward felt himself ever in the Emperor's debt as a result.

As a prelude to closer Anglo–Austrian relations Edward VII paid his first, and only, visit to Vienna as sovereign in August and September 1903. It was the first time an English king had been in Austria since Richard I was captured and interned at Durrenstein on his return from Jerusalem in 1192.

At a banquet at the Hofburg on his first evening, the King delighted his astonished host by announcing his appointment as field marshal of the British army. The gift in itself was not surprising, as the Emperor was already an honorary colonel of the 1st King's Dragoon Guards. What was startling was the way in which it was conferred. Such appointments concerning foreign rulers were usually notified to those rulers' capitals and cleared with military authorities at home in advance. King Edward cared little for such formalities, and with his knowledge of human nature he knew such a gift would be far more effective if bestowed unexpectedly. He was right, for the Emperor was thrilled and could talk of little else for the rest of the evening. Early next day he sent personal telegrams of greeting to all his fellow field marshals in the British army list. The Emperor's personal staff had rarely seen their master unbend so much.

Even so, private conversations between monarchs soon revealed the limits of King Edward's powers. He had two matters to raise with the Emperor. The first was the plight of the former Crown Princess. Since Rudolf's death, Stephanie had been treated as a virtual outcast by her father, who was hated throughout Europe for his infamous treatment of his family and for atrocities in the Congo carried out in his name. When she made a second, happier marriage in 1900 to the Hungarian aristocrat Prince Elmer Lonyay, King Leopold declared it incompatible with his dignity and promptly cut her out of his will. Francis Joseph had never been close to his daughter-in-law, though it was inconceivable to imagine him stooping to such spiteful depths as the King of the Belgians. In fact, despite his dislike of the telephone, he had been persuaded to have one installed on his desk, and to use it in order to send Stephanie his good wishes on her second marriage. Could His Imperial Majesty, King Edward asked, make some gesture to intervene on Princess Lonyay's behalf? It is unlikely that anything or anyone could have moved the notoriously greedy and unpaternal King Leopold in a more charitable direction, but perhaps King Edward did persuade the Emperor to look more kindly on his daughter-in-law. That year she was seriously ill for some time, and he not only enquired regularly as to her state of health, but also sent her doctors, medicine and food from the imperial kitchens, and visited her personally several times. When she recovered he was clearly delighted.[24]

The other subject of discussion which King Edward broached was the Sultan of Turkey's ill-treatment of his Christian subjects in Macedonia, and general instability in the Ottoman empire. He wanted some pressure to be applied to the Sultan, and was impatient at the Great Powers' apparent disinterest. Before leaving Vienna he also mentioned it to Count Goluchowski, urging on him a firm yet peaceful attitude towards Turkey in the Balkans. To the minister, he commented that British and Austrian policy was virtually identical, as he saw it – namely to preserve the status quo in the Near East as long as possible, and thus avoid a war which would have incalculable consequences for Europe. As long as Austria did nothing provocative in the Balkans, it could count on England's support.

After establishing this measure of close personal contact unknown in Queen Victoria's reign, King Edward was determined to make it last. One way in which he felt this could best be done was to consult the Emperor on relatively uncontroversial topics of interest to him. Early in 1904 he asked the military attaché at the British embassy in Vienna to ask the Emperor for his views on arming cavalry with lances, saying he wanted His Majesty's private opinion, not that of leading military circles in Vienna. Francis Joseph was flattered that King Edward should ask his views, and replied warmly with a long letter setting out the pros and cons of equipping cavalry with lances and the possible implications for modern warfare. A way was thus paved for the regular interchange of ideas on similar matters.

To his regret, the King never managed to persuade the Emperor to pay a state visit to London. One was provisionally scheduled for June 1904, but in June the British ambassador to Vienna, Sir Francis Plunkett, reported to Lord Knollys, King Edward's private secretary, that there was no chance. 'There is, I regret to say, no doubt that the Emperor has aged considerably within the last six months, and is obliged to take precautions which are new to him.' Spring reviews in Vienna and Budapest had been cancelled on the pretext that owing to difficulties in the Hungarian parliament, the recruits were incorporated later than usual, but in fact they had been given up to save him fatigue. Since paying a visit to King Oscar of Sweden he had been very tired, and the doctors were uneasy as to the 'consequences of the fatigue and excitement of a visit to London'.[25]

Both sovereigns arranged for their heirs to visit each other's courts. In the spring of 1904, the Prince and Princess of Wales, later King George V and Queen Mary, were entertained at the Hofburg. Their reception at the Vienna railway station, on 18 April, was 'most alarming', according to the Princess. Waiting to greet them were the Emperor himself, several archdukes, members of the British embassy, and a guard of honour. Their arrival at the Hofburg was 'another ordeal', for all the Austrian archdukes stood at the head of the staircase. The Prince and Princess had to say a word to each, the latter finding it 'all delightful tho' tiring, everyone so kind & the Emperor charming'.[26] They had the use of twelve apartments, and dined with the Austrian suite attached to them and their own household, finding the emperor's timetable of dining at 5 and retiring to bed early not quite their style. The Prince found everyone very kind, 'but my goodness this Court is stiff and they are frightened of the Emperor'.[27]

In Austria and Germany, King Edward was suspected of doing his utmost to try and detach Emperor Francis Joseph from the close alliance with Berlin. Such a judgement seems to owe more to hindsight than reality, though in view of the King's increasing distrust of his unstable nephew Emperor William, such a development might not have been altogether unexpected. Francis Joseph, it was said, remained gently but stubbornly resistant to such efforts. However, there was one small liberty which King Edward took with the venerable Habsburg Emperor on his visit to Ischl in August 1908. The imperial carriage drawn by Lippizaner horses was waiting in front of the Hotel Elizabeth to take them for a drive, but the King dismissed the coachman. When the time came for them to make the journey, the only form of transport was a car in which he had secretly intended them to travel. The Emperor was displeased, but as there were so many visitors watching them he could hardly refuse. On their return he commented succinctly to Ketterl that the drive was agreeable enough, but he still preferred his Lippizaner team.[28]

Some time during this visit to Austria, though probably not on this drive, the King appealed to the Emperor to try and use his influence to persuade Emperor William of the danger of unrestricted naval rivalry between Germany and England. It was no more than part of his general effort to enlist a friendly fellow-monarch's help in trying to defuse international tension. Yet Francis Joseph had not the slightest interest in naval matters, and refused to become involved.

From time to time, Francis Joseph had doubts about Francis Ferdinand as heir to the throne. Now in his early forties, the Archduke could be charming in his own family circle, as a devoted husband and father, or as a host showing guests around his treasured rose garden. In general, when away from home, he could be brusque, lacking in grace, and not afraid to show the violent prejudices – anti-Semitic, anti-Magyar and anti-Italian – that could lead to his being regarded as a political liability. In these spheres, it appeared, his wife's reasonable outlook and influence had little effect. Nevertheless, he showed himself more methodical in preparing for the throne than Rudolf had ever been. He built up a personal intelligence service at the Belvedere, and in January 1906 persuaded the Emperor to accept it as a military chancellery. Under the supervision of Major von Brosch, it grew into a team of fourteen officers who prided themselves on having greater knowledge than the Emperor's own advisory body.

While Francis Joseph was sometimes exasperated by his energetic, bustling nephew, he never treated him with anything less than respect. He knew that it was important for his heir to be adequately prepared by being granted access to official papers. Copies of all important documents and despatches were sent regularly from the war ministry to Belvedere. Francis Ferdinand always remained as interested in military affairs as the efficient if unpopular Archduke

Albrecht, who had died in 1895, and in naval matters, ever ready to don an admiral's uniform and launch new battleships or visit the fleet. Even so, the Emperor found him aggressively authoritarian, and looked askance at what was in effect an alternative court in Vienna, where ambassadors were welcomed while carefully keeping in touch with the man expected to ascend the throne before long.

Nevertheless, uncle and nephew shared a common bond in their aversion to Hungary. Both were present at celebrations in Budapest in June 1907 for the fortieth anniversary of the imperial coronation that had followed ratification of the *Ausgleich*. After the special church service, they talked about the proceedings, when Francis Ferdinand said what an effort it was for him to come to Hungary, as he never liked being there. 'I feel the same,'[29] answered the Emperor quietly, his eyes fixed on the ground. Perhaps it brought back bitter memories of Elizabeth, reminding him that she had only seemed happy when she was among the Magyars; perhaps he had never completely been able to forgive and forget their taking up arms against Habsburg rule during the early months of his reign. As for Francis Ferdinand, he had his suspicions that the Hungarians were only waiting for Francis Joseph to die, so that they could offer the Magyar crown to Prince Eitel Frederick of Prussia, son of the German Emperor.*[30]

Sometimes Francis Ferdinand did not hesitate to conceal his distrust of the Prussians. Once a German officers' deputation came to Vienna, and he shook hands and spoke to everyone present except the detachments of Prussian regiments, whom he walked past without comment. When word of this reached Francis Joseph, he gave his nephew a sharp reprimand.

The Emperor was always punctilious about respecting Hungarian susceptibilities. While in the country, he never wore any uniform other than that of a Hungarian field marshal or his own 1st Hussar Regiment, and he always donned it before leaving Vienna, so he would be seen thus attired on his arrival at Budapest. On ceremonial

---

* Prior to her marriage to Prince Otto von Windischgrätz in 1902, it had been rumoured that Elizabeth, daughter of Rudolf and Stephanie, was to be married to Eitel Frederick and that he would be chosen as heir to the Hungarian throne.

occasions there he wore the ribbon of the Grand Cross of the Hungarian Order of St Stephen. At informal receptions following court banquets at Budapest, he always conversed with the Hungarian guests in their own language, even if he knew they were fluent German speakers as well.

It probably never occurred to Francis Joseph that there were dangers inherent in the empire's dependence on him, an old man of nearly eighty, and his continued survival. As head of state he neglected to make provision for a successful governmental system which would function regardless of the personality of his successor. He had long kept Francis Ferdinand out of any position of responsibility, and his half-hearted relinquishing of powers after the heir began to assert himself suggested that he was reluctant to hand over anything of substance. Had he thought to transfer more power to the representative assemblies and governments of his kingdom and empire, all might have been well and good. Yet he remained basically an authoritarian Emperor, firmly adhering to his position as head of state by divine grace.

In the autumn of 1906 Count Goluchowski told the Emperor that he intended to resign the foreign ministry. Francis Joseph chose Baron Aehrenthal, ambassador at St Petersburg, to succeed him. A supporter of closer ties with Russia, Aehrenthal had made it his mission to reclaim for the empire her position as an independent force vis-à-vis the other great European powers, after several decades in which she had seemed like a passive, less energetic junior partner of Germany. It would prove a controversial objective in time.

Despite Francis Joseph's position as senior monarch on the European stage, it was difficult not to be overshadowed by the bustling Emperor in Berlin. Where Francis Joseph was concerned, an interesting personal connection bound them together, albeit loosely. Gisela had inherited the Achilleion at Corfu from her mother, but she regarded it as an encumbrance, an unwanted reminder of times she would rather forget, and in 1907 she sold it to Emperor William. He, his family and suite visited it every April until the war, and sometimes he sailed back from the island to Trieste, breaking his journey in Vienna with a display of enthusiasm which Francis Joseph came to dread.

While William was careful to treat him with due deference and respect, the assertion in his memoirs that Francis Joseph treated him 'almost as if I had been his own son'[31] is surely an exaggeration. The elder man found his showy contemporary in Berlin tiresome at times, resenting his arrogance and the impression he strove to give that he was an authority on everything. Francis Joseph had never really forgiven William for his effrontery in criticising the Austrian troops during his visit to Vienna in the autumn of 1888. He commented privately in a letter to Frau Schratt at least once that the mere thought of Emperor William's forthcoming visit to Vienna was giving him indigestion. A small shooting party would be a pleasant, *gemütlich* (cosy) affair until the Emperor arrived with his large suite, 'and then it will be more awkward and strenuous'.[32]

All the same, Francis Joseph had a certain amount of respect for William, not least for the way in which he had come to terms with the handicap of a lifeless left arm. He admired him for his role in the general development of Germany's economic and military prowess during his reign, and he remained scrupulously loyal to the Austro-German alliance, though he may have regarded the younger man with suspicion, knowing that William and his close friend Count Philip von Eulenburg regarded the senior ruler in Vienna as elderly and progressively enfeebled, and believed he should make no pretensions to leading the Triple Alliance.

Francis Joseph may have had a more charitable view of Emperor William's peaceable intentions than his contemporaries. When his entourage were discussing a controversial, even bellicose, telegram from the sovereign in Berlin to Paul Kruger, President of the Transvaal, during the Boer war in South Africa, he disagreed with those who thought that William was trying to issue a challenge to England, saying he knew 'only too well that the German Emperor's one thought is always the maintenance of peace'.[33]

Yet as men both rulers were very different. As the German Chancellor, Prince Bernhard von Bülow observed, William always wanted to be at the centre of attention, while Francis Joseph kept himself 'so far as his duties as ruler allowed him, well in the background, and never spoke from the stage'.[34] Moreover, William went out of his way to treat Francis Ferdinand and Sophie with all due honours, receiving the Princess as if she was royalty, a civility which did not please Francis Joseph.

In 1908 Austria celebrated the diamond jubilee of the father figure beloved and revered by all. Festivities were planned carefully so as not to tire him, and so every few weeks some ceremony took place. One of the first was on 7 May, when Emperor William led a deputation of German kings and princes to Schönbrunn to greet Francis Joseph. It was as if each of them freely acknowledged that despite the transfer of economic, political and military supremacy from Vienna to Berlin, for the Germans there was still only one Emperor.[35] There were three generations of German princes, William told him in his address, all of whom had looked up to him as a model before being called to high office. 'Our hearts leap as we pay homage to a noble ruler, a faithful ally, a mighty shield of peace.'[36] After he had conveyed their joint congratulations, Francis Joseph received each of them individually. As he felt obliged to change into the uniform of any of their regiments in which he held honorary rank, it was a lengthy ceremony.

Two weeks later, a procession of 82,000 schoolchildren assembled on the lawns at the palace. Remarking with tears in his eyes that the older he became, the more he loved children, the Emperor waved to them from the balcony, deeply moved. Celebrations continued intermittently throughout the year, the most glorious being a costume parade and historical pageant along the Ringstrasse in June, in which 12,000 men from all parts of the empire (except the Czechs, who refused to join in) and 4,000 horses participated. Six centuries of Habsburg martial glory passed in review, to the sound of clarions and drums, from armoured knights to modern howitzers, with the standards that had flown at the great battles of history, from Pavia and Belgrade to Malplaquet and Leipzig. Francis Joseph stood on a dais watching for three hours, tears in his eyes as his pet pony passed by, and as veterans of units with which he had served as a youth moved in procession.

In December, the anniversary month of his accession, younger members of the dynasty serenaded him with garlands and bouquets in the palace's private theatre, and Francis Ferdinand led a deputation of the archdukes and their families assembled in the Hofburg. Only the heir apparent's children, not permitted to bear the name of Habsburg, were absent. Francis Joseph then attended a short gala at the opera, and the Viennese enthusiastically hailed the Emperor who had long since earned their affection and respect.

In the autumn of 1908 Francis Joseph had accepted an invitation to attend the German army manoeuvres at Stettin. As was only to be expected from the Prussian army, the execution of the troops' various evolutions was beyond criticism, which was more than could be said for the quality of refreshment. At midday he was served with some disgusting soup and overcooked beef. Though he never complained about the unexciting but at least palatable fare generally served to him at Vienna, this poorly prepared meal was not acceptable to him. His valet informed the steward and chief cook next morning that his master was accustomed to a more varied menu, but to no effect. For the rest of his time at Stettin, food was brought from the local hotel instead.

When Emperor William attended the Dual Monarchy manoeuvres two years later, he asked for champagne. Beck, now Chief of the Austrian General Staff, was prepared to send for some, but Francis Joseph said bluntly that they did not have champagne at manoeuvres; however, the German Emperor could have as much beer or wine as he liked. Ketterl was pleased that he had had his revenge for the appalling Stettin broth and stew.[37]

One small family difficulty remained unresolved at the time of the jubilee. It was suggested that the Emperor might celebrate his anniversary by revoking the law excluding the children of Francis Ferdinand from the succession. That he did not do so did not bother the heir in the slightest; to him the Habsburg crown was 'a crown of thorns, and nobody who is not born to it shall aspire to it'.[38]

Despite the celebrations, one initiative by the Dual Monarchy during the year would cost them dearly. Momentous changes were taking place in the Balkans, and the Emperor was sure that the best way of maintaining peace in the area was to work closely with St Petersburg, preserving the old Austro–Russian entente. The time had come for the annexation of Bosnia and Herzegovina, and on 6 October 1908 the Emperor signed a proclamation addressed to the people of both provinces saying that, as they deserved an autonomous constitutional government, he had decided that Austria would extend 'sovereign rights' to both provinces. They would be his only territorial gains during his long reign.

He had not anticipated the result, for the timing of the annexation displeased several of the other crowned heads in Europe. In Berlin Emperor William II was deeply offended at not having been taken into his old ally's confidence beforehand. In England King Edward VII, who likewise thought he should have been given some warning, feared that stability in the Balkans would be compromised. British hostility saddened Francis Joseph, particularly as he had always had great respect for the country. The English, he told Joseph Redlich, one of his future biographers, were the most intelligent and efficient politicians, as they always managed to achieve a good compromise between political parties. 'How different from us in Austria!'[39] Anti-Austrian demonstrations took place in a number of Italian cities. Moreover, both lands shared a border with Serbia, which had long coveted them for herself.

The annexation turned Serbia into a sworn enemy of the Dual Monarchy, intent on vengeance. Over the next few years, more and more observers would come to realise that the scene was set for the final battle between Germans and Slavs, and that it could be the start of a greater war than Europe had ever seen before. What they were witnessing was a lighting of the slow fuse which would blow Europe apart.

In March 1909, after pressure from Russia, Serbia agreed to recognise the annexation and to pledge good neighbourly relations with Austria, and the crisis was officially over. Those who dreamed of and aspired to a 'Greater Serbia', the anarchists, officers, lawyers, academics and civil servants, were content to bide their time. Moreover, the annexation had strengthened rather than weakened the Austro-German relationship. William II believed he had halted Austria's slide into isolation, and did not intend to release the Emperor from the bonds of Hohenzollern friendship. On a visit to Vienna he made a speech telling the people of Austria that he had stood 'shoulder to shoulder' beside their Emperor. It irritated Francis Joseph, who looked uneasily on the military stance of his Prussian ally whom he had considered such a staunch man of peace.

TEN

'The Machinations of a Hostile Power'

The end of diamond jubilee year had been marked by demonstrations in Bohemia against the Habsburgs, and nearly a fortnight of martial law in Prague. In February 1910 General Marijan Varesanin, governor of Bosnia, proposed that a senior member of the dynasty should pay a visit to the provinces of Bosnia and Herzegovina. The Emperor was keen to undertake the journey himself, and in March it was announced that he would go at some time between 30 May and 5 June.

Rumours of a conspiracy reached the Austro-Hungarian embassy in Paris during May, with a police informer claiming he had heard southern Slav anarchists talking of a plan to kill the Emperor at Mostar, capital of Herzegovina. The authorities were sure that any attempt on his life was more likely to be made at Sarajevo than in any other town. Closer surveillance of travellers entering the town was ordered, and additional uniformed police were stationed in the streets. Francis Joseph was not unduly perturbed by such threats, which he dismissed as *'un des risques du métier'*. His only reservation about the visit was that the summer heat and dust might be too much for him. However, he made the journey, arriving safely at Sarajevo on the afternoon of 30 May, his train stopping at several stations in Bosnia in order to give his new subjects a chance to see their sovereign, albeit from a safe distance. He stayed in the Bosnian capital for four nights, driving through the city in an open carriage on four occasions, and to the spa at Ilidze in a car. At a military review, he took the salute on horseback.

After his return to Vienna on 3 June, Francis Joseph wrote to Katherine Schratt saying it had gone better than he had expected. One of the senior military commanders, General Michael Ludwig von Appel, called it 'a triumphal progress', and suggested that the heir, Francis Ferdinand, should come to Sarajevo, and bring his wife (since October 1909 Her Highness the Duchess of Hohenberg, and with precedence after the archduchesses) and children to stay at Ilidze, as it would surely give the population much happiness.

Soon after his return, five shots were fired at Governor Varesanin as he rode back to the Konak. He was unhurt and his assailant, Bogdan Zerajic, killed himself with his last bullet. It was later found that he had been shadowing the Emperor during his visit, and had been trailed by three detectives in Sarajevo all the time. A friend of his testified to the fact that, while at Mostar railway station, he was so close to the Emperor in his distinctive white uniform and green-feathered shako, an easy target for would-be assassins, that he could almost have touched him. Yet he admitted he was unable to commit the deed, as he was overawed by the dignity in the elderly gentleman's face. He targeted Varesanin instead and, failing to hit his quarry, killed himself as an act of martyrdom. A schoolboy, Gavrilo Princip, visited Zerajic's grave and swore to avenge his death.

Now in his eightieth year, the venerable Francis Joseph had achieved considerable respect, loved by his subjects and fêted by other rulers. Theodore Roosevelt, a former president of the United States, was received by him in private audience in April 1910, when he allegedly referred to himself as 'the last monarch of the old school' and 'the protector of my peoples against themselves'.[1] Roosevelt came away with the impression that the Emperor was not a very able man, but at least he was a gentleman. He was invited to dine at Schönbrunn, an occasion spoilt only by what Roosevelt saw as the 'atrocious' habit of the Emperor and the others of rinsing their mouths and emptying them into the fingerbowls provided at table.

Francis Joseph was broadminded enough to respect republican forms of government. The United States of America, he could appreciate, was a federation of peoples functioning effectively without any need for a unifying dynasty. Such a concept might work perfectly well for nations of the new world, but not necessarily for Europe, particularly not the old system of the Dual Monarchy which rested on divine sanction. At least once he admitted self-deprecatingly to others that he was something of an anachronism, and politicians were heard to complain that they sometimes suggested proposals, only to be countered by preconceptions which dated back to the era of Schwarzenberg.

It was a state of affairs deplored by the commentator Joseph Baernreither, who wrote in 1913 of the 'wall of prejudices' that cut the Emperor off from any independent-thinking political personalities. All fresh political ideas, he said, were kept from the sovereign by the ring of courtiers, military and medical personnel which surrounded him. 'The powerfully surging life of our times barely reaches the ear of our Emperor as distant rustling. He is kept from any real participation in this life. He no longer understands the times, and the times pass on regardless.'[2] The faithful but far-seeing Ketterl did his best to remedy the situation by bringing his master newspapers and articles which had previously been kept from him, and by telling him things that he would otherwise never have heard.[3] These attempts to draw His Majesty out of the state of splendid isolation imposed on him by the court met with annoyance from Ketterl's colleagues at the palace.

Against this it was arguable that years of experience and fundamental common sense gave Francis Joseph a deeper, more detached insight into human problems than younger ministers or generals could comprehend. But in his last years, he himself realised that he was an elderly man out of time, out of touch and lacking the energy to provide the leadership his empire needed. In some ways he was still the same Emperor that he had been during his early years, proud of the Habsburgs' position in history, afraid of losing wars and therefore provinces. In an age when the peoples of his empire were demanding national equality and representative government, he still hankered after the acquisition of more provinces. The only territories which he had added to his dominions were Bosnia and Herzegovina, thus assimilating South Slavs into the empire, a move that was fiercely resented by Germans and Magyars alike. Thirty years before, Crown Prince Rudolf had predicted that Balkan expansion would prove a mistake, fearing that it was tantamount to putting one foot in the grave.[4] Those who shared his views would probably not have been surprised when events around Bosnia were one day to start the war ultimately destined to destroy the empire.

For many years, it had been customary for Francis Joseph to celebrate his birthday on 18 August every year by hearing low Mass early in the morning in the imperial villa at Ischl, where he continued to spend part of the summer. Afterwards the family and members of his suite gathered to congratulate him in person, and after a family dinner in the afternoon his son-in-law Prince Leopold of Bavaria proposed his health. He would reply to this with his own toast, as he emptied his glass of champagne: 'To the health of my dear family and welcome guests'.[5] In August 1910 there was a larger gathering than usual, with more than seventy members of the dynasty making a special effort to join him in celebrating his eightieth birthday.

Every year on the Emperor's birthday each member of the staff was given a bottle of wine and loaf of bread. Once the director of the Chancellery Office, known behind his back as the 'master of economies', announced his intention of withdrawing this privilege on the grounds that the servants did not use the wine to drink their master's health, but sold it instead. There was such a storm of indignation that the idea was quietly dropped.[6]

Although a lifelong devout Catholic, Francis Joseph was equally tolerant of other faiths, and had no time for religious bigotry. Prejudice against Protestants had no place at his court and among his personal suite. On all his journeys within the empire, in addition to attending services at Roman Catholic churches, he always made a point of visiting those of the Protestant and Greek faiths, as well as mosques and synagogues, and often went to their services as well.

His eldest grandchild Elizabeth, daughter of Gisela and Leopold, found it necessary to tell him a secret which she had not yet told her mother, namely that she had fallen in love with Baron Otto von Seefried zu Buttenheim, a cavalry lieutenant in the Bavarian army and a Protestant. It would not be received well by the family, she feared, because of differences of rank and religion. However, Elizabeth was not an archduchess, and her grandfather saw no reason to withhold his consent to their marriage as she was a fairly junior member of the family. He gave the couple his blessing, granted the Baron a commission in the Austrian army, and the match proved a happy one.

Such leniency was not extended to every member of the imperial house. As Wickham Steed observed, where dynastic interests were not at stake the Emperor could be kindly, patient and courteous. Where he thought they were at stake, he could be hard to the point of callousness.[7] In 1909 Francis Ferdinand's youngest brother, Ferdinand Charles, lost his heart to Bertha Czuber, daughter of a university professor. Forbidden to marry morganatically, he defied the family by doing so regardless. As a result he was expelled from the house of Habsburg, struck off the army list, though he had held the rank of major-general, stripped of his orders and medals, and banished from the empire. 'Herr Ferdinand Berg' thus officially ceased to exist in the eyes of the family.

The Emperor's health was still good, though the onset of old age brought persistent ailments such as bronchial catarrh and asthma. Since his mid-seventies he had regularly suffered from such attacks, ascribed by his entourage to the cold water with which he had himself rubbed down each morning on rising. The court physician, Dr Joseph von Kerzl, advised him to omit this part of his routine, but in vain. In the spring of 1911 he was seriously ill, and when he failed to throw off a persistent cough, his doctors told him he must remain in bed. He still insisted on having the state papers brought to him each morning, but nevertheless Francis Ferdinand was alerted to his uncle's disquieting condition in case it should lead to anything worse.

In the last week of May Sir Fairfax Cartwright, British minister in Vienna, reported to Sir Arthur Nicolson, under-secretary of state for foreign affairs, that while the Emperor was in Hungary 'all manner of rumours are current with regard to the state of his health'. While there seemed to be no cause for alarm, his persistent hoarseness and cough were a matter for concern among his medical advisers. They recommended that he should not return to Schönbrunn, which was too exposed to wind and dust, but instead take up residence in a nearby villa at Wiener Wald, surrounded by fields and forests. They also wanted him to abandon his old routine of spending the summer at Bad Ischl, on the grounds that it was 'unfavourable' to his health. The trouble with His Majesty, according to 'a confidential source', was '"Arterien-Verkalkung" in the throat, which is the result of old age and for which there is practically no remedy except care and avoidance of irritation'.[8]

By October 1911 Francis Joseph was reasonably fit again. In view of his age he could no longer be expected to pay state visits to foreign capitals, and he could be excused from attendance at tedious court balls. Yet that month he travelled the forty miles from Vienna to Schloss Schwarzau, seat of the Duchess of Parma, to attend the marriage of his great-nephew Archduke Charles to Princess Zita of Bourbon-Parma and propose the toast at their wedding breakfast. Charles was the son of Archduke Otto, Francis Ferdinand's younger brother, who had died suddenly in 1906 at the age of forty-one, wracked by disease. Some said syphilis, brought on as a result of his dissolute life, had carried him off, but some attributed his death to cancer of the larynx. As Francis Ferdinand's descendants were barred from the succession, Charles was second in line to the throne, and his marriage was of considerable dynastic significance.

At first the Emperor had looked with scant enthusiasm on the match. The late Duke of Parma's family had included several feeble-minded children, admittedly by his first marriage; and as Zita belonged to a deposed Italian royal house, he felt that she was perhaps an unsuitable bride for a Habsburg archduke who might well inherit the throne. However, Charles was clearly happy with his betrothed princess, and other guests noticed that their Emperor seemed in the best of spirits that day. Nobody had seen him in such a jovial mood for quite some time, and they never did so again.

Nevertheless, during the taking of group photographs after the ceremony it was unusually cold. Nobody had thought to provide the elderly gentleman with a cloak, and afterwards he went down with a severe chill. Coughing heavily and feverish, his health gave cause for concern again that autumn. Dr Kerzl insisted that he would do well to spend most of his time at Schönbrunn, where the air was clearer than at the Hofburg. Not until the following spring did he seem his old self, no longer complaining about the consequences of 'that wretched day at Schwarzau'.[9]

In October 1912 King Nicholas of Montenegro declared war on the Ottoman empire. The fighting was over within two months, with an armistice agreed on 3 December, and peace talks opening at St James's Palace, London, a few days later. Proclaiming that he had always been unlucky in wars, Francis Joseph was determined to keep Austria out of the conflict. He was at odds with the more military-minded in Vienna, led by General Oscar Potiorek, who had succeeded Varesanin as governor of Bosnia-Herzegovina in May 1911, and was pressing for mobilisation and the despatch of more troops to the provinces in case of rebellion. Francis Joseph rejected his request each time, on the grounds that it would be seen as provocative and inflammatory.

On 28 October the ministerial council decided to ask him for a gradual increase of troops, calling up reservists but being careful not to intensify the crisis by ordering full-scale mobilisation. The greatest priority was given to Bosnia-Herzegovina and southern Hungary, but by the end of November the increase of troops in Galicia, facing the Russians, was causing alarm in Cracow and Lvov. Francis Ferdinand favoured peace at first, but when the armistice was signed, he was perturbed by reports of patriotic belligerence in Belgrade, and gave serious consideration to the idea of a pre-emptive strike. He had long been critical of general staff planning in the army, and on 7 December he recommended to the Emperor that Conrad von Hötzendorff should be reinstated as Chief of the General Staff. In time, both uncle and nephew would regret his return to the centre of affairs. The Emperor needed to remind Hötzendorff that it was not for him to try and interfere in foreign policy affairs, on the grounds that he himself as Emperor made it; 'in this sense My minister of foreign affairs is conducting My policy'.[10]

Leopold von Berchtold, who had succeeded Aehrenthal as foreign minister earlier in the year, was anxious about the mood in Belgrade, as well as pro-war hysteria in much of the press. On a private visit to Francis Ferdinand at the Belvedere, he found the heir keen on an immediate attack on Serbia and Montenegro. Later that day, at Berchtold's request, the Emperor presided over a meeting of ministers at Schönbrunn. Neither Hötzendorff nor the war minister, General Alexander Krobatkin, were present, so it was not technically a war council. In Krobatkin's absence the case for military action was presented by Francis Ferdinand, while Berchtold proposed that they should hold back until they knew the results of the St James's Palace Conference which was about to take place in London. The Austrian finance minister in turn argued that the imperial economy could ill afford the cost of such a campaign. As a result, the Emperor decided that they should give full support to the peace talks in England, and no military action should be envisaged at present.

Francis Ferdinand accepted his uncle's decision, and supported Berchtold. A dissatisfied Hötzendorff refused to accept the verdict, and insisted that only a short victorious campaign against Serbia and Montenegro would allow the Dual Monarchy to impose an acceptable settlement in the western Balkans. Krobatkin agreed with him. At the end of the month Berchtold sought another audience with the Emperor, but found him adamant in his support for peace. Bulgaria's refusal to cooperate at the conference table led to a further outbreak of fighting in the Balkans from early February to April 1913, after which the diplomats resumed peace talks in London. The Austrians found themselves largely outvoted at the conference, and by the end of April Francis Joseph authorised Potiorek to proclaim a state of emergency in Bosnia-Herzegovina, thus putting the army on a war footing in both provinces.

The strain imposed on Francis Joseph by the perpetual state of crisis was considerable. By now he generally visited the Hofburg only for official business and the increasingly infrequent ceremonial occasions. He spent a few days at Wallsee with Valerie and her family in the winter of 1912/13, but otherwise he was rarely seen in public.

Still he found comfort in the company of Katherine Schratt, now a widow of nearly sixty. She spent some of her time abroad, gambling at Monte Carlo and driving around in an automobile, much to his consternation. Nevertheless, when she was in Vienna they still saw each other, and it was rumoured by some that they were husband and wife. Such a theory surely owes more to gossip and excited imagination than reality, as the Emperor was far too conscious of his imperial dignity to contemplate marrying an actress. In any case, it beggars belief that he would have considered it for a second in view of his nephew and heir's own morganatic match.

However, the octogenarian ruler and his middle-aged companion clearly benefited from each other's company. It is hard not to look indulgently at the time they must have spent together, he brushing his hair or combing his luxurious side whiskers immediately before her visits, perhaps in order to avoid a gentle nagging about not looking smart enough, she making sure he had a warm rug beside his iron bedstead, or a dressing gown when it turned chilly. (Emperor William I was reputed to have once scoffed that Hohenzollerns did not wear dressing gowns, but no parallel remark about the Habsburgs has been attributed to his contemporary in

Vienna.) When his doctor ordered Francis Joseph to desist from smoking strong cigars, one of his few indulgences, in order to keep bronchitis at bay, Katherine found him some milder ones instead. On summer evenings she would invite him to a private dinner party at her house at Gloriettegasse, where the entertainment included a quartet playing Strauss waltzes or Lehar operetta melodies in the garden.

Still the Austro-Hungarian empire remained vulnerable to scandal. In the spring of 1913 Hötzendorff was warned by German counter-intelligence that the chief of staff to a regiment of the army corps in Prague, Colonel Alfred Redl, was a Russian spy. Redl was confronted in a hotel room by a small specially authorised group of officers, left alone with a loaded revolver, and did the honourable thing. After he had done so, it was found that he had been blackmailed by the Russians because of his homosexuality and a taste for the good life. Yet within days there were alarming stories in the press about corruption, sexual perversion and treachery in the army and high society. Francis Joseph agreed that it was only right that Redl should have been encouraged to take his own life, because if he had been brought to trial it would have undermined confidence in the military establishment. Francis Ferdinand thought the issue had been badly handled, and resented Hötzendorff's complicity in Redl's suicide.

The Emperor and his heir clearly disagreed on other issues, as well. Francis Ferdinand was much the better-informed on many matters pertaining to the empire, as he did not have to rely on what a small circle of advisers chose to tell him. The heir had built up an elaborate network of unofficial informers who could be relied on to keep him in touch with military affairs and with the aspirations of the different minority groups throughout the Dual Monarchy. It was regrettable that the Emperor rarely consulted him, but chose to work in isolation. Sometimes, it seemed to those around him, it was only necessary for him to hear Francis Ferdinand's views on a subject to make him want to do or order the very opposite.

Much as he might resent his sovereign's old-fashioned obedience for tradition down to the last letter, the heir held his uncle in great respect. Had there been better communication between them, Francis Joseph might have persuaded him to modify his prejudices against the Magyars and convinced them of their strengths as well as their weaknesses.

The Duchess of Hohenberg's lack of precedence at court still irritated her husband. In May 1911 Sir Fairfax Cartwright had written to Arthur Nicolson of efforts by others to effect a reconciliation between sovereign and heir after an unpleasant scene in January on the matter of her precedence at a court ball. The Archduke, the ambassador was told,

> behaved in so violent a manner that the Emperor, speaking of the Archduke's conduct to intimate friends, declared that he feared the Archduke's mind was becoming affected, and His Majesty is said to have even hinted that the moment might soon come when the necessity would arise of having to exclude the Archduke from succession to the Throne. It was this scene, I am informed, which decided the Emperor not to send the Archduke to London to represent His Majesty at the Coronation festivities.*[11]

Notwithstanding any misgivings about his nephew, in August 1913 Francis Joseph appointed him inspector-general of the monarchy's armed forces, a post only held once previously, by the ever-efficient if unpopular Archduke Albrecht.

Despite his advancing years, the Emperor was determined to participate in ceremonial occasions as long as his health permitted. In October he took the salute at a military parade in Vienna celebrating the centenary of the battle of Leipzig, a memorable allied victory over Napoleon Bonaparte.

To some, it seemed as if such a parade might be a prelude to a renewed outbreak of fighting. Serbia was flushed with success after a small but significant victory over Bulgaria during a short military campaign in the summer, and was now falling out with Montenegro over territorial differences. A secret society, the Black Hand, had been established among army officers in Belgrade in 1911 with the

---

* The coronation referred to was that of King George V and Queen Mary in London in June 1911, at which the Emperor was represented by Archduke Charles.

aim of uniting the Serb minorities in the Habsburg and Ottoman empires with those in Serbia itself.

Once more the Emperor's warlike spirit was aroused. He was losing patience with the Serbs, and believed that the time had come to administer a swift pre-emptive strike. Francis Ferdinand urged caution, largely on the grounds that the army was in no condition to undertake a campaign, but the Emperor's view prevailed. He authorised Berchtold to send Serbia an ultimatum, handed on 18 October to Nikola Pasic, prime minister and foreign minister in Belgrade, giving them eight days to evacuate Albanian territory or face the consequences. Realising that there would be no military help from Russia, Pasic gave way, and the ultimatum was complied with. The Black Hand viewed their prime minister as a weakling whose commitment to the cause of Serbia was in question, but the day of reckoning would soon come.

Yet it was generally assumed that the Emperor would see his days out without witnessing any further major European conflict. His first English biographer, Francis Gribble, who completed a life of him in 1913 and published it early the following year, commented in his final chapter that the elderly ruler who had just passed his eighty-third birthday and the sixty-fifth anniversary of his accession prayed that there would be peace in his time. 'Most likely he will get his way. There prevails throughout Europe, as well as throughout Austria, a sentimental feeling that he has suffered enough, and that it would be cruel to disturb his last days with war or civil commotion.'[12]

While Emperor Francis Joseph had mixed feelings about his difficult but capable heir, he was impressed with the way in which Francis Ferdinand had discharged his military duties. Ironically, the Emperor's promotion of his nephew sealed the latter's fate. One of the new inspector-general's first decisions, taken after consultation with Hötzendorff, was to hold the main summer manoeuvres for the following year in Bosnia, which he would be obliged to attend. In March 1914 it was announced that the Archduke would be at manoeuvres in the Bosnian mountains in June, and then pay a state visit to Sarajevo, accompanied by the Duchess of Hohenberg. Three years earlier he had considered a similar journey, but had second thoughts after being warned that the Serbs would surely make an attempt on his life. Members of the Black Hand were urging all patriotic Serbs to take 'holy vengeance' on the Habsburg dynasty, and he was told that his life might be threatened if he went. While insisting that it was his duty, sometimes he gave the impression that he would rather not tempt providence and go to Bosnia.

Whether he would be in a position to make the visit was initially in some doubt. In April Francis Joseph fell seriously ill with chronic bronchitis, and daily bulletins on his health were issued by Dr Kerzl for over a month. At one stage Francis Ferdinand was on full alert, staying with his family at Konopischt in case the worst should happen, ready to cancel his itinerary altogether if his uncle's health worsened. In Belgrade the conspirators whispered among themselves that their weapons would not be needed after all. If Emperor Francis Joseph was so ill, they said, his heir would not be coming to Bosnia that summer. Not until 23 May were the bulletins discontinued, and though officially out of danger the Emperor was still weak. For once he was unable to carry out his normal work of reading and approving reports of ministerial council meetings within the usual fortnight. Had he not recovered, the lives of his heir and consort would have been spared – and those of many others in the next four years as well.

By the end of May Francis Joseph was clearly himself again. Both men met a couple of times in the first days of June for their regular audience, and Francis Ferdinand was still vacillating over whether to attend the Bosnian manoeuvres or not. Reports had been received of the possibility of a conspiracy to murder him, and he was also unsure whether he would be able to endure the intense midsummer heat in Bosnia. What passed between them was never recorded for certain, though according to Hötzendorff, on 4 June the Emperor advised his heir to do as he wished, and certainly did nothing to dissuade him. He even agreed that the Duchess of Hohenberg could accompany him, more or less as an equal, though in accordance with Habsburg protocol she was still obliged to travel separately from her husband and by a different route.[13] It was the last time uncle and nephew ever came face to face.

The Emperor remained at Schönbrunn while Francis Ferdinand and his family spent a few days at Konopischt, where he entertained

Emperor William II, with whom his friendship was deepening, and immediately afterwards Count Berchtold and his wife. Towards the end of the month, the Emperor was planning to leave for Ischl, while Francis Ferdinand set out for Bosnia. He had a premonition that he might not return alive; a couple of weeks before his departure he had warned his astonished heir, Archduke Charles, that he would soon be murdered, and told him where to look in his desk for 'papers which concern you' to take and read after his death.[14]

All the same, security precautions were curiously relaxed, and Margutti was aghast to receive printed programmes that week giving every precise detail of the couple's itinerary. Telling the public, and therefore the terrorists, about every step of the Archduke's schedule, he said, 'was really playing with fire'.[15] During the Emperor's visit in 1910 a complete garrison had lined the streets, several hundred suspected subversives were taken into custody, and many more placed under temporary house arrest. This time the garrison troops remained on manoeuvres, and the one infantry battalion in Sarajevo was kept in barracks. At the same time, Governor Potiorek gave no impression that he had realised the significance of the date chosen. Sunday 28 June was Serbia's National Day, the anniversary of the battle at Kossovo in 1389 at which the Turks had destroyed medieval Serbia, a day of national mourning and vengeance; and, more recently, the first anniversary of vengeance fulfilled, namely Serbian victory in the second Balkan war.

Francis Joseph intended to leave for Ischl in the middle of July, in accordance with the routine he had followed for the last few years. He had told his aides that he had no intention of altering the date, as there were so many claims on his attention with state affairs. They were surprised, therefore, when he announced at less than a day's notice that he intended to go on 27 June. For him to change his plans like this was almost unprecedented. The only reason, they thought, was that he wanted to be away from Vienna when his heir returned from Bosnia, so he would not have to have a face-to-face meeting with him. It seemed that the Emperor was still less than well disposed towards the nephew designated as his successor, and had been irritated by plans in the programme treating the Duchess of Hohenberg as a future empress. Too old and weary to insist on getting his way any more, he simply preferred to avoid confrontation.

On 23 June, Francis Ferdinand and Sophie said farewell to their children and left Konopischt for the last time as they set out on their fateful journey. The military exercises in Bosnia were over by midday on 27 June, and the Archduke sent the Emperor a telegram to let him know that the bearing and efficiency of the army corps had been outstanding. The following day, he said, he would visit Sarajevo, and leave in the evening.

Early on Sunday afternoon a telephone call was received at the Kaiservilla at Bad Ischl. Count Paar had been on duty when tragic news arrived from Mayerling in 1889 and again from Geneva in 1898. It fell to him to break tidings to the Emperor a third time of violent death within the family.

As part of their programme, on the morning of 28 June Francis Ferdinand and Sophie took their places in the motorcade through Sarajevo to inspect the forces, attend a reception in the city hall, and visit a folk museum. It was a day of blazing sunshine, with no breeze to offer them any respite from the heat.

About ten minutes after the motorcade had entered the city, a bomb was thrown at the car by Nedjelko Cabrinovic, a member of the Black Hand. It passed behind Sophie, who was slightly grazed by the fuse cap and severely shaken. The car behind them was wrecked; the occupants and several onlookers were injured, though none fatally. Francis Ferdinand arrived at the city hall angry and unnerved after their narrow escape, but having vented his fury on the unfortunate mayor he regained his composure. After listening to the mayor's speech and replying with a stiffly worded message of thanks, the Archduke enquired after those who had been wounded, with a view to visiting them later in hospital. He sent a telegram to the Emperor, telling him not to take too seriously any reports about the bombing incident as he was unhurt. When told that Cabrinovic had jumped into the river but been dragged out and arrested by police, he remarked through clenched teeth that they would be less likely to lock the fellow up than award him the Medal of Merit. There was some discussion about altering the rest of the day's itinerary; should the museum trip be deferred, or should everything be cancelled? It was assumed that as the assassination attempt had failed, it was unlikely there would be any more attempts on the heir's life. At least there would be no harm in a drive down the Appel Quay to have lunch with the governor at his residence.

The processional route was altered at such short notice that nobody thought to inform the driver of the leading car. At a crucial turning, he was ordered to change direction. As he stopped to reverse and the cars came to a halt, another member of the Black Hand, Gavrilo Princip, stood on the corner watching. He had been thrown into a panic by Cabrinovic's failure, and feared he would be seized for questioning because of his complicity in the plot. Now he unexpectedly found the Habsburg target and his wife within a few feet of him. Drawing a loaded pistol from his pocket, he stepped into the street and fired twice. The police reached him just as he was about to turn the gun on himself.

As the chauffeur turned the second car around, a thin stream of blood spurted from the Archduke's mouth. Sophie cried out, 'In God's name what has happened to you?' She then collapsed between his knees. Count Franz Harrach thought she had fainted from fear, and only later did he see that she had also been shot.[16] She died almost at once. Francis Ferdinand made a valiant effort to prevent her from falling, entreating her to live for the sake of their children. Muttering feebly, 'It is nothing', several times, he began to lose consciousness, and slumped forward. By the time the cars reached the governor's residence, he was dead as well.

It was by no means the first time a European crowned head, consort or heir had fallen victim to assassins within the preceding four decades. Apart from Empress Elizabeth in 1898, the grim roll call had also included Tsar Alexander II of Russia in 1881; King Humbert of Italy in 1900; King Carlos of Portugal and his heir the Duke of Braganza in 1908; and King George of Greece in 1913. Only eleven years earlier, King Alexander and Queen Draga of Serbia had been butchered in a palace revolution at Belgrade with several of their relations, servants and ministers. At first glance the events at Sarajevo appeared as just another grim reminder of royal and imperial mortality.

In his succinct way, King George V of England, who had entertained Francis Ferdinand and Sophie on what almost amounted to an unofficial state visit less than a year previously, probably summed up matters better than anyone else when he noted in his journal that it was a 'terrible shock for the dear old Emperor'.[17] Paar's record of his master's words on being brought the news – saying that 'the Almighty does not allow Himself to be challenged with impunity', and that 'a higher power has restored the old order which I unfortunately was unable to uphold'[18] – has passed into history, though the phrases may seem too stilted to be credible. That the Archduke had let the Habsburgs down by persisting in contracting an unsuitable marriage had always rankled with Francis Joseph, but he had never ceased to respect his nephew's abilities.

Many people in high places knew that the violent removal of Francis Ferdinand would have a major impact on the empire, even if they did not foresee the precise course of events. Some thought the assassination of the heir and his wife 'a happy dispensation for Austria', while others maintained that had he lived, he would have brought an end to the stagnation of Francis Joseph's regime, which had 'become untenable through weakness and planlessness', and endeavoured to put the Dual Monarchy on a sounder footing, both internally and externally.[19] Stephanie, Countess Lonyay, the woman who might have become Empress of Austria-Hungary, was sure the couple had been sent to their deaths. The assassinations, she later said, could not have happened without the government's knowledge. The Emperor was well aware of the risk his nephew was taking, but he 'simply looked on'.[20]

Valerie hurried to the palace to be with her father, and found him 'amazingly fresh', though tears came to his eyes when he spoke of the poor orphaned children. Yet it came as no surprise to her that he was not personally stricken, and too honest to make any pretence of emotion. When she told him that Charles would 'do well', he looked at her and said solemnly that for him it was a relief from a great worry.[21] This did nothing to lessen his concern for his great-nephews and great-niece. For the first time in their lives, he asked for the young Princes and Princess of Hohenberg to be brought to him, and explained as gently as he could what had happened to their parents. In his old age he had become increasingly fond of younger members of the family, and now he made an effort to spend time with those who had suffered more deeply than anyone else from the shocking blow.

A telegram had also been sent to Archduke Charles, son of the late Archduke Otto and next in succession to the throne, who was with his wife Zita and family at Reichenau, their country home about thirty miles south-west of Vienna. Equally shocked, he contacted his great-uncle and was asked to join him in Vienna. On meeting him at Schönbrunn, Emperor and heir had an emotional reunion, and according to Zita (who was not present at the scene), it was then that the older man burst into tears for the first time since being given the news. 'I am spared nothing,' he told Charles, adding, 'At least I can rely on you.'[22]

The coffins of the murdered couple were brought back from Sarajevo to the coast by rail, then by sea to Trieste aboard a battleship, and by rail again to Vienna, on the evening of 1 July. European crowned heads, including the dead couple's close friend Emperor William II, and King Albert of the Belgians, were planning to attend the funeral in person. It was open to doubt whether an archduke and his morganatic wife would be given full honours at their burial, but the question was neatly avoided by an announcement that the Emperor's poor health precluded him acting as host to European sovereigns and their representatives.

Although not specifically mentioned at the time, there was another pressing reason for not inviting foreign potentates or their representatives. To do so would present them – particularly emissaries from England, Russia and Italy – with an opportunity for a discussion of the Austrian attitude to be taken towards Serbia in the light of the outrage. Neither of the minister-presidents nor the senior ministers of the Dual Monarchy wished to be drawn on the matter before they had had ample time to consider the matter.

The obsequies in Vienna would therefore be limited to a single day. Interment would be in the family crypt at Artstetten, Francis Ferdinand's estate in Lower Austria, which he had had built five years previously, aware that his wife would never be allowed to rest beside him in the imperial vault beneath the church of the Capuchins. There was to be a lying-in-state and a service in Vienna. Prince Montenuovo, an old personal foe of the late Archduke (and ironically born of a morganatic marriage himself), was put in charge of the arrangements, and ordered that Sophie's coffin should not be brought to the service but left at the station. The woman who had literally died for her country was granted no insignia on her coffin, apart from the gloves and fan of a lady-in-waiting. Only personal intervention by the new heir Charles to Francis Joseph made sure there would be a joint service.

Next morning the chapel was opened to the public for a few hours. (Some accounts said four, others only two.) At midday a large crowd was still waiting to be admitted, but the doors were firmly closed to them. A requiem was held that afternoon, lasting barely an hour, attended by ministers, generals, members of the diplomatic court as well as the family. The Emperor remained impassive throughout. Francis Ferdinand's secretary watched him carefully during the ceremony, and saw no sign of emotion or sorrow on his face; 'with the same unmoved expression he used to display to his subjects on any occasion, he let his eyes roam over the gathering of mourners'.[23] After being told that the service was at an end, he turned quickly without another glance at the caskets and left the chapel.

That evening the hearses bearing the coffins left the Hofburg and were taken on their last journey to Artstetten, with no military parade and only a minimal escort. The minister of war had ordered a reluctant Montenuovo to agree that commanding officers of units in the Vienna garrison might turn out their troops to line the route, and over 100 members of the aristocratic families who had served the Habsburgs for generations joined the cortège at the outer gateway of the Hofburg, to walk bareheaded behind the hearses on their long journey to the station. It was partly out of respect to the murdered heir, but also partly a gesture of defiance against the court chamberlain and his third-class burial for the man who was evidently more popular than he had supposed. The coffins reached Artstetten early next morning, after a hazardous journey in a thunderstorm and torrential rain, having narrowly avoided being tipped into the Danube while being ferried across the waters. A simple service for the couple was held in the village church, attended by their children, Francis Ferdinand's stepmother Maria Josepha (who absented herself from court for the next few months in view of the shabby treatment shown to her stepson and his wife in death), Charles, Zita and other close friends and members of their entourage.

Berchtold, a close friend of Francis Ferdinand, had previously been regarded as one of the doves among the Emperor's advisers. But soon after the assassination he decided that a tough response, including military action against Serbia, was called for. If Austria failed to act decisively, it would seem like a renunciation of its position as one of the great powers. His advice, coupled with growing evidence of complicity by the Serbian government in the shooting, persuaded Francis Joseph that something would have to be done about the Serbs. It was apparent that the double assassination had not been a spontaneous act but a carefully planned operation, as reports from General Potiorek in Sarajevo indicated high-level involvement of military officials in Belgrade. He needed to know from Count Tisza how the Hungarians would react to any military confrontation. Tisza favoured what he called forceful diplomatic pressure on Serbia, but deplored any moves which might involve a risk of war.

Francis Joseph agreed that the time for military action had not yet arrived, but on 2 July he wrote to Emperor William II, declaring that those responsible in Belgrade had to be punished, and that Serbia had to be eliminated as a political force. At first he avoided any use of the word 'war'. The letter was entrusted to a personal envoy, Count Alexander Hoyos, and presented to the Emperor in Berlin on 5 July, one week after the murders. Hoyos remained in Berlin for two days of discussion with senior policy makers at the Wilhelmstrasse. His comments suggested that Berchtold was more bellicose than his Emperor, and may have created the impression in Berlin that if a general European war was inevitable, it should be sooner rather than later, at a time when Germany could rely on the Dual Monarchy to accept the full commitments of their military alliance. On the evening of 6 July, Berchtold received a telegram informing him that Austria-Hungary could rely on German support with regard to any action against Serbia.

On the morning of 7 July Francis Joseph resumed his interrupted holiday at Bad Ischl, staying in the Salzkammergut for the next three weeks. During the crises which had led to war in Europe in 1859, 1866 and 1870 he had been in constant touch with his generals or ministers if not both. Now, while they conferred feverishly in Vienna over the implications of Serbia's behaviour and the support they might expect to receive from the other European powers, he remained away from the epicentre with only a small personal staff. Perhaps he had accepted that he was powerless to influence events or maintain control any longer. His prime ministers in Austria and Hungary, plus Berchtold and Hötzendorff, could be allowed to wield power between them.

All the same, it required the Emperor's authority to take the decisive step. Berchtold went to Bad Ischl on 8 July to consult him on the wording of a harsh ultimatum to Serbia, the expectation being that it would be rejected and that a localised war would be the result. Only Tisza had counselled caution at the meeting which agreed on such a course of action. On discussing the matter with Berchtold, Francis Joseph agreed that the ministers must present a united front, and he believed that a peaceful solution of the crisis would be worthless without a positive guarantee that the Pan-Serbian movement would be suppressed on the initiative of Belgrade. After taking soundings from his colleagues and the Magyars, Tisza realised that Hungary was ready for war.

On 19 July Berchtold convened a council of ministers at his home. It was resolved that a strongly worded ultimatum should be presented to Belgrade, giving Serbia forty-eight hours to accept the Austro-Hungarian demands, and providing for mobilisation within a week if necessary. At Bad Ischl Francis Joseph discussed the matter with Paar, still convinced that any war would remain localised, and confident that Serbia would give way under pressure. On 21 July Berchtold returned to the Kaiservilla and presented him with a copy of the ultimatum, which was believed at the time to have been approved and revised by Emperor William and Baron Heinrich von Tschirschky, German ambassador in Vienna.[24]

Francis Joseph was surprised by the severity of the impositions, which included demands that the Serbian government must give a formal assurance that it would condemn and forbid all Serb propaganda directed against Austria-Hungary; that a declaration expressing condemnation would be published on the front page of the official journal on the following Sunday, and that it would express regret that Serbian officers and officials participated in anti-Austrian propaganda; that any Serbian publications which incited hatred and contempt of Austria-Hungary be suppressed; and that representatives of Austria-Hungary would assist Serbia in stamping out 'the movement directed against the territorial integrity of the Dual Monarchy and take part in the judicial proceedings on Serbian territory against persons accessory to the Sarajevo crime'.[25] Despite Francis Joseph's reservations, the ultimatum was presented to the government at Belgrade on 23 July.

When Francis Joseph received the Duke of Cumberland to luncheon two days later, he was noticeably ill at ease, his mind evidently absorbed by the crisis. The Serbs rejected the ultimatum, and on being handed the message by Margutti, he muttered to himself that breaking off diplomatic relations did not necessarily signify war. After consulting Berchtold, he agreed to sign the mobilisation order for war against Serbia and Montenegro. Later that evening he saw Katherine Schratt, and he told her sadly that he had done his best but feared this was the end. To Hötzendorff he said that 'if the monarchy must perish, it should at least perish with decency'.[26] He had long believed that the empire was a volcano which throughout his reign had been waiting to explode. Perhaps, after sixty-five years of living in its shadow, he felt powerless to resist the inevitable.

Nevertheless, he had been assured by the military command that Serbian resistance would be negligible and that the country would be overrun within two or three weeks. War was officially declared on Serbia on 28 July. When Paar saw the document, he muttered incredulously that 'men of eighty-four years of age don't sign war proclamations!'[27] Next day Francis Joseph issued orders for the court to return to Vienna, and published a proclamation to his subjects. In it he said how much he had wanted to devote his remaining years 'to working for peace and to protecting my peoples from the heavy burdens and sacrifices of war'. This had been made impossible as 'the machinations of a hostile Power, moved by hatred, compel me after many long years of peace to take up the sword to preserve the honour of my Monarchy, to defend its integrity and its power'.[28]

Having signed the declaration of war against Serbia, and in effect the death sentence of the old order in Europe, the Emperor left Bad Ischl on 30 July. That same day Russia ordered general mobilisation, and twenty-four hours later the governments of Austria-Hungary and Germany put their armies on a war footing. On 1 August fighting broke out along Germany's eastern frontier, followed by an invasion of Luxembourg and Belgium. With great reluctance, and under German pressure, Francis Joseph agreed to declare war on Russia on 6 August. Regretfully he took off his Order of St George, presented to him by Tsar Nicholas I in 1849 during the early months of his reign and which he had worn with pride ever since. He was equally dismayed when Britain joined France in declaring war on Austria-Hungary on 12 August, even though there was no conflict of interest between Vienna and the western powers, the Austro-German alliance apart. Committed to the partnership with Germany, both empires were resolved to stand or fall together.

ELEVEN

'Why Must it Be Just Now?'

When hostilities broke out in Europe Francis Joseph was almost eighty-four. Having declared war, in practice he ceased to be anything more than the titular ruler of the Austro-Hungarian Empire. From that point, all military power was concentrated in the army high command, led by Hötzendorff, as chief of the general staff. As the Emperor believed that at least one member of the dynasty should be responsible for leading the men into battle, the task fell to Archduke Frederick, nephew of Archduke Albrecht.

A British correspondent in Vienna at the time, speaking to the editor of an Austrian journal, observed that the crowds enthusiastically supported war against Serbia, little knowing what they had let themselves in for. The Austrian journalist replied that the man in the street thought the Serbs would be taught a good lesson if only a small fleet of Danube monitors was despatched to within shooting distance of Belgrade. Defeating a small insolent Balkan state was one thing, 'but when it comes to the Russians it will be a different matter'. The Emperor, both men felt, 'had always been for peace and wished to end his days in quiet'. Had it not been for the assassinations at Sarajevo, he would probably never have consented to war against Serbia. Much as he had been angered by the Archduke's action in taking his wife, who had no sovereign rights, on a semi-regal tour in provinces whose loyalty was dubious at best, and despite his personal antipathy to the late heir, he was made to feel that such a gross insult to the imperial house could only be avenged in blood.[1]

At first his new heir Charles was attached to the Austro-Hungarian headquarters, but as the next Emperor, it was imperative that he should not be posted anywhere where his life might be endangered. After a few weeks he asked for a new and more mobile role as the link between the Emperor and his armies, a request which was duly granted. When not visiting the battlefields, he remained in Vienna, generally at the Hofburg, where he received copies of all the reports submitted by the ministers to the Emperor himself. Francis Joseph devoted part of each day to a personal tutorial in which he would teach his heir the arts of government and the benefit of advice accumulated over his sixty-five years of rule. Each night or morning, Charles was handed some files to study; he would report on any decisions he had taken or recommended, and the Emperor would question him on his reasons and comment on any conclusions reached.[2]

Sometimes Charles would bring his eldest son Otto to see his great-great-uncle. The little boy, who was two years old in November 1914, was a comfort to the elderly sovereign in his last years. From Paris Katherine Schratt had brought Francis Joseph a small casket containing a music box from which sprang a toy nightingale, with a very lifelike sound. It always stood on the table where he kept his cigars, and he enjoyed listening to it so much that when alone he would often wind it up for company. When Otto came to see him, he had to wind it up over and over again to keep the boy amused, until at length he had to suggest that the bird was becoming hoarse from singing too long.[3]

At his time of life, there was no possibility of the Emperor taking command of his troops in person. More than once he wished he could be with his army, but knew he was much too old. As an Emperor in time of national conflict his roles were limited to the customary tasks of administrative routines in studying the papers, and reading reports from the battlefronts in Galicia and Serbia. They offered him scant encouragement, and he realised that the war was going badly for the Dual Monarchy. Francis Ferdinand's persistent warnings that the Austrian army was grossly inferior to those of the other continental powers, especially in artillery, had been largely disregarded; the lessons of 1866 were never learnt.

Hötzendorff proved an unreliable commander, and despite assuring the Germans that in the event of war with Russia, most troops would be sent to Galicia – an undertaking repeated by Francis Joseph in a personal message to William II – he still ordered maximum concentration against Serbia. It meant needless changes in plans and war strategy which cost the Dual Monarchy dearly, culminating in defeat by Russian forces at the battle of Lemberg in September. General Potiorek had hoped to present a defeated Serbia to the Emperor as an eighty-fourth birthday present on 18 August, but by that time his troops were no longer making progress against the Serbs.

General Arthur von Bolfras, head of the military chancellery, kept the Emperor regularly informed on all matters to do with the policy and conduct of the war. Francis Joseph was angered by confidential accounts of desertions from the Czech regiments, dissatisfied with the conduct and strategy of his general staff, and told others that he wished the Austrian army was under German leadership. When Zita congratulated him in mid-August after they received news of an Austro-Hungarian victory against the Russians, he said sadly that in the past his wars had begun with victories, only to finish in defeats. His people would say that he was old and could not cope any longer, 'and after that revolutions will break out and then it will be the end'.[4] He was powerless to do anything. Having handed over authority to the high command, he felt it was not his place to interfere in matters affecting the conduct of the forces.

By now the Emperor rarely left Schönbrunn, where Prince Montenuovo ordered the park next to the palace to be closed to the public for security reasons. There might be popular demonstrations against the war and perhaps even the imperial crown, and it was important that the sovereign should see or hear nothing of them. As a result, the Viennese saw so little of their Emperor that there were rumours he was completely senile or even dead, and the fact was being kept secret. His apartments were on the northern front of the palace, and usually in shadow, so in the cold damp autumn and winter they were not suitable for a man in his mid-eighties.

As he had always lived frugally, there was little more he could do in the way of self-sacrifice. However, from the first day of the war he stopped eating white rolls, asking that only black bread should be served at his table. Even when children or other guests were invited, this rule was not relaxed. Only when he became prone to serious digestive problems did his physician persuade him to have white bread, if not white rolls, baked for his consumption.[5]

Christmas 1914 was spent at Schönbrunn, a joyless affair at which not even the presence of his daughters and some of the grandchildren could cheer the Emperor up. He could not help but compare their present unhappy situation with the cheerful festivities they had enjoyed at Wallsee in previous years.

In October 1914 the Italian minister for foreign affairs, San Giuliano, had died. He had been a keen supporter of the Triple Alliance, but his successor Giorgio Sidney Sonnino did not share such loyalties, and his appointment convinced Francis Joseph that Italy would abandon her neutrality and soon join their enemies. Discouraged by the course of the war, Berchtold resigned his office in January 1915 and went on active service as a staff chaplain. On 8 March the Emperor presided over a ministerial council for the last time, to discuss the Italian situation. Sonnino was demanding territorial gains from the Dual Monarchy as the price of continued neutrality, and a treaty signed in London in April offered Italy more land in the event of an allied victory over Germany. As a result the Italian government declared war on Germany and Austria-Hungary a month later.

This escalating conflict was a far cry from the localised campaign against Serbia which Francis Joseph had almost certainly envisaged, and had certainly been persuaded to endorse, the previous summer. According to the Russian press, by the spring of 1915 he was so anxious to prevent further bloodshed during his lifetime that he appealed to Pope Benedict XV to act as mediator in Berlin, 'in order to overcome the Emperor William's obstinate desire to continue the war regardless of consequences', and after this failed, to act in a similar capacity in Petrograd with a view to concluding a separate peace with Russia. As part of the peace settlement, he was prepared to surrender Bosnia, Herzegovina and Galicia.[6] Military circles, however, were not optimistic about any initiative from Vienna, as long as the Austro-German armies remained so closely interwoven, with all campaign plans dictated by the high command in Berlin. Austria-Hungary was very much the junior partner in the alliance.

While the Emperor regularly saw his ministers and generals, he received very few visitors from abroad. One exception was Field-Marshal August von Mackensen, one of the senior German commanders, whom he met shortly before the latter embarked on a successful campaign to invade Serbia in September 1915. Francis Joseph invited him to dine, spent many hours in his company, and said afterwards that 'with men like that one never goes wrong'.[7] It seemed the Emperor was seeking what comfort he could, now that his empire's destiny was firmly wedded to that of Germany, in a cause that looked ever more doomed.

On 24 June 1915 he came out on to the palace balcony to acknowledge cheers from a crowd celebrating the recapture of Lemberg from the Russians. With him came Zita, who had moved into the palace with the Emperor while Charles was away, and her eldest son Otto.

In October Tsar Ferdinand of Bulgaria entered the war on the side of the Central Powers, prompting Francis Joseph to remark that if 'the Bulgarian' was joining them it must be because he thought they were winning.

By the end of November the Austro-Hungarian, German and Bulgarian armies had overrun Serbia, thus fulfilling one of the main Viennese war aims. But the Emperor recognised that this had been achieved largely with the help of other powers, and under the German leadership which he so admired yet realised sadly was so much superior to anything the Austrians could provide. Offset against that was a disastrous offensive against Russia which ended in failure, and a poor harvest in Hungary which was making the Austrian provinces largely dependent on German bread. The Dual Monarchy had become ever more reliant on German military and economic resources in general, and was gradually losing its independence of action.

On 18 August 1916, the Emperor's eighty-sixth birthday was celebrated as usual, with a solemn Mass in the chapel at Schönbrunn, and a great luncheon was held at the ministry of war with the military cabinet. While guests were under no illusions as to the progress of the conflict, they did their best to bring some cheer to the occasion. When Krobatin proposed his sovereign's health, all those present joined in enthusiastically. As the band struck up the Austrian national anthem and those of their allies, he remarked sardonically that if only their enemies celebrated occasions of such a nature, and their band had to play the anthems of their partners in arms, it would take them more than an hour to get through. It was unlikely that anyone needed reminding of the delicate situation in which the Central Powers found themselves.

Yet at one point during the day, probably in the morning, the Emperor found time to continue working at his desk as he had done for so many years. There is something rather touchingly pathetic in the thought that he spent at least part of his last birthday working on, or at least reading through, a plan for revision of the Austrian imperial constitution in peacetime.[8] By the time peace came, the Habsburg empire would be no more.

Meanwhile, Russian successes in Galicia and the Bukovina were bringing the Dual Monarchy close to defeat. On 27 August Roumania entered the war on the side of Italy and France, and quickly overran Transylvania, much to the shock of the Austrian and Hungarian forces. German troops once again came to their salvation by halting the Russian front and the Roumanian advance, yet the price was to be even greater German dominance. In September the Emperor had to agree to a joint high command of the Central Powers, headed by William II and his commanders, Generals Paul von Hindenburg and Erich von Ludendorff, who thus had total leadership of all German and Austrian forces at the front.

It was not the only unpalatable news Francis Joseph had to face that autumn. He was convinced that his prime minister, Count Karl Stürgkh, was keeping from him bad news about the state of things in Vienna, particularly the shortage of bread, milk and potatoes. A starving people, he knew, would not put up with much more. Declaring that he could not let his empire go to hopeless ruin, he pledged himself to call an end to the conflict by the spring of 1917.[9]

On 21 October Stürgkh was lunching in a Viennese hotel when Friedrich Adler, son of the socialist leader and a journalist by profession, walked up to him and fired three shots at point-blank range, killing him instantly. Adler made no effort to resist arrest, and when police officers questioned him as to his motives, he said calmly, 'I have to account for this before the court.'[10] (Adler was found guilty of murder in May 1917 and sentenced to death, but this was later commuted to a prison sentence.)

At around the time of the assassination, there were riots in Vienna, with food shops plundered and ransacked, and a crowd marched to the gates of Schönbrunn Palace. The Emperor saw them from his window, and demanded to know what was going on. Rather hesitantly, Ketterl told him that his people were angry because of the shortage of food. Children were being sent home from school, some of them fainting through weakness. The Emperor's household would not let him drive through the streets, because they did not want him to see the queues which formed for hours in order to buy provisions from the dwindling stocks still left in the shops. Furious at having to find out such information from his valet rather than being informed by ministers, the Emperor gave the ministers a very uncomfortable time the next day. If his people were really suffering from famine and poverty, he told them, it was their responsibility to make peace at any cost, even without consulting their German partners if necessary. Blind adherence to the time-honoured alliance must not take precedence over the welfare of his subjects, otherwise anarchy would break out and revolution would overwhelm the empire while the armies were at war.

Early in November a correspondent with *The Times*, D. Thomas Curtin, reported that Austrian dissatisfaction with Germany was widespread, but the people had no way of voicing it as the Reichsrat had been silent since the beginning of war. This he blamed squarely on the government, the ruling classes and above all the Emperor, who between them 'dared not trust a meeting of the 13 races in that polyglot Empire', and he said that the Austrians felt they had been used as a catspaw to pull Germany's chestnuts out of the fire. An Austrian officer told him that the army had 'smashed Serbia for the Germans, and all we got in return was a few pigs'; they had destroyed Montenegro, captured northern Albania, borne the brunt of a great part of the Russian attacks, lost thousands of their best troops against the Italians, 'and it is about time we came to terms with Russia, and if necessary with Italy'. A Hungarian deputy declared that Austria would be only too glad to give Italy the Trentino if they could retain Trieste, but Austria, utterly exhausted, was in a mood to give up anything.[11]

Ernst von Körber, formerly minister of finance, was appointed as Stürgkh's successor. On his first day in office, Körber found the Emperor in a state of considerable excitement over friction between the German and Austrian high commands and their respective governments, on the matter of the future of Poland. Francis Joseph asked him to accept a proclamation just issued by the German army and about to be promulgated by both Emperors, solemnly promising the Poles the future unity and independence of their state in union with Austria-Hungary and Germany. Körber objected on the grounds that this would create resentment among other groups in the empire, and was on the point of refusing when the aged Emperor implored him, with uplifted hands, to give way. Knowing that his sovereign was not well, and fearing that he might have a sudden stroke if thwarted, he gave way.

Until his last weeks, Francis Joseph told his entourage that he was well simply because he refused to be ill – indeed, he must not be ill. Once he told Ketterl the story of the sovereign (unnamed) whose physician drew a salary only so long as his master was well, but did not get a farthing if the ruler's ill-health made his presence necessary, on the grounds that 'the best police force is the one that keeps order so efficiently that its intervention is never needed'.[12] However, the 'Arterien-Verkalkung' on which his entourage had remarked some five or six years earlier gradually developed into chronic catarrh. By the autumn of 1916 he was increasingly tired, dispirited, and prone to his old enemy bronchitis. Fits of coughing and fever alarmed his doctors, and early in November pneumonia was diagnosed. His ever-faithful Margutti continued to bring him his documents each day, and read him some aloud, but found that he no longer seemed to understand them as before.

A telegram was sent to Charles, who was in eastern Saxony visiting the eastern front, to warn him that he should prepare himself for the inevitable end. He returned to Schönbrunn to find the Emperor much better than he had expected. Katherine Schratt made the journey from Hietzing, where she was presiding over a convalescent home for wounded officers, but she found him too weak to follow her conversation or answer her much of the time. Gisela and Valerie had planned to come and see him together, but hesitated in case he would draw the obvious conclusion – that they were expecting to join a deathbed vigil. Instead Valerie came on her own, staying in the palace so that she and Erszi, now Princess von Windischgrätz, could be on hand to look after him. He resisted their pleas that he should go to bed, telling them that he would cough less if he was sitting upright. There was still work for him to do, he said, especially studying reports from the Roumanian front, and recruitment papers. When it was suggested that a group of nuns should nurse him he refused, saying that the three servants who had faithfully served him in health should also care for him in sickness.[13]

By early November he was coughing badly at night, but the doctors were reassured to find that his heartbeat and breathing were still regular. On 17 November *Vossische Zeitung* announced that on 2 December, the sixty-eighth anniversary of the Emperor's accession, he would issue a proclamation greatly increasing the rights of sovereignty exercised by his heir Archduke Charles, who would 'have charge of affairs of the realm conjointly with the Emperor'. That this announcement was made simultaneously with bulletins referring to His Majesty's 'slight cold' did not pass unnoticed.[14] Many readers must have doubted whether the Emperor would live to see another anniversary.

On 18 November his doctors prescribed him a glass of strong white wine and two small glasses of champagne as a tonic. Two days later he admitted that he was very tired, and went to bed early. He was roused at his usual hour on the morning of 21 November, and though clearly feverish, insisted on working at his papers as he had done for so many years. Archduke Frederick visited him, and they spent nearly an hour in conversation. Charles and Zita arrived just before midday, and were surprised to find him still at his desk. He had a temperature of 102, but was still working on documents about recruitment. Putting his work aside briefly, he talked to them and they thought his speech seemed normal, despite fever and weakness. He was very happy to have received the blessing of the Pope, he told them, and their army's recent victories in Roumania had brought him great joy. They left, unaware that a crisis was imminent. Others around him thought he knew that he was dying; he admitted sadly that although he had taken over the throne under the most difficult conditions, he was leaving it under even worse ones. Though he would have liked to spare Charles such a fate, he had every confidence in him; 'he is made of the right stuff, and will know how to cope'.[15] Gisela had been warned that the end was approaching, and put in a discreet appearance among the throng.

That evening he finally admitted that the effort was becoming too much. At around 7 p.m. he laid his pen down at his desk for the last time, and allowed Ketterl to help him to bed. As news spread to the outside world that he was slipping away, large crowds assembled near the cathedral, outside the newspaper offices, and at the gates of Schönbrunn. Valerie had been at the palace for several days, and soon after darkness fell she left for the station at Vienna to meet one of her daughters off the train, only to be recalled immediately by one of her father's couriers. It was this action which made the multitudes realise how serious the situation must be.

Before being left to sleep, the Emperor told everyone that he had not yet finished his work, and must be woken again next morning at his customary hour of 3.30. Ketterl made him a cup of tea and helped him sip from it, as he muttered feebly, 'Why must it be just now?'[16] Recognising that his master's time had nearly come, Ketterl summoned a court chaplain to administer the last rites, and Valerie read the prayers for the dying. One more fit of coughing turned into the death rattle as the sick man sank back against his pillows, while family, court dignitaries and others, gathered round. Shortly after 9 p.m. he passed away.

Ketterl dressed his master for the last time in his field marshal's uniform, and on his breast pinned the Order of the Golden Fleece, the War Medal, the Officers' Service Cross and the jubilee medals struck for the anniversaries of 1898 and 1908. Charles and Zita had been summoned, but they arrived too late to see him breathe his last. As everyone filed out of the death chamber, nobody seemed to know what to say or do. For a few moments there was complete silence, until one of the courtiers walked up to Charles, and with tears in his eyes, made the sign of the cross on his forehead.

One of the first actions of Charles as Emperor was to respect the close friendship of some three decades enjoyed by the deceased, and he led Katherine Schratt to his deathbed where she laid two white roses on his chest. She had last visited him two days earlier, and knew she would probably not see him again alive. Having received a telephone call from Montenuovo to inform her that the Emperor had gone, she was shocked to receive another invitation saying that His Majesty wished her to come to the palace. In her grief, it took her a moment to realise that they had a new sovereign.

For Gisela and Valerie, it was to be their last meeting in Vienna. Sadly, their father's death did not bring the sisters any closer. He had died wearing his wedding ring and signet ring. Both of them wanted the latter as a keepsake, and quarrelled bitterly over who had the better claim. It was removed from his finger, but in the end they agreed reluctantly that it should be replaced and buried with him.

The people of a hungry, war-weary Vienna, facing a bitterly cold winter, might have been excused for being in no mood to mourn their Emperor. Even so, none but his oldest subjects could remember a time when he had not reigned over them. Francis Joseph had become part of the very fabric of the empire, and to some, his death during a bitter winter when the war was going badly must have seemed like a heavy curtain coming down on the world they had known. His body lay in state for three days at the palace; according to protocol, an emperor could not be buried until nine days after death, and the funeral took place on 30 November.

Many of the troops were engaged on one of three battle fronts. A single battalion was left in Vienna, apart from the Life Guards who were to escort the hearse. It was therefore decided that, in the army's absence, the people should have their chance to salute their late sovereign. The coffin was not taken directly from the Hofburg chapel to the Cathedral of St Stephen, but instead along a route through much of the city. A short service in the cathedral was attended by Emperor Charles, Empress Zita, and their heir, four-year-old Archduke Otto. Afterwards they were joined by King Ludwig III of Bavaria, King Frederick Augustus of Saxony, Tsar Ferdinand of Bulgaria, and Crown Prince William of Germany, representing his father the Emperor,* to follow the funeral chariot on foot in procession from the cathedral to the Kapuzinergruft, the crypt of the Capuchin church, where over 140 members of the dynasty were entombed in the imperial vault.

Two days later a final requiem was said in the Hofburg chapel, attended by the imperial family and court dignitaries. Appropriately, it was the sixty-eighth anniversary of that December day when Emperor Ferdinand had laid aside the imperial crown in favour of his eighteen-year-old nephew.

---

* Emperor William II had been to Vienna two days previously to pray with Charles at the bier of Francis Joseph, but did not attend the funeral, ostensibly 'for security reasons'.

The Emperor who had been heard to tell those around him that he had been spared nothing was at least granted two privileges. He had died of natural causes, yet had not lived long enough to see the final downfall of the Habsburg realm.

It was clearly the end of an era. In London *The Times* noted that the death of Francis Joseph removed 'a figure that seemed to have become a permanent figure of the political configuration of Europe'. It also appreciated that Austria did the bidding of Berlin, and considered it impossible to apportion responsibility for what it called a 'criminal policy', the outbreak of war in the continent. At his age, he was probably incapable of resisting pressure which a younger man might have withstood. Had the Serbian crisis occurred a few years earlier, a more forceful Francis Joseph could have helped to prevent the inexorable slide into war, for which he was surely less to blame than the German Emperor, the military party in Berlin, and their accomplices in Austria-Hungary. When he was laid to rest, it was concluded, everyone would

> reflect that an era which might have been a great era in Habsburg history has closed amid ruin, bankruptcy, blood and tears; but in these reflections there will be place for human compassion with the lot of a man who came as a stripling to the throne, who saw brother, wife, son and nephew perish by violence, who lost the fairest provinces of his empire, and who must have ended a long and chequered reign with forebodings of disaster to his House and his dominions graver than any which even he had known.[17]

The French press was more blunt. In Paris, *Débats* acknowledged that although the late Emperor had seemed inclined towards peace after the assassinations at Sarajevo, he let himself be persuaded that the conflict with Serbia could be localised. As often before in his reign, he began something without regard for the consequences, and would therefore share with Emperor William II 'responsibility for the barbarities which have devastated Europe for the last two years'.[18]

Aged twenty-nine at the time of his accession, Charles had been left an unenviable legacy. He was as committed to peace as his great-uncle had been, yet some of the empire's elders believed his cause was already doomed. Dr Lammasch, a law professor in Vienna, thought him unfitted by character to deal with the situation. The young Emperor, he said, was too good-natured and too human. 'He does not trust himself to use his authority, and boldly act the part of traitor today to his country in order that he may be her saviour tomorrow.'[19]

Charles valued good relations with Germany, and had the utmost respect for Emperor William, but knew that he was dominated by the Prussian military establishment, and committed against his better judgement to the almost hopeless cause of total victory at any cost. He was also aware that German victory would mean domination of the Dual Monarchy by Berlin, and that any major military success by the Germans could mean the end of Austria as they knew it.

In March 1917 the Bolshevik revolution took Russia out of the war, removing an enemy from Austria's eastern front, but prospects were still ominous for the Austro-Hungarian empire. The Italian campaign was a heavy drain on resources, and the United States of America entered the war on the side of the entente powers. British and French forces never clashed except for occasional naval encounters in the Adriatic Sea; the only allied power seriously engaged against the Dual Monarchy was Italy. Charles decided to launch a new peace initiative; through his brothers-in law, Princes Sixtus and Xavier of Bourbon-Parma, he contacted the French president, Raymond Poincaré, and his prime minister Aristide Briand. They assured him they did not seek the destruction of the Habsburg monarchy, only the return of Alsace-Lorraine, which had been in German hands since the end of the Franco-Prussian war in 1871, and unconditional guarantees of Belgian and Serbian independence. Pressed by Prince Sixtus, Charles agreed to these conditions in writing, assuring them that he would take up the issue of France's demands for the restoration of their territory with his allies.

A change of administration in France followed, with the pro-Austrian government of Aristide Briand replaced by that of the less sympathetic Alexandre Ribot. Talks with David Lloyd George, British prime minister, concluded that no immediate response to Vienna was possible. Italy would have to be consulted first, and as the Italians had been brought into the war largely with promises of territorial gains at Austria's expense, the plan seemed doomed. In May Charles wrote to Sixtus reiterating opposition to any form of peace in which Italy did not participate, but holding out hope for an Italian peace overture in which she might be prepared to compromise on her annexation demands. The understanding reached in Austria-Hungary with France and England on many essential points, he believed, would help them to overcome any obstacles that remained in the way of 'an honourable peace'.[20]

Charles had reckoned without Germany's blind faith in eventual victory. Count Ottokar Czernin, Austrian minister of the exterior, believed that any separate Austrian peace would amount to betrayal of their ally. Yet Charles knew time was running out, and feared that a combination of hunger and war-weariness could lead to revolution in Austria. In March 1918 Czernin, deciding to stake everything on German military success, declared that Austria-Hungary would never abandon Germany, provoking the French government into publishing Charles's letter of March 1917 to Prince Sixtus. Czernin asked Charles to deny publicly having written it and was promptly asked to resign, but Charles's authority had been dealt a severe blow, as Emperor William was mortified to learn that he had willingly endorsed France's demand for Alsace-Lorraine. The Dual Monarchy was now even more irrevocably committed to Berlin's war strategy; worse still, his capitulation before the entrenched power of German and Magyar opinion had destroyed any faith that the entente powers ever had in the new Emperor, and with it the monarchy's chances of salvation through a compromise agreement with the western powers. German military victory would come at a cost; Charles and Czernin's successor, Istvan von Burian, were asked to agree to a political alliance, a military treaty, and a customs union, if they were to dispel doubts raised by the Sixtus letter. Germany now intended to dominate Austria-Hungary economically as well as militarily.

By late summer the tide was turning against Germany and its allies. With mutinies, deserting regiments, failed offensives and mounting casualties, the cause of the Central Powers was as good as lost. Charles renounced the German alliance, and signed an armistice with Britain and France on 4 November, but it was too late. Five days later he was presented with a document of abdication, technically a manifesto agreed jointly by members of the last imperial cabinet and socialist ministers of the new republic, requiring the Emperor to recognise in advance any new constitution that might be decided upon, and to relinquish all participation in affairs of state. In effect, the last ruler of the Habsburg dynasty was being asked to renounce his power but not his crown. That evening he left Schönbrunn for his private hunting lodge at Eckartsau, north-east of Vienna. By Christmas he was under pressure to leave Austrian soil or give up the crown.

Prince Sixtus feared the revolutionary government in Austria might fall into the hands of the extreme left, and with the precedent of the imprisonment and butchery of ex-Tsar Nicholas II and his family the previous year, it was imperative that the family should be escorted to safety. In the spring of 1919 Charles and his family left Austria, after signing a document known to posterity as the 'Feldkirch manifesto'. It was to demonstrate that he had merely undertaken an act of voluntary self-banishment, and to declare the republican government 'null and void' for him and the house of Habsburg. They settled first at Chateau Wartegg, near the Austrian border, moving later to Villa Prangins on Lake Geneva. In 1921 he made two abortive attempts to regain his throne in Hungary, after which the Swiss government asked him and his family to leave the country, and they were despatched to exile in Madeira. Charles had never been strong, and within weeks a severe cold developed into bronchitis. He died on 1 April 1922, aged thirty-four.

Emperor Francis Joseph had presided over an empire which has been described as 'a dynastic accident brought together by marriage, death and family fortune', as opposed to the British empire, which was 'won primarily through conquest and settlement'.[21] Some three centuries before his reign, the Holy Roman empire had been an essential bulwark against the Ottoman threat to central Europe. Later, it came to embody the hopes and prayers of those countries which saw it as a benign power preventing French domination of Europe.

Its collapse in 1918, or more accurately the collapse of the Habsburg empire, left a huge vacuum in central Europe, ready to be filled by either Russia or Germany, vying for European domination. A redrawing of national boundaries at the Treaty of St Germain in

1919 resulted in the creation of Czechoslovakia, which included the industrial centres of the old empire. The new, much smaller Austria was now a predominantly agricultural country with a semi-industrial capital, Vienna, home to one-third of the country's population. The country's new boundaries made trading difficult, and political differences between the socialist capital and the more conservative countryside threatened its internal stability. The national problems solved by the new settlement had been replaced by another problem, in that the majority of Austrians were Germans and sought union with Germany itself, for political and economic reasons. Such a union, or *Anschluss*, was prohibited by the Treaty of St Germain.

Destruction of the empire in 1918 had thus removed the chief agent of European stability, and left Austria vulnerable to its vastly more powerful neighbour Germany, with consequences leading to an even more devastating European conflict in the Second World War. In April 1945, as five years of hostilities were drawing to a close, Winston Churchill declared that the war 'should never have come unless, under American and modernising pressure, we had driven the Habsburgs out of Austria and Hungary and the Hohenzollerns out of Germany. By making these vacuums we gave the opening for the Hitlerite monster to crawl out of its sewer onto the vacant thrones.'[22]

The historian A.J.P. Taylor saw it differently. Europe, he wrote a few years later, was to find unity as Greater Germany, the only way in which it could become a world power, 'capable of withstanding the other two'. The legacy of German defeat, he noted, 'was Bolshevism and American intervention in Europe' and 'a competition between communism and liberal democracy'[23] which would dominate much of the rest of the twentieth century. The post-Second World War landscape of Europe only changed in 1990 with the fall of Soviet Russia and the reunification of West and East Germany, the latter of which had been under the communist yoke. It was the year Taylor died, and one year after the death of Zita, the last Empress, who had passed away at the age of ninety-six.

If measured in terms of wars fought and won, Emperor Francis Joseph's long reign was hardly a striking success. In personal terms, his life was tragic. Yet for almost seventy years he personified his empire, just as Queen Victoria was the embodiment of Great Britain and the British empire for a slightly shorter span. The dashing young man of 1848, on whom so many hopes had rested, became a legend in his own lifetime and beyond. On 18 August 1930, the centenary of his birth, memorial services were held in the Viennese churches, and thousands came to pay homage at the Capuchin crypt where he was buried. There were celebrations throughout other towns of the Austrian republic, especially Bad Ischl, where members of Austrian hunting clubs and ex-servicemen's associations gathered to remember their late sovereign. On the Sirinskogel, the hillside opposite the villa where he had stayed every summer for more than half a century, the initials F.J. were traced in electric lights.[24]

Emperor Francis Joseph of Austria-Hungary, the last monarch of the old school, as he had called himself, was a ruler of paradoxes. He was the sovereign who tried to subjugate Hungary, only to become its constitutional monarch, and held steadfast to the Austro-German alliance despite his personal antipathy to the brash upstart Emperor William II. He was the autocrat schooled in absolutist convictions, who became a supporter of universal male suffrage. He was the ruler who helped to sustain peace for many years, yet ironically in the last years when his power was slipping away from him, he signed the document that helped to unleash the forces setting in motion the First World War.

Notes

Abbreviations

PRO – Public Record Office
QVJ – Queen Victoria's Journal
RA – Royal Archives

Chapter 1

1 Palmer, p. 8
2 Brook-Shepherd, *Royal Sunset*, p. 118
3 Redlich, p. 22
4 Gribble, p. 64
5 Haslip, *Imperial Adventurer*, p. 25
6 Crankshaw, p. 104; Corti, *Von Kind Zum Kaiser*, p. 25
7 Ashley, vol. I, p. 103
8 Haslip, *Imperial Adventurer*, p. 15
9 Tschuppik, *Reign of Francis Joseph*, p. 8
10 Ibid (all Tschuppik references below are to this title unless stated otherwise)
11 Redlich, p. 18
12 Tschuppik, p. 15
13 Morton, p. 41
14 Redlich, pp. 32–3

Chapter 2

1 Haslip, *Imperial Adventurer*, p. 38
2 Redlich, p. 51, Tsar Nicholas I to Empress Alexandra 23.5.1849

3 Crankshaw, p. 67
4 Haslip, *Lonely Empress*, p. 33
5 Listowel, p. 44
6 Redlich, p. 49, Prince Schwarzenberg to Prince Metternich 29.7.1850
7 RA VIC/I 27/64, memo by Ernest, Duke of Saxe-Coburg Gotha 17.2.1852
8 Crankshaw, p. 87
9 Redlich, p. 91
10 Ketterl, p. 28
11 Redlich, p. 246
12 Redlich, p. 116, Otto von Bismarck to Leopold von Gerlach 25.6.1852
13 Redlich, p. 14
14 Tschuppik, p. 100
15 Gribble, p. 69
16 Ibid
17 Gribble, p. 67
18 RA QVJ 23.2.1853
19 *Letters of Queen Victoria*, I, ii, pp. 447–8, King Leopold to Queen Victoria 3.6.1853
20 Tschuppik, p. 102
21 Corti, *Elizabeth*, p. 22 (all Corti references below are to this title unless stated otherwise)

22 Corti, p. 36
23 RA VIC/Y.98/27, Queen Victoria to King Leopold 28.8.1853
24 Corti, p. 38
25 Corti, p. 39
26 Corti, pp. 44–5
27 Corti, p. 46
28 *The Times*, 24.4.1854
29 Tschuppik, *Elizabeth*, p. 23
30 Palmer, p. 77, Archduchess Sophie's journal 24.4.1854
31 Palmer, p. 78
32 Corti, p. 55

Chapter 3

1 RA QVJ 29.4.1854
2 Redlich p. 165–6
3 De Burgh, p. 33
4 Redlich, p. 253, Peter von Meyendorff to Count Nesselrode 1.6.1854
5 RA QVJ 5.7.1854
6 Corti, p. 57
7 Redlich, p. 159
8 PRO FO7/461/21505, Lord Russell to Lord Clarendon 6.3.1855; Crankshaw, p. 128
9 RA VIC/Y80/103, King Leopold to Queen Victoria 6.2.1857
10 Corti, p. 73
11 Corti, p. 76
12 Marek, p. 122, Archduke Maximilian to Emperor Francis Joseph 10.4.1858
13 Ibid., Archduke Maximilian to Emperor Francis Joseph 7.1.1859
14 RA VIC/Add I 15/82, Queen Victoria to Emperor Francis Joseph 22.2.1859
15 Corti, p. 79
16 Ibid.
17 Ibid.

18 Corti, pp. 80–81
19 Ketterl, p. 193
20 RA QVJ 14.7.1859
21 RA QVJ 18.7.1859
22 Listowel, p. 261
23 Haslip, *Imperial Adventurer*, p. 21
24 Redlich, p. 246
25 Crankshaw, p. 181, Emperor Francis Joseph to Archduchess Sophie 21.10.1860; Burckhard, Karl J., *Briefe des Staatskanziers Fürsten Metternich-Winneburg an den oesterreichischen Minister des Aussern Grafen Buol-Schauenstein aus den Jahren 1852–1859*, Munich, 1934, p. vi
26 Haslip, *Lonely Empress*, p. 138
27 Martin, vol. V, p. 223
28 PRO F30/22/40, Julian Fane to Lord Russell 13.9.1860
29 PRO F30/22/98, Lord Russell to Julian Fane 21.9.1860
30 *Letters of Queen Victoria*, I, iii, p. 409, Queen Victoria to Lord Russell 21.9.1860
31 Crankshaw, p. 181; Schnurer, p. 232

Chapter 4

1 Marek, p. 135
2 RA VIC/Z 14/22, Crown Princess of Prussia to Queen Victoria 17.12.1862; Corti, *English Empress*, p. 99
3 Bridge, p. 5
4 Haslip, *Lonely Empress*, p. 170
5 Queen Victoria, *Dearest Mama*, pp. 262–3, Queen Victoria to Crown Princess of Prussia 5.9.1863
6 *Letters of Queen Victoria*, II, i, p. 108, memo 3.9.1863
7 Tschuppik, p. 123

8 Tschuppik, p. 133
9 Brook-Shepherd, *Austrians*, p. 85
10 Gribble, p. 139
11 Brook-Shepherd, *Austrians*, pp. 93–4
12 Corti, p. 122
13 Palmer, pp. 146–7, Emperor Francis Joseph to Archduchess Sophie 22.8.1866
14 RA QVJ 7.12.1866
15 Cassels, *Clash of Generations*, p. 41, Emperor Francis Joseph to Empress Elizabeth 7.8.1866
16 Ibid, pp. 41–2, Emperor Francis Joseph to Empress Elizabeth 20.8.1866
17 Bled, p. 148
18 Corti, p. 140
19 Corti, pp. 144–5

Chapter 5

1 Corti, p. 146
2 Corti, pp. 149–50
3 Corti, p. 151
4 Corti, p. 152
5 Haslip, pp. 178–9; Listowel, p. 20
6 Morton, p. 238
7 Tschuppik, p. 307
8 Ketterl, p. 31
9 Ketterl, pp. 45–6
10 Margutti, p. 34
11 Marek, p. 203, Marie Festetics diary 28.11.1873
12 Cassels, *Clash of Generations*, p. 2
13 Cassels, p. 3
14 Palmer, p. 194; Brook-Shepherd, *Royal Sunset*, p. 136
15 Palmer, p. 172
16 Gribble, pp. 155–6
17 Cassells, *Clash of Generations*, p. 20
18 Bülow, 1897–1903, p. 162
19 Haslip, *Lonely Empress*, p. 239

20 Palmer, p. 178
21 Margutti, p. 52
22 Queen Victoria, *Darling Child*, p. 44, Crown Princess of Germany to Queen Victoria 25.5.1872
23 *The Times*, 2.5.1873
24 Queen Victoria, *Darling Child*, p. 89, Crown Princess of Germany to Queen Victoria 26.4.1873
25 Queen Victoria, *Darling Child*, p. 90, 8.5.1873
26 William II, *My Early Life*, p. 73
27 Haslip, *Lonely Empress*, p. 250
28 Corti, p. 188
29 Haslip, *Lonely Empress*, pp. 254–5
30 Corti, p. 193

Chapter 6

1 Palmer, p. 189, Empress Elizabeth to Crown Prince Rudolf January 1874
2 Obolensky, p. 47
3 RA Add.MS. A.3/123, Prince of Wales to Queen Victoria 26.1.1869; Magnus, p. 101
4 Corti, p. 238
5 Palmer, p. 217
6 Hamann, pp. 10–11; Beller, p. 136
7 Palmer, p. 220
8 Margutti, p. 89
9 Cassels, *Clash of Generations*, p. 125
10 Listowel, p. 91, Crown Prince Rudolf to Latour 4.9.1883
11 Stephanie, p. 146
12 Palmer, p. 235
13 Corti, p. 290
14 Palmer, p. 235

Chapter 7

1 Haslip, *Lonely Empress*, p. 348
2 Listowel, p. 147
3 Stephanie, p. 208

4 Listowel, p. 131
5 RA QVJ 23.4.1888; *Letters of Queen Victoria* III, i, p. 414
6 Barkeley, p. 195; Stockhausen, p. 117
7 Brook-Shepherd, *Uncle of Europe*, p. 77
8 Corti, p. 299, Archduchess Valerie diary 9.12.1887
9 Lonyay, p. 241
10 Paget, *Embassies*, vol. II, p. 465
11 Paget, pp. 465–6
12 Judtmann, p. 233
13 RA VIC/Z 498/20, Lord Salisbury to Queen Victoria 31.1.1889
14 Judtmann, p. 142
15 Morton, p. 246
16 Anon, p. 163
17 Judtmann, p. 186–7
18 Margutti, p. 74
19 Judtmann, p. 241, Emperor Francis Joseph to Emperor William II 31.1.1889
20 Judtmann, p. 242
21 Ketterl, p. 191
22 Palmer, p. 262
23 Judtmann, pp. 146, 150
24 Palmer, p. 265
25 *The Times*, 7.2.1889
26 Haslip, *Emperor and Actress*, p. 114
27 Margutti, p. 98
28 Margutti, p. 74
29 Haslip, *Emperor and Actress*, p. 107
30 Pauli, pp. 30–31
31 Pauli, pp. i, 31–2
32 Crankshaw, p. 291, Archduke Albrecht to Archduke Francis Ferdinand 18.10.1889

Chapter 8

1 Gribble, p. 274
2 Marek, p. 361
3 Paget, *Embassies*, vol. II, p. 494
4 Haslip, *Emperor and Actress*, p. 124
5 Marek, p. 361
6 Palmer, p. 270
7 Redlich, p. 448
8 Palmer, p. 277
9 Haslip, *Emperor and Actress*, p. 122
10 Haslip, *Emperor and Actress*, p. 125
11 Ibid
12 Ketterl, p. 24
13 Ketterl, pp. 21–3
14 *Letters of Queen Victoria* III, iii, p. 36, Queen Victoria to Lord Salisbury 21.3.1896
15 Corti, p. 355, Empress Elizabeth to Archduchess Valerie, April 1895
16 Gribble, p. 272
17 Praschl-Bichler, p. 63
18 Gribble, p. 281
19 Cassels, *Archduke and Assassin*, p. 28
20 Corti, p. 355, Emperor Francis Joseph to Empress Elizabeth December 1895
21 Ibid., p. 362
22 Tschuppik, p. 350
23 Corti, p. 368, Emperor Francis Joseph to Empress Elizabeth 17.7.1898
24 Corti, p. 375, Emperor Francis Joseph to Empress Elizabeth 1.9.1898
25 Ibid., Emperor Francis Joseph to Empress Elizabeth 9.9.1898
26 Corti, p. 384
27 Bülow, 1897–1903, p. 234
28 Gribble, pp. 161–2
29 Marek, p. 375
30 Pauli, p. 90
31 RA VIC/Add I 88/74, Sir Horace Rumbold to Queen Victoria 19.9.1898

32 Margutti, p. 58
33 Ketterl, p. 65
34 Ibid

Chapter 9

1 Haslip, *Emperor and Actress*, p. 225
2 Cassels, *Archduke and Assassin*, p. 38
3 Gribble, pp. 12–13
4 Cassels, *Archduke and Assassin*, p. 39
5 Cassels, *Archduke and Assassin*, p. 43
6 Pauli, p. 151
7 Haslip, *Emperor and Actress*, p. 221
8 Margutti, pp. 131–2
9 RA VIC/Add I 88/83, Sir Horace Rumbold to Queen Victoria 9.9.1900
10 Ketterl, p. 85
11 Haslip, *Emperor and Actress*, p. 211
12 Ketterl, p. 84
13 Ketterl, pp. 163–4
14 Ketterl, p. 27
15 *The Times*, 8.3.1929
16 Margutti, p. 49
17 *The Times*, 18.8.1930
18 Ketterl, p. 47
19 Ketterl, p. 34
20 Margutti, p. 50
21 Margutti, pp. 196–7
22 Redlich, p. 482
23 Ketterl, p. 186
24 Margutti, pp. 103–4
25 RA/VIC/W.44/91, Sir Francis Plunkett to Lord Knollys 24.4.1904
26 Pope-Hennessy, p. 385
27 Gore, p. 189
28 Ketterl, p. 201

29 Margutti, p. 212
30 Ketterl, p. 122.
31 William II, p. 230
32 Haslip, *Emperor and Actress*, p. 197
33 Margutti, p. 221
34 Bülow, 1897–1903, p. 148
35 Brook-Shepherd, *Austrians*, p. 136
36 Paoli, p. 229
37 Ketterl, p. 170
38 Crankshaw, p. 354; Funder, p. 496
39 Redlich, p. 519

Chapter 10

1 Marek, p. 414
2 Beller, p. 188; Hamann, *Meine liebe*, p. 530
3 Ketterl, p. 46
4 Beller, p. 189; Hamann, p. 218
5 Margutti, p. 183
6 Ketterl, p. 49
7 *The Times*, 18.8.1930
8 PRO FO/371 1047, Sir Fairfax Cartwright to Arthur Nicolson 25.5. 1911
9 Margutti, p. 154
10 Bridge, p. 4; Hötzendorff, Conrad von, *Aus meiner Dienstzeit*, Vienna, 1921, II, 282
11 PRO FO/371 1047, Sir Fairfax Cartwright to Arthur Nicolson 25.5.1911
12 Gribble, pp. 341–2
13 Brook-Shepherd, *Austrians*, p. 151
14 Brook-Shepherd, *Last Habsburg*, p. 27
15 Pauli, p. 275
16 Cassels, *Archduke and Assassin*, p. 179
17 Gore, p. 287
18 Margutti, pp. 138–9
19 Crankshaw, p. 388

20 Pauli, p. 273
21 Haslip, *Emperor and Actress*, p. 263
22 Brook-Shepherd, *Last Habsburg*, p. 3
23 Pauli, p. 292
24 *The Times*, 17.11.1916
25 *The Times*, 25.7.1914
26 Jaszi, p. 424
27 Margutti, p. 323
28 Crankshaw, p. 404; *Wiener Zeitung* 29.7.1914

Chapter 11

1 *The Times*, 9.9.1914
2 Brook-Shepherd, *Last Habsburg*, p. 43
3 Ketterl, pp. 103–4
4 Brook-Shepherd, *Last Habsburg*, p. 29
5 Ketterl, p. 245
6 *The Times*, 3.4.1915
7 Redlich, p. 531
8 Marek, p. 462
9 Margutti, p. 362
10 *The Times*, 23.10.1916
11 *The Times*, 4.11.1916
12 Ketterl, p. 249
13 Ketterl, p. 251
14 *The Times*, 18.11.1916
15 Brook-Shepherd, *Last Habsburg*, p. 46
16 Ketterl, pp. 251–2
17 *The Times*, 22.11.1916
18 *The Times*, 23.11.1916
19 Margutti, p. 136
20 Brook-Shepherd, *Last Habsburg*, p. 87
21 Lieven, *Habsburg Empire*
22 Winston Churchill, 8.4.1945, various quotation websites – original source and context uncertain, thought to be in private conversation at home
23 Taylor, p. 568
24 *The Times*, 19.8.1930

Bibliography

Letters

Royal Archives, Windsor: Queen Victoria's Journal; miscellaneous correspondence and memoranda, 1852–1904

Public Record Office, London: correspondence between Lord John Russell and Lord Clarendon, 1855; Lord John Russell and Julian Fane, 1860; Sir Fairfax Cartwright and Arthur Nicolson, 1911

Books

The place of publication is London unless otherwise stated

Anon, *Recollections of a Royal Governess*, New York, Appleton, 1916

Ashley, Evelyn, *The Life of H.J. Temple, Viscount Palmerston, 1846–65: with Selections from his Speeches and Correspondence*, 2 vols, Bentley, 1876

Barkeley, Richard, *The Road to Mayerling: Life and Death of Crown Prince Rudolph of Austria*, Macmillan, 1958

Beller, Steven, *Francis Joseph*, Longman, 1996

Bled, Jean-Paul, *Franz Joseph*, Blackwell, 1992

Bridge, F.R., *The Habsburg Monarchy among the Great Powers, 1815–1918*, Oxford, Berg, 1990

Brook-Shepherd, Gordon, *The Last Habsburg*, Weidenfeld & Nicolson, 1968

—— *Victims at Sarajevo: The Romance and Tragedy of Franz Ferdinand and Sophie*, Harvill, 1984

—— *Royal Sunset: The Dynasties of Europe and the Great War*, Weidenfeld & Nicolson, 1987

—— *The Last Empress: the Life and Times of Zita of Austria-Hungary, 1892–1989*, HarperCollins, 1991

—— *The Austrians: a Thousand-year Odyssey*, HarperCollins, 1996

Bülow, Prince Bernard von, *Memoirs*, 4 vols, Putnam, 1930–1

Cassels, Lavender, *Clash of Generations: A Habsburg Family Drama in the Nineteenth Century*, John Murray, 1973

—— *The Archduke and the Assassin: Sarajevo, June 28th 1914*, Frederick Muller, 1984

Corti, Conte Egon Caesar, *Elizabeth, Empress of Austria*, Thornton Butterworth, 1936

Bibliography

—— *Von Kind Zum Kaiser: Kindheit und erste Jugend, Kaiser Franz Josephs I, und seiner Geschwister*, Graz, Verlag Anton Pustet, 1950

—— *The English Empress: a Study in the Relations between Queen Victoria and her Eldest Daughter, Empress Frederick of Germany*, Cassell, 1957

Crankshaw, Edward, *The Fall of the House of Habsburg*, Longman, 1963

De Burgh, A., *Elizabeth, Empress of Austria: a Memoir*, Hutchinson, 1899

Funder, Friedrich, *Vom Gestern ins Heute. Aus dem Kaiserreich in die Republik*, Vienna, Herold, 1952

Gore, John, *King George V: A Personal Memoir*, John Murray, 1941

Gribble, Stephen, *The Life of the Emperor Francis Joseph*, Eveleigh Nash, 1914

Hamann, Brigitte (ed.), *Majestät, ich warne Sie: Geheime und private Schriften*, Vienna, Amalthea, 1979

—— *Meine liebe, gute Freundin! Die briefe Kaiser Frans Josephs an Katharina Schratt*, Vienna, Uberreuter, 1992

Haslip, Joan, *The Lonely Empress: A Biography of Elizabeth of Austria*, Weidenfeld & Nicolson, 1965

—— *Imperial Adventurer: Emperor Maximilian of Mexico and his Empress*, Weidenfeld & Nicolson, 1971

—— *The Emperor and the Actress: The Love Story of Emperor Franz Josef and Katharina Schratt*, Weidenfeld & Nicolson, 1982

Hyde, H. Montgomery, *Mexican Empire: The History of Maximilian and Carlota of Mexico*, Macmillan, 1946

Jaszi, Oszkar, *The Dissolution of the Habsburg Monarchy*, Chicago, University of Chicago Press, 1961

Judtmann, Fritz, *Mayerling: the Facts behind the Legend*, Harrap, 1971

Ketterl, Eugen, *The Emperor Francis Joseph I: An Intimate Study*, Skeffington, 1929

Listowel, Judith, *A Habsburg Tragedy: Crown Prince Rudolf*, Ascent, 1978

Lonyay, Count Carl, *Rudolf: The Tragedy of Mayerling*, Hamish Hamilton, 1950

Magnus, Philip, *King Edward the Seventh*, John Murray, 1964

Marek, George R., *The Eagles Die: Franz Joseph, Elizabeth, and their Austria*, Hart-Davis, MacGibbon, 1975

Margutti, Lieutenant-General Baron von, *The Emperor Francis Joseph and his Times*, Hutchinson, 1921

Martin, Theodore, *Life of HRH The Prince Consort*, 5 vols, Smith & Elder, 1874–80

Morton, Frederic, *A Nervous Splendor: Vienna 1888/1889*, New York, Little, Brown, 1979

Obolensky, Dmitri, *Bread of Exile: a Russian Family*, Harvill, 1999

Paget, Walburga, Lady, *Embassies of Other Days*, 2 vols, Hutchinson, 1923

—— *In My Tower*, 2 vols, Hutchinson, 1924

Palmer, Alan, *Twilight of the Habsburgs: The Life and Times of Emperor Francis Joseph*, Weidenfeld & Nicolson, 1994

Pauli, Hertha, *The Secret of Sarajevo: The Story of Franz Ferdinand and Sophie*, Collins, 1966

Pope-Hennessy, James, *Queen Mary, 1867–1953*, Allen & Unwin, 1959

Bibliography

Praschl-Bichler, Gabriele, *Historische Photographien aus den Alben des Kaiserbruders Erzherzog Ludwig Viktor*, Vienna, Amalthea, 1999

Redlich, Joseph, *Emperor Francis Joseph of Austria: A Biography*, Macmillan, 1929

Schnurer, Franz, *Briefe Kaiser Franz Josefs am seine Mutter 1838–72*, Munich, 1930

Schweinitz, Hans Lothar von, *Denkwürdigkeiten des Botschafters General von Schweinitz*, Berlin, 1927

Sinclair, Andrew, *Death by Fame: A Life of Elisabeth Empress of Austria*, Constable, 1998

Stephanie of Belgium, Princess, *I Was To Be Empress*, Ivor Nicholson & Watson, 1937

Stockhausen, Juliana von, *Im Schatten der Hofburg. Gestalten, Puppen und Gespenster. Aus meinen Gesprächen mit Prinzessin Stephanie von Belgien, Fürstin Lonyay, der letzten Kronprinzessin von Osterreich-Ungarn*, Heidelberg, Kerle-Verlag, 1952

Taylor, A.J.P., *The Struggle for Mastery in Europe 1848–1918*, Oxford, Oxford University Press, 1954

Tschuppik, Karl, *The Empress Elizabeth of Austria*, Constable, 1930

—— *The Reign of the Emperor Francis Joseph 1848–1916*, Bell, 1930

Van der Kiste, John, *Windsor and Habsburg: The British and Austrian Reigning Houses 1848–1922*, Gloucester, Sutton, 1987

Victoria, Queen, *The Letters of Queen Victoria: a Selection from Her Majesty's Correspondence between the Years 1837 and 1861*, ed. A.C. Benson and Viscount Esher, 3 vols, John Murray, 1907

—— *The Letters of Queen Victoria, 2nd Series: a Selection from Her Majesty's Correspondence and Journal between the Years 1862 and 1885*, ed. George Earle Buckle, 3 vols, John Murray, 1926–8

—— *The Letters of Queen Victoria, 3rd Series: a Selection from Her Majesty's Correspondence and Journal between the Years 1886 and 1901*, ed. George Earle Buckle, 3 vols, John Murray, 1930–32

—— *Dearest Mama: Private Correspondence of Queen Victoria and the Crown Princess of Prussia, 1861–1864*, ed. Roger Fulford, Evans Bros, 1968

—— *Darling Child: Private Correspondence of Queen Victoria and the Crown Princess of Prussia, 1871–1878*, ed. Roger Fulford, Evans Bros, 1976

William II, Emperor, *My Early Life*, Methuen, 1926

Websites

Lieven, Dominic, *The Habsburg Empire*, Fathom Knowledge Network, 2002 http://www.fathom.com/feature/122075/

Journals

European Royal History Journal
Royalty Digest
The Times
Weiner Zeitung

Index

Index